SUBTLE TOOLS

Subtle Tools

THE DISMANTLING OF AMERICAN DEMOCRACY FROM THE WAR ON TERROR TO DONALD TRUMP

KAREN J. GREENBERG

PRINCETON UNIVERSITY PRESS

PRINCETON & OXFORD

Copyright © 2021 by Princeton University Press

Princeton University Press is committed to the protection of copyright and the intellectual property our authors entrust to us. Copyright promotes the progress and integrity of knowledge. Thank you for supporting free speech and the global exchange of ideas by purchasing an authorized edition of this book. If you wish to reproduce or distribute any part of it in any form, please obtain permission.

Requests for permission to reproduce material from this work should be sent to permissions@press.princeton.edu

Published by Princeton University Press
41 William Street, Princeton, New Jersey 08540
99 Banbury Road, Oxford OX2 6JX

press.princeton.edu

All Rights Reserved

First paperback printing, 2023
Paperback ISBN 9780691216577

The Library of Congress has cataloged the cloth edition as follows:

Names: Greenberg, Karen J., author.
Title: Subtle tools : the dismantling of American democracy from the War on Terror to Donald Trump / Karen J. Greenberg.
Other titles: Dismantling of American democracy from the War on Terror to Donald Trump
Description: Princeton : Princeton University Press, [2021] | Includes bibliographical references and index.
Identifiers: LCCN 2021012538 (print) | LCCN 2021012539 (ebook) | ISBN 9780691215839 (hardback) | ISBN 9780691216560 (ebook)
Subjects: LCSH: United States—Politics and government—2017– | War on Terrorism, 2001–2009—Political aspects. | Executive power—United States. | Trump, Donald, 1946– | Administrative agencies—United States—Reorganization. | September 11 Terrorist Attacks, 2001—Influence. | Terrorism—United States—Prevention—Political aspects. | Political culture—United States. | Law—Political aspects—United States—History—21st century. | BISAC: POLITICAL SCIENCE / Security (National & International) | LAW / Government / General
Classification: LCC E912 .G75 2021 (print) | LCC E912 (ebook) | DDC 306.20973—dc23
LC record available at https://lccn.loc.gov/2021012538
LC ebook record available at https://lccn.loc.gov/2021012539

British Library Cataloging-in-Publication Data is available

Editorial: Bridget Flannery-McCoy, Alena Chekanov
Jacket/Cover Design: Pamela L. Schnitter
Production: Erin Suydam
Publicity: James Schneider, Kate Farquhar-Thomson
Copyeditor: Theresa Malhame

This book has been composed in Arno

For Danny

What rough beast, its hour come round at last, may be slouching toward Washington to be born?

ARTHUR SCHLESINGER JR. (1986)

CONTENTS

SUBTLE TOOLS

INTRODUCTION

The Subtle Tools

Terrorist attacks can shake the foundations of our biggest buildings,
but they cannot touch the foundation of America.

GEORGE W. BUSH, SEPTEMBER 11, 2001

ON SEPTEMBER 11, 2001, Manhattan's twin towers collapsed into rubble.
Within hours, the edifice of American democracy began to fracture as
well. Some were quick to foresee the scale of change the destruction
would yield. Many officials inside the White House agreed with the CIA
director George Tenet's pronouncement that "all the rules have
changed."[1] According to a PEW Research Poll taken at year's end, "opinion leaders in every region agree that Sept. 11 marked the beginning of
a new chapter in world history." Approximately 78 percent of U.S. respondents believed that "a new era" had been "opened up."[2] Donald
Trump, then a mere bystander to politics, predicted, "This country is
different today and it is going to be different than it ever was for many
years to come."[3]

These first impressions turned out to be right. Over the course of the
next two decades, a vastly different America has taken root. Slowly but
inexorably, basic building blocks of the country have been undermined
and at times destroyed. In the name of retaliation, "justice," and prevention, fundamental values have been cast aside, among them the right to
be safe from abusive power by the state. Americans have been stranded,

neglected, and—in the name of security—their guarantees of security have eroded.

This transformation was set in motion immediately after the attacks of 9/11. Within eighteen months, three acts of Congress would transform the country. The first was the September 2001 Authorization for the Use of Military Force. The second was the October 2001 USA Patriot Act, and the third, one year later, was the creation of the Department of Homeland Security, brought into being by the Homeland Security Act.[4] I will focus on each in the chapters to come.

All lined up as prelude to November 2002, the first mid-term election since the Great Depression election of 1934 in which the president's party maintained control of both houses of Congress. The 2002 election set these legislative changes in stone and fixed the country on the course it has pursued to this day—away from liberalism and toward self-serving greed and the perpetuation of injustice and inequality.

These trends were certainly not new in the history of the country, or even in the recent past. Together, these measures would reinforce a history of discrimination and racial injustice that dated to the country's founding and echoed the abuses of executive power that occurred with escalating frequency into the twentieth century: the Watergate scandal, the concealed efforts to escalate the war in Vietnam, the secret deal trading arms for hostages in the Iran–Contra affair, and the economic policies of the Reagan years that endeavored to reverse the New Deal and its economic and social safety nets, continued into the Clinton era. Yet while the war on terror was not the first time an administration would sidestep the law and the Constitution, such departures from law gained terrifying momentum after the attacks of 9/11.

By 2008, the policies of the war on terror had taken an immense toll. The wars in Afghanistan and Iraq together cost almost half a million lives.[5] The creation of an indefinite detention regime at Guantanamo and the use of torture to extract information from "high value detainees" at CIA black sites had taken the country down a path that alarmed defenders of the rule of law and those once dependent on the United States as an ally in the struggle for human rights worldwide. American citizens' trust in government had been fractured due to revelations of surveillance policies and the expansive use of law enforcement powers in investigations that had initially been launched against suspected terrorists but over time targeted many others.

When Barack Obama was elected president in 2008, optimism abounded over the opportunities to reverse course on post–9/11 policies. Obama's election heralded "a change in the direction and tone of the country" and a "bitter setback" for the interests that had flourished through the Bush years.[6] Obama's anti–Iraq War campaign rhetoric and his opposition to the legal and policy exceptions made in the name of that war gave hope to critics of the war on terror. He came into office with promises to close the detention facility at Guantanamo Bay, to diminish the dependence on secrecy and institute policies that emboldened transparency, to restore the clear prohibition on torture, and to generally move the country in a direction that adhered to constitutional principles and protections.

Yet making progress proved harder than Obama had anticipated. As he would write over a decade later in his memoir, *A Promised Land*, he at times underestimated the virulence of the political opposition he would encounter.[7] Closing Guantanamo eluded his efforts as he made the calculation that passing the Affordable Care Act took precedence over the controversy closing Guantanamo was certain to unleash. His attempts to end the military presence in Iraq and Afghanistan—already known as the "forever war"—were unsuccessful. Moreover, it seems, having been persuaded by some of the security-versus-liberty arguments that those inside his own cabinet embraced, he even expanded parts of the war-on-terror arsenal—most notably the use of drone strikes with much greater frequency and against an expanding number of countries. By 2016, despite the promises of the Obama administration to wrench back some of the Bush-era deviations from the jaws of democracy's detractors, the country was still living in the thrall of the institutional and cultural changes that 9/11 and the 107th Congress had wrought.

One reason was that beneath these more overt policy choices of the post–9/11 era, including the decision to go to war in Iraq and the weakening of civil liberties in the name of national security, lay a less visible but equally destructive set of practices. These less visible means were what I call the "subtle tools" of the war on terror, which bestowed powers without immediately calling attention to themselves. More crushingly than any one policy or piece of legislation, the subtle tools forged out of the wreckage of 9/11 have acted as a corrosive blanket smothering the good out of a democracy in turmoil.

The first of the subtle tools was the degradation of language, the starting point for political dishonesty and power mongering, and the platform upon which undemocratic and unlawful policies have been fashioned. After 9/11, language that was fuzzy, imprecise, and confounding obtained a secure foothold in government discourse. Over time, that linguistic imprecision enabled another subtle tool—confusion and imprecision in the roles and responsibilities of the institutions of government, which I term "bureaucratic porousness." The third subtle tool, by definition hard to detect, was secrecy and the withholding of facts. The fourth and final tool, one that went hand in hand with devalued language and obfuscatory truth, was the abandonment of legal and procedural norms for lawmaking, oversight, judicial review, transparency, and many other elements of governance.

With these subtle tools in hand—imprecision and vagueness in language, secrecy and the hiding of facts, bureaucratic porousness, and abandonment of norms—the presidency after 9/11 expanded to exercise unprecedented levels of power, the public was deprived of information at record levels, and accountability was essentially removed as a mechanism within the halls of power and replaced by impunity. In each step, the institution most clearly tethered to the law—the Department of Justice—played a role. Enabled by this crucial ally, these tools were in place by the time Trump came into office, and they enabled the final transformation of the culture of governance in America.

Historians often describe the shape of American history in cyclical terms. Some liken it to a pendulum swing or an ebb and flow. The historian Arthur Schlesinger Jr., building on the outlines provided by his father Arthur Schlesinger Sr. in the 1940s and by Henry Adams in the first decade of the twentieth century, posited the "cyclical hypothesis" about the course of America's history: A "pattern of alternation ...

between negative and affirmative government," between conservative and liberal governments in roughly thirty-year cycles, between periods of "deregulation, devolution and privatization" and periods in which the United States takes "the lead in the search for remedies against war and terrorism and weapons of mass destruction, against poverty and disease."[8]

However, years later, the younger Schlesinger saw a potential interruption of this cyclical motion. "The 1990s," he wrote, "have plainly not been the liberal era forecast by the cyclical hypothesis."[9] The conservative cycle had outlasted the predications of his cyclical theory, taking the country on "a scary voyage into uncharted waters."[10] As the Civil War, the Industrial Revolution, the 1960s, and the end of the Cold War had disrupted the cycles, so the newly technical age—which he termed the era of the "Computer Revolution"—was to his mind to blame for the stalling of the pendulum swing. Appealing to the humanist tradition, Schlesinger worried about the derailment of both politics and culture. Writing in 1999, he listed the challenges as "war and terrorism . . . weapons of mass destruction . . . poverty and diseases" as well as racial divides, environmental concerns, and the need for reforms in education and the economy. But Schlesinger refused to concede defeat: "The cycle, though derailed, is not necessarily dead."[11] Whether the cycles would return, he was not sure. But the historian in him gave way to the mystic, as he landed upon the image that the end of the cycles evoked for him. "What rough beast, its hour come round at last, may be slouching toward Washington to be born?" he asked, paraphrasing from "The Second Coming," W. B. Yeats's famous ode to civilization's demise.[12]

I believe Schlesinger was right. The cycles—the pendulum swings— are today perilously close to stasis. A completely new direction is now in place, wherein the mandate of security has successfully unmoored fundamental liberties and given permanence to a new version of democracy, one that has infiltrated American institutions, laws, public culture, and economy—in sum, the culture of governance. The legacy of the war on terror has spawned a full-throated embrace of a new national vision, one with roots deep in the American past yet with many novel features, among them a weakening of the separation of powers doctrine, a degradation of rights to and of citizenship, an increasing lack of independence on the part of the courts, and the willful destruction of professionalism in government, each of them forcefully launched in the wake of 9/11.

Armed with the subtle tools forged in the wake of 9/11, Donald Trump's presidency threatened to put the final brakes on this pendular movement. While the changes after 9/11 might organically have been curtailed as the era of terrorism wound down, the rise of Trump and the interests he helped promote have impeded any such change. He turned wholeheartedly to the subtle tools, which were brought to his attention by those in agencies that had mastered them during the war on terror: the Department of Homeland Security and the Department of Justice. Made aware of their existence, Trump instinctively understood their power to sow political disruption and undermine U.S. institutions, law, and policy. He took these tools, already destructive, and sharpened them into weapons.

Some of this was bound to occur. In fact, many transformations unleashed by 9/11 had been tried and tested in the past, and many of the political interests and personalities that had helped bring Trump to power harkened back to the times when presidential power had overstepped the lawful limits of their power—including the conservative law group the Federalist Society, and longtime Republican insiders such as William Barr. But the past failures had given rise to new strategies. The indictments and convictions of top officials after the Watergate and Iran–Contra scandals revealed the subtle tools at play, but poorly used. Those who championed these tools were better prepared now.

Seen in this context, President Trump, his administration, and the policies they spawned are the consequence not only of 9/11 but also of its frustrated precedents. Trump did not create a brand-new agenda; he merely provided a new and powerful chapter of the story that had limped through the latter twentieth century and taken on a powerful energy after 9/11.

The subtle tools—and their consequences—have yet to receive the scrutiny they deserve. Historians, journalists, and public intellectuals have cataloged some of the more overt products of these tools in action, among them the decision to invade Iraq, the implementation of illegal and unconstitutional policies of surveillance at home, the use of torture abroad, and the erosion of trust between the body politic and the government. But it was the subtle tools, and their first fruits, that tilled the ground for these more consequential turns in the course of American politics and governance. Although they had been used in some fashion earlier, they were brandished after 9/11 with heightened energy, vaster application, and an understanding that used in coordination with one another, their power could prove limitless. Without these tools, refashioned and strengthened to meet the 9/11 moment, the consequential reversals of liberal democracy could not have been accomplished. Without them, Schlesinger's cyclical pattern might not have been interrupted. Without them, the path to Donald Trump might never have been laid.

As the third decade of the twenty-first century dawns, we must come to terms with the damage that our democracy has suffered and the perils that lie ahead. This has been an extraordinary two decades in the nation's history. We need to grapple not only with the transformation that has taken place before our eyes, in policies that deviate far and wide from principles of liberty and justice, but also with the unseen, beneath-the-surface changes to the culture of governance that enabled those policies to come into being in the first place. It is my hope that by recognizing these subtle tools, and the power their owners can wield, we can deepen our understanding of the dysfunctional culture of governance that evolved in the years after 9/11. Perhaps then we can embark on the corrections needed to restore our cherished traditions of law, justice, and governance. As George Orwell reminds us, in the very diagnosis lie the rays of hope for the future, for "to think clearly is a necessary first step towards political regeneration."[13]

1

Ground Zero

Let us just pause for a minute and think through the implications of our actions today so that this does not spiral out of control. . . . Let us not become the evil that we deplore.

CONGRESSWOMAN BARBARA LEE, SEPTEMBER 14, 2001

IN THE FIRST HOURS of shock and confusion following the September 11 attacks on Manhattan's twin towers, observers cast around in search of words to describe the magnitude of the devastation they were witnessing firsthand. However seemingly permanent the Manhattan skyline, however seemingly secure the country's Capitol, weaponized planes had reduced downtown New York City to rubble, had severely damaged the Pentagon, and had cost the lives of nearly three thousand people. Buildings lay in ruin. Hidden and half-buried body parts, which would come to fill more than two thousand bags, were strewn everywhere. The fear that more buildings could collapse, as a third building did later that morning, hovered over the scene.

On September 12, the *New York Times* reported a term that workers who were digging among the ruins had started to use: "Ground Zero." By the next day, the quote marks around the term had disappeared. Lower Manhattan, the *Times* reported, had been "rechristened" Ground Zero. It seemed appropriate to a flattened landscape whose recovery was hard to envision in the days to follow.[1]

8

Up until then, Ground Zero had called to mind a very different moment in time. In 1945 Robert J. Oppenheimer and his fellow scientists at the Manhattan Project had coined the term to denote the first nuclear test in Alamogordo, New Mexico. The nuclear explosion, equivalent to 20,000 tons of TNT, had lit the sky countrywide with an intensity brighter than the sun. To one observer at the epicenter of the explosion, the blast's blinding light seemed "like the end of the world."[2] In fact, it presaged a new beginning. From the ashes of Los Alamos, the atomic age was born.

On 9/11, "Ground Zero" took on a new meaning. It was not just the physical space of destruction in Lower Manhattan; it was shorthand for the challenge of recovering from the attacks. In an instant, a new age had come to the United States. The first Ground Zero had launched the nuclear age. The second would launch the Global War on Terror.

As Donald Trump, then a New York City businessman and real estate developer, predicted, the recovery would be transformative. Two days after the 9/11 attacks, he envisioned not only "a whole different skyline" but "a whole different city and world."[3]

He was right. From its very beginning, the recovery efforts held the seeds of a vast transformation. The need for unlimited powers, equal to the devastation connoted by "Ground Zero," infused the plans of policymakers. In this urge for dramatic action, language—instead of being wielded as a tool for specifying and delimiting experience—became instead a tool for imprecision and vagueness in the service of unbridled authority.

The power of language to make—or undo—a nation has long been recognized. The Founding Fathers used exquisitely exact language to design the structures and laws for their "city on the hill." They considered precision, and the near religious avoidance of vagueness, to be a foundational requirement for the drafting of the constitution for the new democracy. They set out "express" terms, stipulations, restrictions, and delegations, and specified "powers," "exceptions," "limits," "enumerations" and "tenures" pertaining to the authorities mentioned throughout.[4]

James Madison in Federalist, no. 37, counseled that "perspicuity, therefore, requires not only that the ideas should be distinctly formed, but that they should be expressed by words distinctly and exclusively appropriate to them." Acknowledging that "unavoidable inaccuracy" can at times occur in the face of "the complexity and novelty of the objects defined," he nonetheless urged his colleagues to avoid as much as possible "vague and incorrect definitions" and to guard against "indistinctness" and "obscurity."[5] And while the words of the Founding Fathers often promised more than the underlying reality—as in the use of "all men are created equal" to mean only white men—the dangers of imprecision loomed large in their imaginations.

Fifty years after the founding, Ralph Waldo Emerson reminded his fellow citizens that purity in language was a sign of the presence of nature's true spirit. He warned of circumstances in which "the corruption of man is followed by the corruption of language," a time when "duplicity and falsehood" would replace "simplicity and truth."[6]

A century and a quarter later, Arthur Schlesinger Jr. returned to the themes that Emerson had raised. It was 1974, and the Watergate investigation had led to the indictment of President Nixon's closest aides and campaign managers. His vice president had resigned to avoid corruption charges. The president himself was facing an impeachment trial in the Senate that was expected to result in a guilty decision. In a speech titled "Politics and the American Language," Schlesinger contrasted the "noble language" of the Founding Fathers—"lucid, measure and felicitous prose, marked by Augustan virtues of harmony, balance and elegance"—with the "linguistic pollution" and "semantic malnutrition" of his times. He chastised his fellow writers for using "words altogether adrift from meanings," an "alchemy that changes words into their opposites."[7]

Schlesinger was channeling George Orwell, who in 1946 had explored the symbiotic relationship between language and politics in his iconic essay "Politics and the English Language." "The present political chaos," he wrote, watching Europe succumb to fascism, "is connected to the decay of language."[8] Orwell thought the "decadence in language" was "probably curable." Less confident than Emerson and Orwell, Schlesinger still longed for a future in which leaders would "make language a means not of deception but of communication, not an enemy but a friend of the reality principle."[9] That was not what the future held.

War by Any Other Name

In the frantic mood of the first days following the attacks, one of the first concepts to fall into the realm of vague and uncertain meaning was "war." As a shell-shocked public listened in on the evening of the attacks, President George W. Bush spoke in bellicose, breast-beating language. "We stand together to win the war against terrorism," he told the nation. In response to the "evil acts" of our "enemies," and the "mass murder[s]," he acknowledged that "a great people has been moved to defend a great nation." Bush promised an armed response: "Our military is powerful and it's prepared." Two days later, he called the attacks "more than acts of terror; they were acts of war."[10]

The nation's lawmakers concurred. The weaponized planes that hit New York City, Washington, DC, and the fields outside of Shanksville, Pennsylvania had been an "act of war," equal to that suffered on December 7, 1941, when the Japanese bombing of Pearl Harbor precipitated U.S. entry into World War II. More than sixty senators spoke from the Senate floor on September 12, many repeating the words FDR had chosen to encapsulate the magnitude of the attack on Pearl Harbor: "the day of infamy."[11] Voices united in search of a route to war.

This new "day of infamy" necessitated an aggressive response, they argued. "Bin Laden is at war with the United States," Arlen Specter, a Republican senator from Pennsylvania announced, "it is time that we reciprocate."[12] Republicans and Democrats alike echoed Specter's sentiment. North Dakota's Democratic senator Byron Dorgan named the enemy: "We must now wage war on terrorism." He was not the only one to invoke this ambiguous adversary. Quoting liberally from poets and philosophers alike, from Shakespeare to Clausewitz, the country's elected politicians agreed with Nebraska senator Chuck Hagel, who as a young man had volunteered for service in Vietnam despite a draft board recommendation that he attend college instead, when he said, "We are at war with the scourge of our time: terrorism." (A dozen years later, Hagel would be called to serve as the secretary of defense, supervising the war on terror that would still be raging when he took up the position). Senator Mary Landrieu and others echoed his sentiment.

"The American people," Landrieu declared, were "called to war."[13] Maine's senator Susan Collins spoke for many: "Our determination to winning the war on terrorism must have the same high priority that we gave to winning World War II."[14]

Unsparing as the nation's lawmakers were with the words of war, they were loath to make a formal declaration of it. Adhering to Congress's constitutional role in authorizing a declaration of war—reinforced by the 1973 War Powers Act, passed in reaction to what many senators saw as presidential overreach by Johnson and Nixon in commencing and prosecuting the war in Vietnam—the White House drafted a proposal and passed it to Congress within twenty-four hours. But Bush and his advisors did not ask to declare war. Instead, the White House asked for an Authorization for the Use of Military Force. The AUMF, as it was known, was passed by Congress on September 14 and signed by the president on September 18.

Between both chambers, there were 518 votes in favor—and only one nay, from California congresswoman Barbara Lee.[15] In an impassioned speech on the House floor, she expressed her "sorrow for the families and the loved ones who were killed and injured this week. Only the most foolish and the most callous would not understand the grief that has really gripped our people and millions across the world." She acknowledged the resolution would pass. But, she explained, she was opposed to it:

> This unspeakable act on the United States has forced me, however, to rely on my moral compass, my conscience, and my God for direction. . . . I am convinced that military action will not prevent further acts of international terrorism against the United States. . . . However difficult this vote may be, some of us must urge the use of restraint. Our country is in a state of mourning. Some of us must say, let us step back for a moment. Let us just pause for a minute and think through the implications of our actions today so that this does not spiral out of control.

She ended with a warning: "As we act, let us not become the evil that we deplore."[16]

Lee's was a voice of caution that stood alone in Congress. On five separate occasions in the future, she would push to sunset the resolution, but to no avail.

If there is an Ur document in the war on terror and its legacy, it is the AUMF. Riddled with imprecision, its terminology was geared to codify expansive powers. The president could "use all necessary and appropriate force" with no limits specified and could do so against a nameless set of enemies—"those nations, organizations, or persons he determines planned, authorized, committed, or aided the terrorist attacks that occurred on September 11, 2001." The battlefield, like the enemy, was nameless. The president was also authorized to use force against those who "harbored such organizations or persons, in order to prevent any future acts of international terrorism against the United States by such nations, organizations or persons."[17] Nor was there a mention of what could signal the end of conflict.[18] In sum, it was to be a war with neither temporal nor geographical boundaries, and lacking definitional limits when it came to the enemy.

Few were surprised by the fact that the White House had proposed this authorization for the use of force rather than a full-throated declaration of war. Presidents throughout history have been reluctant to invoke such declarations, and since Truman's initiation of the Korean War without congressional approval—the first overseas conflict for which the United States did not invoke a declaration of war—the pattern of the president assuming the power to go to war without actually declaring it as such had been set for the modern era.

But the war with al Qaeda was different from those that had preceded it. None of the undeclared wars of the past century had occurred after the country had been attacked at home. "Our nation has been put on notice," President Bush said in reminding the country of that difference. "We're not immune from attack."[19]

The AUMF thus stood in stark contrast to the declaration of war that had followed the original "day of infamy." The joint resolution after Pearl Harbor empowered FDR to wage war against a specific enemy: Japan. It declared "that a state of war exists between the Imperial Government of Japan and the Government and people of the United States." As new enemies came on board throughout Europe, specific declarations of war were issued for each country, patterned precisely on the declarations of war against Japan. The goals, these declarations stated, was "to bring the conflict to a successful termination."[20]

The failure to specify the enemy was a departure from custom as well. In authorizations of force that followed World War II, the enemies were named. Even the Gulf of Tonkin Resolution that began the Vietnam War, one of the most criticized authorizations in the history of American warfare, included more specific language than the AUMF (despite its later use for vast, open-ended, and secretive aims). It pledged to "assist any member or protocol state of the Southeast Asia Collective Defense Treaty requesting assistance in defense of its freedom."[21] No such clarity was included in the AUMF.

In its imprecision, the resolution unleashed the possibility of expansive powers for the president and his administration. Even before its passage, lawmakers were quick to sound the alarm against what they sensed to be an inherent danger in the imprecision of the AUMF's language. An original draft from the White House included a sentence authorizing the president to "deter and preempt any related future acts of terrorism and aggression against the United States"—in other words, to attack enemies beyond those involved in the attacks.[22] Wisconsin senator Russell Feingold later summed up the opposition to the original draft that he along with Senator Joe Biden of Delaware and Senator Carol Levin of Michigan shared. They warned of the use of "open-ended terms like *terrorism* rather than focusing the language on those who had actually attacked us." [23]

Second-term senator Feingold, an outspoken advocate of constitutional protections and chairman of the Constitution Subcommittee of the Judiciary Committee, continued to raise the alarm as the bill worked its way to passage. The inclusion of "unnamed aggression" could be seen as blanket authority for "future acts" of warfare. For him, it was "a first sign" that the response to 9/11 might be "heartbreakingly reckless."[24] Even as the fires where the planes had crashed were still burning, Feingold focused on the loopholes that the open-ended, unspecified authorities could exploit—especially the last sentence that gave the president permission to counter threats not specifically connected to 9/11, in a preemptive fashion, against virtually any target considered to be a potential enemy. He was determined to have the sentence struck.

Feingold succeeded. The final wording of the AUMF as passed consisted of "comparatively narrow wording."[25] The remainder of the brief 312-word joint resolution adhered to its original form. But the passage's removal did not address the resolutions' overall imprecision. The AUMF remained vague, and as such, it provided a green light for sprawling, unnamed powers for the president. It was a blank check for the president, as Barbara Lee, along with Senators Patrick Leahy and Arlen Specter, reminded the House and Senate respectively. Yet despite these warnings about its vagueness, Congress passed the AUMF in record time, with only Lee's nay vote.

The vote approving the resolution set the nation on a course that was antithetical to the spirit of law as a doctrine based on precision and limits and was inattentive to the constitutional principle of the balance of powers. It was thus the first of many pieces of legislation, endemic to the war on terror, that would embrace imprecision as a means of expanding authorities. Its vagueness led not only to temporally and geographically unrestrained warfare—a global battlefield with no end to the struggle in sight—but also to the aims of the war itself. In the AUMF's imprecise, vague, and overly broad language, the first subtle tool of the war on terror showed its power. It would become the signature of government policy in the war on terror, and far beyond.

Secret Authorization

But the vague and broad powers assumed by the president proved to be even wider than those known to Congress. Unbeknownst to Feingold and the members of Congress, the passage Feingold had succeeded in removing from the final resolution was revived behind closed doors.

John Yoo was a young and ambitious lawyer at the Department of Justice's Office of Legal Counsel (OLC), closely allied with Vice

President Dick Cheney's legal adviser David Addington. A Yale Law School graduate and former clerk for the conservative Justice Clarence Thomas, Yoo had been in place at the OLC for only two months prior to 9/11. Yet in a memo titled "The President's Constitutional Authority to Conduct Military Operations against Terrorists and Nations Supporting Them" that circulated seven days after the AUMF was passed by both chambers of Congress and was seen only by a few administration officials, Yoo provided a very different interpretation of the Constitution than that which counseled some restraint on the president even in times of war.[26] The AUMF by his reading was an act of propriety and statesmanship, not a constitutional requirement. The president actually did not need Congress's approval to go to war.

Yoo ignored the prevailing legal doctrine that the president had the power to act as commander in chief to conduct war, but Congress had the power "to declare war" as specified in Article I of the Constitution. He not only declared this reasoning null and void, but added further that the president had the authority to act "preemptively against terrorist organizations or the States that harbor or support them, whether or not they can be linked to the specific terrorist incidents of September 11"—the very notion Feingold had wrested out of the authorization.[27] Yoo was referring to the theory of the unitary executive that originated during the founding period, which privileged executive power, especially in matters involving national security. As Yoo explained in the memo, "the centralization of authority in the President alone is particularly crucial in matters of national defense, war, and foreign policy choices, where a unitary executive can evaluate threats, consider policy choices, and mobilize national resources with a speed and energy that is far superior to any other branch."

Armed with this memo, the Department of Justice secretly authorized the president to act unilaterally and preemptively in the war on terror, and to do so beyond the minimal restrictions of the AUMF—namely, its tie to the 9/11 attacks—and beyond the exercise of purely military operations. The secret revision of the AUMF provided a hint of much more potent reinterpretations of language and law to come;

the passage that had been deleted would remain alive in the minds of those supervising the war effort.

The second subtle tool of the Bush administration's war on terror was now in play—secrecy—often at the hands of the Department of Justice and in the name of the unitary executive. As the *New York Times* journalist and author Charlie Savage summed it up, "Yoo penned one secret memorandum after another claiming that the president, as commander in chief, had the constitutional authority to lawfully take actions that were seemingly prohibited by federal statutes and treaties."[28] The subtle tools of linguistic imprecision and secrecy set the pattern for the war to come.

President Bush acknowledged the novelty of the war that the AUMF authorized in a broadcast to the nation on September 20. Addressing a joint session of Congress, Bush delivered a speech that was lauded on both sides of the aisle. "On September the 11th, enemies of freedom committed an act of war against our country." The United States, he told the nation, would respond in kind. "Our war on terror begins with al Qaeda, but it does not end there. It will not end until every terrorist group of global reach has been found, stopped and defeated." Like the attacks of 9/11, the response would be unprecedented in size and scale.

It would be "a lengthy campaign unlike any other we have ever seen." He elaborated, "This war will not be like the war against Iraq a decade ago, with a decisive liberation of territory and a swift conclusion." Nor would it resemble "the air war above Kosovo two years ago, where no ground troops were used and not a single American was lost in combat." Instead, the president declared, "Our response involves far more than instant retaliation and isolated strikes." The war would be long, indeterminate, and expansive.[29]

And it was. Over time, the war on terror came to be a "long war," an "endless war," and a "forever war," spawning others directly or indirectly, while the breadth and scope of its geographical and political aims were criticized as "mission creep," insufficiently tethered to the authorities granted in the AUMF. By the middle of 2019, the AUMF had been invoked forty-one times to justify the use of U.S. military activities in eighteen countries—not accounting for any instances and locations that might have been classified. It had been used against half a dozen different terrorist groups, including ISIS (the Islamic State of Iraq and Syria), which did not exist when the AUMF was passed.[30]

The imprecision not only allowed the war on terror to engulf a vast geographical and temporal scope but it also confused the aims of military engagement. For those tasked with fighting the war, it bred confusion and frustration on almost every level, from tactical to strategic to behavioral norms. The aims of the war were one of the many items excluded from the AUMF's language, a lapse which quickly posed problems. When Brigadier General Stanley McChrystal arrived in Afghanistan in 2002 (where he would later serve as the general in command of U.S. and NATO forces), "he wasn't sure," as the journalist Steve Coll explains, "whether the force's mission was going to be nation building or continuing the pursuit of remnants of al Qaeda and the Taliban."[31] Soldiers in the battlefield were confused as well, including about the application of the rules for the treatment of prisoners taken in the war. "It's extremely hard to wage war with so many undefined rules and roles," one officer explained, as he later tried to defend his role in connection with the deaths of two detainees in custody at Bagram Air Base in Afghanistan in 2002.[32]

So, too, there was imprecision in terms of who could be detained in U.S. custody and how they would be treated. Instead of relying on specific determinants of guilt, the United States and its coalition allies detained hundreds of persons—many of whose names and conduct were unknown to the United States—based only on general notions of proximity to conflict zones or relationship to other suspects. Just how little the United States knew about these individuals was apparent the day the first twenty detainees arrived at the newly opened Guantanamo Bay Detention Facility on January 11, 2001. Documents and "pocket litter"— papers, notebooks, pictures, wallets, passports and more— accompanying them, potentially containing evidence about the guilt or innocence of each, were mixed together in "plastic bags full of stuff that wasn't associated with one single person," as one intelligence officer recalled, with the information on each individual indistinguishable from the information on another.[33] Distinctiveness, clarity, and the legal procedures that could follow were thereby compromised from the start.

The mission of Guantanamo Bay was as imprecise as the language and terminology of the authorization under which it was established. Founded as a place to hold detainees from the war on terror in indefinite detention, the camp occupied a fuzzy, undefined legal space. This imprecision was intentional and spoke directly to the determination to evade both U.S. and international law. Prisoners had clear rights, defined by international humanitarian law. Common Article 3 of the Geneva Conventions—the treaties championed by the United States in the post–World War II era that bound nations to lawful treatment of combatants and noncombatants during wartime—defined the standards for the humane treatment of prisoners of war. In theory, by issuing an authorization instead of a declaration of war, the administration had already begun skirting the obligations of international law.

Yet to make sure the clear protections of the international treaties did not pertain to Guantanamo Bay, Defense Secretary Donald Rumsfeld went further and forbade the word "prisoner" to be used to refer to the war on terror captives held there. Instead of "prisoners," the captives would be labeled "detainees" and were therefore presumably outside the legal controls of international conventions regarding the treatment of prisoners of war. But this was not enough; a new term of art was further devised to define these prisoners: "enemy combatant." Under the international law of armed conflict, the term "lawful belligerents" defined a category of captive to whom the protections of the laws of war applied. But this new, essentially definitionless category of "enemy combatant," and its twin "unlawful enemy combatant," created a wide-open space for novel policy, including indefinite detention without due process and the use of "enhanced interrogation techniques," another semantic creation intended to disguise the policy of torture undertaken at secret CIA detention facilities around the world.

This imprecise language confused both those on the ground at Guantanamo and those overseeing detention facilities in the theaters of war. The first commander at Guantanamo Bay Detention Facility, Brigadier General Michael Lehnert, remembered being in the dark about the mission there. "What was the purpose of the detention camp?" he asked himself. What rules controlled the treatment of those in detention?[34]

The same confusion held at prisons in Iraq. Reservist Brigadier General Janis Karpinski, responsible for Abu Ghraib and other prisons holding detainees from the war in Iraq, rued the lack of clear policy guidance for operating and managing the detention facilities.[35] A subsequent report on Department of Defense (DOD) interrogation policies found them "inadequate" and "poorly defined," and compromised by the "absence of specific guidance."[36] It was a confusion that would serve the Pentagon well in defying legal limits previously established for the detention and the treatment of prisoners.

The Legacy of the AUMF

The vagueness and imprecision of the 2001 AUMF provided the template for many future policies and pieces of legislation, including the 2002 AUMF, passed on October 16, 2002, which set the stage for the Iraq War.[37] Although the 2001 AUMF was already expansive in its lack of definitions and limits, and although it would be applied in future years to more and more terrorist organizations and geographical locations, legislators sought a second authorization, specific to a nation-state, for the war in Iraq. But even in its geographical specificity, the 2002 AUMF lacked clarity. Like its predecessor, it contained neither temporal constraints nor any sense of the concessions or formal procedures that would bring an end to the war. By including elements of the imprecision of the original AUMF in the 2002 AUMF, the Bush administration continued a pattern that would appear in much of the war on terror policy to follow, thus further weakening the legitimacy of the laws that had predated the war on terror and its unique circumstances.

By the time President Obama came into office, the imprecision and accompanying expansiveness that characterized the AUMFs had manifest themselves in numerous breaks with law and custom. A graduate of Harvard Law School and for twelve years a lecturer in constitutional law at the University of Chicago, Obama recognized the power of the language that had been adopted to elide precision and allow legal overreach, and he endeavored to remove some of the vaguer, open-ended language of his predecessor. He insisted on retiring the more editorial terms such as "war on terror," "enemy combatants," and the associated term "Long War" from the administration's lexicon, as well as the nebulous but emotionally loaded "Islamist extremist terrorism" and the sweeping term "radical Islam."[38]

However, his administration did not return to the definitive vocabulary established by traditional law and jurisprudence. Rather, Obama's administration substituted new, generic terminology: "Overseas contingency operations" replaced the "war on terror"; "unprivileged enemy belligerents" replaced "enemy combatants"; and the more ideologically neutral "terrorists" and "violent extremists" replaced "Islamist extremist terrorism" and "radical Islam."[39] Notably, the new terms were still disappointingly imprecise.

Eventually, Obama also tried to rein in the policies that the open-ended terms had unleashed, beginning with the military presence that the AUMF had set in motion—but not before having amplified the U.S. military commitment. When Obama came into office, he inherited roughly 30,000 troops in Afghanistan and just under 150,000 in Iraq. Obama escalated troop numbers in Afghanistan over the course of 2009 by approximately 50,000. In December of that year, he delivered a speech at West Point in which he announced his intention to send another 30,000 troops to Afghanistan. He acknowledged that his decision to scale up the troop numbers flew in the face of his campaign promises. "I do not make this decision lightly," he told the cadets, "I make this decision because I am convinced that our security is at stake." He promised, however, that "after eighteen months, our troops will begin to come home."[40]

The drawdown occurred along the lines he had defined, and by the time he left office, 8,400 troops were in Afghanistan—several thousand more than he said he would have preferred.

Similarly, with respect to Iraq, Obama pulled back from the end-the-wars platform that had ushered him into office. George W. Bush had signed a status of forces agreement for the beginning of a phased withdrawal in June 2009, with the objective of a complete withdrawal by December 2011. Obama postponed the withdrawal's beginning by ten months, but kept the final date for withdrawal intact and emphasized that the remaining troops that would focus on "training, equipping, and advising." Although he did remove combat troops entirely by the end of 2011, the achievement was short-lived; by 2016, another 5,000 troops had been dispatched to Iraq to confront the challenges ISIS presented in the region.[41]

By the time he left office, Obama's efforts to reduce U.S. troops in Iraq and Afghanistan had been realized, but the objective of complete withdrawal eluded him.

Obama likewise sought to bring greater precision to the legal terminology surrounding detention. On March 13, 2009, the Department of Justice, in a brief filed in a habeas case brought by several Guantanamo detainees, recast the war-on-terror detention authority, announcing that international law, alongside presidential powers authorized by the 2001 AUMF, would, according to a DOJ press release "inform the statutory authority conferred by Congress."[42] In other words, international law—called "quaint and obsolete " by Bush's White House counsel and deemed unpatriotic by some members of Congress—would be considered in future decisions relative to the war efforts. Furthermore, Obama refined the definition of the enemy to "provide that individuals who supported al Qaeda or the Taliban are detainable only if the support was substantial," rather than those who, as in the past, might be detained for proximity to or incidental association with al Qaeda. Detention under Bush, evident in the absence of any procedures for putting individuals in Guantanamo Bay, had required little more than a nod of approval by an American officer or official.[43]

When Obama entered office, 242 detainees remained in custody at Guantanamo Bay. He had promised that on the first day of his presidency he would close Guantanamo within one year. He constituted task forces to review the evidence against each detainee to determine whether they should be released, charged and tried, or remain in detention, and backed by an act of Congress, new rules for the military commissions were established. But the military commissions that presided over these trials were still able to use evidence based on information obtained during the torture of the defendants, or provided by others who had been tortured. Nonetheless, the military commissions made little forward progress. All told, there had been eight convictions, half of which had been obtained during Bush's tenure, and three of which had later been reversed entirely, with another partially reversed. The proceedings against the accused 9/11 co-conspirators, the most important case in the military commissions, had stumbled along, unable to proceed to trial as the Obama years came to an end. Ultimately, while 197 detainees were transferred, repatriated, or resettled out of Guantanamo during Obama's time in office, it was still open with 41 men remaining when Trump came into power.[44]

Meanwhile, relying upon the 2001 AUMF, the Obama administration increased U.S. counterterrorism efforts across the Middle East, Africa, and Central Asia. It also lengthened the list of targeted groups, most prominently with respect to ISIS, the terrorist group that emerged out of war-torn Iraq. Less organized and more readily accessible to followers than al Qaeda had been, ISIS quickly reached out and found followers around the globe. To counter ISIS and other new groups, the Obama administration in this instance abandoned efforts at more circumspect language and adopted its predecessor's use of generic, capacious terminology. The enemy was expanded early in Obama's term to include al Qaeda's "associated forces," a term meant to capture splinter groups and newly emerging ones; it also invoked yet another undefined category to justify the broadened interpretation of the resolution that had been rushed to passage in September 2001.[45]

The greater scope of targets and geography was particularly apparent when it came to drone warfare, in which lethal aerial drones were used to target and kill suspected terrorists. The program, which developed mainly under President Obama, peaked in frequency in 2010. Indulging in the limitless geographical breadth of the AUMF, drone strikes proliferated in conflict zones outside of the hot battlefields. By conservative estimates, Obama launched approximately 600 strikes in Pakistan, Yemen, and Somalia and another 300 in Libya.[46] More inclusive estimates put the number of strikes upwards of 1,800. Notably, a U.S. drone strike killed Anwar al-Awlaki and Samir Khan—both American citizens—in October 2011 and another strike killed Awlaki's 16-year-old son—also an American citizen—two weeks later. The killings illustrated further the expansion of the government's claims of authority to use of lethal force in the name of national security.[47]

Although his rhetoric about the war on terror suggested both legal and operational restraint, Obama proved reluctant to surrender the flexibility that vague language provided for the presidential exercise of elastic powers. As documents released in 2013 revealed, the Obama team relied on its own definition of the word "imminence" to justify the lethal drone strikes. In their hands, the word was recast to mean not that which was immediately threatening but rather that which was potentially harmful in the future. As it had during the Bush administration, the Department of Justice aided in this legal elasticity; a 2011 white paper defended the broader interpretation of the word "imminent" and explained that the idea of an "imminent threat of violent attack against the United States does not require the United States to have clear evidence that a specific attack on U.S. persons and interests will take place in the immediate future."[48]

In May 2013, Obama endeavored publicly, and in a document classified at the time, to signal his intention to rein in the targeted killing program.[49] His new policy, first sketched out in a fact sheet and released in full only in 2016, stipulated that except for in "extraordinary cases" the United States would use lethal force only when the target posed a "continuing, imminent threat to US persons" and "near certainty" that civilians would not be harmed or killed as a result of the strikes.[50] The policy seemed to work; during Obama's second term, according to U.S. reports, the percentage of civilian casualties from drone strikes decreased precipitously.

Thus, though promising restraint, Obama ultimately refused to let go of imprecise language and its potentially expansive applications. Much as the new guidance honored the idea of specificity, the actual restraints amounted to less than what had been promised. As the then deputy legal director of the American Civil Liberty Union's (ACLU's) staff member Jameel Jaffer pointed out, many of the terms of the fact sheet that attempted to redefine the targeted killing policy were themselves "vague, elastic and even contradictory."[51] "Indefeasible," he pointed out, joined "imminence" as a vast and amorphous term.

Against the backdrop of rhetoric promising curtailment and his intentions to rein in the broad powers embraced by the Bush administration, the fuzzy contours of America's engagements in the war on terror nonetheless remained. By the time Obama left office in January 2017, the United States was engaged in the longest war ever in U.S. history.

When Trump assumed office in January 2017, the 2001 AUMF, fifteen and a half years old, was still in place in the original form in which it had been passed. It had come up for amendment or reconsideration four times in the years before Trump took office, and would do so another three times during his presidency. Although amendments sunsetting it passed the House on several occasions, proponents of that termination were unable to garner enough votes to pass the Senate. This remained the case in 2020, even though in spring 2019, Trump had felt confident enough to declare an end to the war against ISIS, tweeting, "They are now being beaten badly and at every level," boasting along with Vice President Mike Pence that the United States had "crushed the ISIS caliphate." The White House spokeswoman Sarah Huckabee Sanders echoed their words. ISIS had been "100 percent eliminated."[52]

Trump leaned into the AUMF in the tradition of his predecessors, exploiting its imprecision, and stretching its elasticity even further. Whereas Obama had struggled to draw some clear lines for restraint amid the vague terms of the resolution, Trump, repeating the authorities for expansion cited by Obama, was comfortable in the breadth and scope it allowed him. On March 12, 2018, the State Department issued a memo that set out Trump's intended extension of the theater of war formerly claimed under the AUMF, adding Niger to the list.[53] Trump also substantially escalated the numbers of drone strikes.

It was not just the potential for adding geographical scope that caught Trump's attention. It was the ever-expansive definition of the enemy allowed for in the 2001 authorization and throughout the laws and policies that followed. When it came to the enemy, the absence of a definition suited Trump well. On the campaign trail and in the transition period after his election to the presidency, he vowed to keep Guantanamo open and "load it up with some bad dudes."[54] In his 2018 State of the Union speech, President Trump made good on his earlier rhetoric and revived the terms that his predecessor had attempted to excise from the national security lexicon, reintroducing the term "enemy combatant." "Terrorists," he informed the nation, "are not criminals. They are unlawful enemy combatants." Toward that end, he revoked President Obama's 2009 executive order ordering the closure of Guantanamo. Trump's new executive order authorized new additions to the detention facility: "The United States may transport additional detainees to U.S. Naval Station Guantanamo Bay when lawful and necessary to protect the Nation."[55] His speech would not be the last time he would use the term "enemy combatant" for those he deemed to be enemies of the United States; in the days to come, he would extend its use to illegal immigrants.[56] Once language and policy had been launched in the service of expansive authorities, they could not easily be reined in.

Through three presidencies, the immortality of the AUMF seemed assured. In July 2020, a bipartisan bill was introduced in Congress in an effort "to limit further expansion of the 2001 AUMF, and for other purposes." The purpose of the bill was to underscore the specific separation of powers outlined in the constitution, which had been disregarded in the seemingly endless growth of executive power in the name of the war on terror and the AUMF. "Together" lawmakers wrote, "we are united by a core principle: Article 1, Section 8, Clause 11 of the U.S. Constitution makes clear that the authority to declare war resides with the Congress and Congress alone."[57] Some feared that Donald Trump would try to broaden the AUMF's authorities even further with countries such as Iran, as we will learn in this book.

The effort to halt the ever-expanding use of this authorization was too little too late. The bill languished, referred to the House Committee on Foreign Affairs, where it remained.[58]

The significance of the AUMF extended well beyond its immediate focus of war. In its elastic, open-ended terminology, it provided a template for the laws and policies to follow in the service of the war on terror. In its metaphoric quality, as a war on an idea as well as a war without a specific enemy in a specific time and place, it created a baseline for activities far afield from the customary battlefield encounters that had traditionally defined war. The AUMF thus introduced imprecision as an invaluable tool for shaping law and policy after the attacks of 9/11. Within days of the AUMF's successful passage, the lure of imprecision would make itself felt again, this time in the restructuring of both law and government, further solidifying the template that the forty-fifth president would later exploit.

2

The Patriot Act

If this bill is passed, it will perhaps be the most devastating one,
certainly the most far-reaching one . . . one that all of us in this body
will rue to our dying day.

DONNA CHRISTIAN-CHRISTENSEN
NONVOTING MEMBER, HOUSE OF REPRESENTATIVES
OCTOBER 12, 2001

ON SEPTEMBER 19, 2001, one day after President Bush signed the Authorization for the Use of Military Force (AUMF), the Department of Justice presented Congress with the early versions of what would become the USA Patriot Act, initially introduced as The Anti-Terrorism Bill.[1] USA Patriot Act was the acronym; the full name was the Uniting and Strengthening America by Providing Appropriate Tools Required to Intercept and Obstruct Terrorism Act of 2001.[2] Recognizing the need for new "tools" in the war on terror, its path to passage, specifying legal tools for law enforcement and intelligence policies, relied heavily on the use of the subtle tool of imprecise language that had been honed during the debates over the AUMF. It relied as well on two additional tools—secrecy, which had reared its head in the legal memos behind the expansive reading of the AUMF, and the disruption of procedural norms. As the AUMF aimed to sanction elastic, sprawling powers in prosecuting war abroad, so the Patriot Act mirrored its efforts in the name of law enforcement and intelligence authorities at home.

The Patriot Act

The professed goal of the Patriot Act was to prevent terrorism. In the words of Ohio congressman Michael Oxley, "September 11th ushered in a new era in American history. We are vulnerable here at home, not just to the fanatics who hijacked those planes, but to other terrorists who have access to biological, chemical, and maybe even nuclear weapons. This threat will not end in 2 years, 5 years, or 10 years."[3] The Patriot Act was meant to avert another, even larger terrorist attack, and the fear of al Qaeda was soon amplified into a perceived threat from unnamed "other terrorists," possibly with weapons of mass destruction, extending far into the future. As the act wound its way through the legislative process, some worried that its powers might result in applications and consequences that challenged standing law, constitutional principles, and the original focus on suspected terrorists.

Some of the legal reforms introduced in the draft Anti-Terrorism bill, submitted by the Department of Justice, were relatively non-controversial—long-sought commonsense updates to laws that had not yet been amended to account for new technologies that had made electronic communications possible. In fact, even voicemails remained outside the purview of law enforcement prior to 9/11. Overall, the draft bill, twenty-four pages in length, authorized open-ended, undefined powers, creating a path for numerous vast and unnamed possibilities and creating almost infinite possibilities in the name of keeping the country safe.[4]

The draft bill called for, among other things, removing limits on unwarranted surveillance, extending secret "sneak and peek" searches that did not require giving notice to the person being searched, lowering the thresholds for criminal investigations (digital and physical), and expanding other powers.[5] Each of these reforms to existing law weakened the clear barriers preventing abuses of power against individual suspects, opening the door to using powers claimed as counterterrorism measures for widespread law enforcement and intelligence collection purposes. It was, Senator Russell Feingold feared, an attempt to bring into law a veritable "wish list" of powers that intelligence and law enforcement officials had long sought, only to be restrained by constitutional protections, as well as some newer requests.[6]

For example, officials within the Department of Justice had been working during the summer of 2001, before the terrorist attacks, to loosen the restrictions on the sharing of information between the intelligence community and law enforcement when it came to international threats—a change that threatened to turn intelligence capacities authorized for the foreign sphere onto domestic targets. In addition, the limits on Fourth Amendment protections had long been sought by law enforcement. Other provisions of the Patriot Act sought by law enforcement for years included greater access to the transactional records of phone and internet communications. The Patriot Act allowed freer collection of this information and extended it to include, for instance, the subject line of an electronic communication. Some saw it as a "blank warrant," others as a "general warrant," not limited to any one place, in contravention of prior practices.[7]

As with the AUMF, the lack of clarity and the expansiveness of the law would serve as the doorway to misuse and abuse of the statute.

Despite the fears swirling in Congress in the fall of 2001, lawmakers in both houses joined Senator Feingold in expressing concern about the vagueness of the proposed bill and its potential application to suspected criminal activity far afield from terrorism. For Feingold, chairman of the Senate Judiciary Committee's Subcommittee on the Constitution, the substitution of a "vague and limitless grant of power" was nothing but "a vast expansion of government fishing expeditions," a form of "bait and switch" in which authorities that were initially justified in the name of countering terrorism would come to apply to criminal investigations generally.[8]

Opponents of these new powers for law enforcement, citing civil liberties concerns, were strongly urged by their colleagues to put their hesitations aside; national security was at stake. Along with their doubts, lawmakers were also asked to dispense with customary process. They were instructed to pass the draft bill submitted by Ashcroft's Department of Justice by week's end—two days later—a "plainly impossible" time frame in the minds of Feingold and many others in the Senate. In the House of Representatives, Wisconsin's Jim Sensenbrenner and Michigan's John Conyers, the chair and ranking member, respectively, of the House Judiciary Subcommittee on Crime, Terrorism, Homeland Security, and Investigations, studiously went to work trying to add language that would specify limits to the increased powers being proposed.

On October 1, the subcommittee finished its bipartisan revision of the Ashcroft proposal. It reportedly reflected a good deal of compromise on both sides. The expectation was that the new 124-page draft, more than four times the length of the proposed version, would get widespread support as it had garnered unanimous support in committee with a vote of 36–0.

But the subcommittee's draft never got a chance to come to a vote. Behind the scenes, the attorney general secretly and aggressively intervened. Debate on the subcommittee's balanced draft was scheduled for the next morning, October 2. On the evening of October 1, Attorney General John Ashcroft, lawmakers reported, "snuck up here to have a meeting," and essentially "hijacked" the Judiciary version of the bill and "destroyed" it. At 3:43 a.m. Ashcroft submitted a new draft that he and others had prepared in the early morning hours.[9]

Ashcroft Intervenes

At 8:00 a.m. on the day the vote was to take place, lawmakers found a brand-new and highly altered version on their desks. The switched-out version was much like the one that had originally been presented to Congress. It was, in Conyers's words, "a tale of two bills."[10] The House members could hardly contain their disbelief at the underhandedness with which Ashcroft had subverted the customary process of drafting and voting on a bill. As Michigan representative John Dingell explained, the new version "suffered some extraordinary changes." Ashcroft had "substituted an entirely different bill."[11]

The replacement draft, along the lines of the original proposal, was masterful in its attempts to restore that proposal. Reflecting the general nature of the changes, the Ashcroft draft pulled back on some of the sunset clauses. Of concern to many was the change in a two-year sunset clause for the weakening of Fourth Amendment protections in the area of foreign intelligence collection. "We wanted to make sure that we force ourselves to review" the relevant FISA (Foreign Intelligence Surveillance Act) provision, Congresswoman Zoe Lofgren explained, "so that the freedoms of Americans are not destroyed as we fight to destroy the terrorists."[12] The Ashcroft draft had extended the sunset to five years. The new draft also watered down warrant requirements, weakened judicial oversight for wiretaps, and authorized uses that had previously been illegal.

The methods put forward in the Ashcroft draft were familiar to those who had witnessed the AUMF's road to passage. The Ashcroft revisions unwaveringly invoked confusion, indistinction, and vague authorities. The new language blurred the distinctions between terrorists and those who associated with them, between terrorist suspects and nonterrorist suspects, between individual suspicion and group suspicion, between judicial search orders pertaining to individuals and those pertaining more broadly to groups. In the words of New York congressman José Serrano, the new draft contained "troubling provisions that expand government's power to invade our privacy, imprison people without due process, and punish dissent. The fact that some expansions of these powers may be used in any criminal investigation, not just an investigation of terrorism, particularly seems like overreaching." Michigan congresswoman Carolyn Kilpatrick echoed Serrano. The bill now granted the government "unbridled powers," including "broad sweeping powers to investigate not only terrorism, but all crimes."[13]

The lawyers among the lawmakers may have known that the bill tread on contested ground. In the application of the law, there is a general caution about overly generalized, excessively vague language. James Madison voiced this concern in Federalist, no. 62: "It will be of little avail to the people, that the laws are made by men of their own choice, if the laws be so voluminous that they cannot be read, or so incoherent that they cannot be understood."[14]

Vagueness had emerged over the twentieth century as a basis for challenging laws considered so imprecise as to be unconstitutional and impossible to apply with fairness or to understand with clarity. In the early decades of the twentieth century, the concept of "void for vagueness" took hold, at times successfully, to challenge the overly broad application of criminal statutes. Though cases involving fair notice defined these cases generally, in the latter twentieth century the void for vagueness doctrine had been applied on the grounds of discriminatory enforcement of the laws.[15] The doctrine as it has evolved holds that laws need to be written clearly in order to ensure that they are understood properly by those subject to them, and applied properly by law enforcement authorities: the lack of clarity should not be used as an excuse for arbitrary and discriminatory enforcement. For example, in a 1972 Supreme Court case *Papachristou v. City of Jacksonville* the court ruled that a vagrancy law was void for vagueness because it criminalized "persons wandering or strolling around from place to place without any lawful purpose or object." The court considered that the vagueness of the statute "encourages arbitrary and erratic arrests and convictions."[16]

The Patriot Act proposal pushed aside this quiet but steady call for clarity in the annals of American law that had been underscored by the void for vagueness doctrine. The susceptibility of antiterrorism laws to being overly vague and broad, as well as misused in discriminatory ways, was an apt lens for judging the Patriot Act and calling for clarity of language throughout. For example, the Patriot Act failed to define what did and did not constitute support for terrorism in ways that could avoid the claim of vagueness. It amended preexisting legislation, notably the 1965 Immigration and Nationality Act, to include measures aimed at countering terrorism, but the absence of any clarifying language in the Patriot Act itself was instructive as to the role breadth and imprecision would play going forward.

Sensing the immediate misgivings of some lawmakers about the expansiveness of the bill, the White House insisted that the vote happen immediately. Senators and Representatives expressed outrage about the substituted draft and the heavy hand of Ashcroft's duplicitous move, pointing out, along with California congresswoman Maxine Waters, that "we had a bipartisan bill and John Ashcroft destroyed it."[17] Nonetheless, the pressure to rush to a vote was, in Feingold's words, "relentless."

Submitted to the Senate on October 24, the new version was scheduled for a vote on October 25. Rushed through to a vote, the bill was never taken up in committee. Feingold tried to introduce several amendments, but was voted down in his attempt, as South Dakota senator Tom Daschle pushed the bill to a vote.[18] The senators were being asked to vote on a bill, as New York congressman Jerrold Nadler put it, "virtually sight unseen."[19]

Most did not read the bill, and admitted as much. Rushed to the floor for a vote, without any Senate judiciary markup, without any amendments, it was, to Feingold's mind "a non-negotiable document" moved through to a vote with "legislative greased lightning."[20] Feingold was the single "No" vote in the Senate. "Well, I read the bill," Feingold explained later. The House voted 357–66 with 9 not voting. Disappointed, Conyers summed up the bill's course to passage, "What you need to know is that the Patriot Act that I sponsored is not the Patriot Act that passed."[21]

Once again, on this occasion evident in real time, the Department of Justice had intervened in secret to bring about the result it sought. The combination of subtle tools proved powerful. In addition to the use of vague language and secrecy, yet another subtle tool had been added and used effectively—the interruption of customary practice, both in the interference with the Sensenbrenner and Conyers draft and with the rush to vote on a bill many legislators had not even read. It was a tool that would take on a life of its own, enabled by imprecision in language and by secrecy, and in the days to come, emerging in particularly dangerous ways in the hands of Donald Trump.

The Patriot Act in Action

The doubts of those who worried about imprecision as a gateway to the abuse of power were immediately borne out, as the law turned into a massive dragnet for enforcement and intelligence agencies. Under a series of provisions, officials authorized the bulk collection of telephone records, business records, and communications alleged to be carried out by foreign agents or those working as agents of a foreign power. The powers granted, elastic and vast, were too tempting to ignore.

A telling example of the expansive authorities resulting from the Patriot Act occurred over the use of National Security Letters (NSLs), an investigative tool that had first been authorized by Congress in 1986. NSLs are letters issued by the FBI demanding personal information from third parties, including financial records, credit reports, telephone and email communications data, and internet searches. The Patriot Act authorized agents to issue such letters without the procedural safeguards that had been in place before 9/11 and without close judicial supervision, as had been required previously. The Patriot Act held that a target no longer had to be a foreign power or the agent of a foreign power (as had been specified in the Foreign Intelligence Surveillance Act of 1978); under the new law, records could be obtained from individuals other than the target of an investigation, provided the information was deemed "relevant."[22] Prior to the passage of the Patriot Act, NSLs required certification by a senior FBI Headquarters official. Now, special agents in charge of the field offices could issue them.

Not surprisingly, the lowered threshold led to an exponential increase in the issuing of NSLs. In 2000, the FBI issued 8,500 NSL requests, often more than one contained in each letter. In 2004, under the new authorities of the Patriot Act, the bureau issued more than 56,000. In 2005, it issued 47,000. In addition, due to sloppy record keeping that led to inaccuracies in the database that was intended to keep track of the NSLs, the bureau acknowledged it was "inaccurate and does not include all national security letter requests" issued by the FBI.[23]

In addition to its enlargement of law enforcement's counterterrorism activities, the Patriot Act was used for purposes far afield from those for which it had been created. By 2003, the Patriot Act was found to have been used to investigate not just suspected terrorists but "suspected drug traffickers, white-collar criminals, blackmailers, child pornographers, money launderers, spies and even corrupt foreign leaders."[24] As the *New York Times* illustrated, the statute was used to seize funds from a U.S. investor accused of stealing from his clients who had fled to Belize, to investigate money launderers in Latin America not suspected of terrorism, and to imprison a young woman traveling with her family on a cruise ship who had written threatening notes in an attempt to get the ship to turn back so she could be reunited with her boyfriend.[25] A 2004 Department of Justice report confirmed the broad uses of the Patriot Act for drug smuggling, money smuggling, and financial crimes found not to be related to terrorism.[26]

It was being used in just the way its critics had warned it would be—an open-ended invitation for new police powers to be expanded in unprecedented ways. In one example of the breadth of the application of the NSL authority, NSLs were issued to libraries asking for lists of books that certain individuals had borrowed. In addition, librarians were forbidden to publicly note that they had been served with the NSLs. The library records policy became a symbol of the overall policy in which breadth and secrecy were signature components.

In 2005, when the Patriot Act came up for reauthorization, Congress, following up on allegations of the misuses of NSLs, asked for inspector general reports on them from 2003 to 2005. According to these inspector general audits of the Patriot Act, the overreach based on unspecific language was not just about the target of prosecutions but also about the methods of investigation.[27] As a 2009 ACLU report summarized, "FBI agents repeatedly ignored or confused the requirements of the NSL authorizing statutes, and used NSLs to collect private information against individuals two or three times removed from the subjects of FBI investigations."[28] The 2007 audit revealed that 22 percent of the audited files contained unreported legal violations on the part of law enforcement and that NSLs were increasingly used to gather information on U.S. persons (57 percent in 2006, up from 53 percent in 2005). The audit also revealed that high-ranking FBI officials improperly issued eleven "blanket NSLs" in 2006 seeking data on 3,860 telephone numbers.[29] As Feingold, Conyers, Vermont senator Patrick Leahy, and others had feared, breadth had become the modus vivendi of the act.

When it came to terrorism per se, the act's language unabashedly encouraged the expansive use of authorities. Under the Patriot Act, the material support statutes—the primary vehicles used to prosecute crimes involving terrorism—included not only financial and operational support to terrorists but also "expert advice and assistance." Nor was the designation "terrorist" specified in limited and definable ways. As the noted civil liberties and constitutional law expert David Cole testified before the Senate in 2005, "the Act defines terrorist organization so broadly that it includes any group of two or more individuals that has ever used or threatened to use a weapon against person or property (except for mere personal monetary gain)."[30] Committee chairman Arlen Specter, senator from Pennsylvania and former assistant district attorney in Philadelphia, agreed, noting that in its first years, the vast "catch-all category" authorized "sneak and peek" searches into anyone said to be "seriously jeopardizing an investigation." In Specter's words, it was "so broad that there are justifiable concerns that it can include practically anything."[31]

Over the course of two presidencies, the Patriot Act was renewed several times, each time with revisions, each time bringing Congress's further assent to embracing the subtle tool of imprecision and the far-reaching application it engendered. In 2005, the revisions included some added minimal protections regarding the use of NSLs and the bulk metadata collection program. For the most part, however, Congress revised the act with the controversial provisions largely intact.[32] In 2011, the Patriot Act passed again, continuing controversial authorities regarding business records, roving wiretaps, and surveillance of "lone wolf" suspects.[33]

Four years later, in 2015, the Patriot Act came under scrutiny by a federal court. Pointing in particular to the misuse of language and its application to implement broad policies, the Second Circuit appellate court declared illegal elements of the legislation that had been initiated in 2002.

The road to this ruling began on June 6, 2013, when Edward Snowden released secret government documents revealing that the National Security Agency (NSA) had been collecting vast troves of information on all Americans. According to the documents, the excessive, warrantless collection and retention of the information resulted from an abuse of the word "relevance." According to a three-judge panel in the Second Circuit, the government's "expansive concept of 'relevance' is unprecedented and unwarranted."[34]

The court corrected the linguistic usage of another term as well—"investigation"—quoting the *Oxford English Dictionary*'s definition and rebuking the government, claiming that "the government's approach" essentially reads the "authorized investigation" language out of the statute. Indeed, the government's information gathering under the telephone metadata program was inconsistent with the very concept of an "investigation."[35] The judge highlighted the discrepancy between the proper use of the term, meaning to "examine (a matter) systematically or in detail," and the government's launching of "general counterintelligence efforts," activities too sweeping to pass muster. "The records demanded," the court explained, went far beyond "suspects under investigation," and even beyond those in contact with suspects. The possible targets were potentially infinite. "They extend to every record that exists, and indeed to records that do not yet exist." The theory of relevance, the court explained, included the reasoning by the government that "there might at some future point be a need or desire to search them in connection with a hypothetical future inquiry."[36]

One of the war on terror's signature subtle tools—imprecise language—was now rebuked on the grounds that it had been used to exercise overly broad powers. Wielded in combination with the secrecy under which these collections were made, the subtle tools had damaged democratic practices in ways that proved hard to miss.

The court's decision, coupled with the government reports concluding that the bulk collection of phone records had not thwarted any specific acts of terror, led ultimately to the expiration of those elements of the Patriot Act. On June 2, 2015, Congress passed the replacement legislation—the USA Freedom Act.[37] It revised Section 215, the provision authorizing the bulk collection of phone detail records. The renewal passed with other controversial authorities intact but without authorization of the bulk warrantless collection that had occurred during the first thirteen years of the act's existence.

Importantly, although the Patriot Act's vague language in the service of expansive authorities received some pushback, the damage was done. The lesson had been learned here, as with the AUMF. Fuzzy, vague language, once in place, could unleash vast, invasive government powers for long periods of time. Moreover, even expired powers could be tapped for revival, as the Trump administration would endeavor to do.

The Patriot Act under Trump

Sixteen months into the Trump presidency, the rogue nature of the call records program reared its head once more. Despite the court ruling on its illegal usage and despite the newly restrained call records program contained in the Freedom Act, its usage had persisted. A report from the Office of Civil Liberties, Privacy and Transparency within the Office of the Director of National Intelligence (ODNI) documented this continued use of widespread, unauthorized collection of phone records. The DNI report blamed the violations on "technical errors." The Trump administration had initially quietly disbanded the Freedom Act's call record program due to the reported violations. Then in 2019, the administration had asked formally for the revival of the program.[38] But the revival did not come to pass and the program was permitted to expire in March 2020. The administration abandoned its support for the program's renewal based on Trump's fears that it could be used against him and individuals within his administration. The USA Freedom Reauthorization Act of 2020 passed without the revival of the call detail records program.[39]

Other overly broad parts of the Patriot Act also successfully caught the attention of the Trump administration. Under the Patriot Act, the window was opened up for preventive, indefinite detention when it came to noncitizens whom the government deemed might cause a danger. It authorized the attorney general to detain foreign nationals without charge for seven days, and thereafter for an indefinite period of time without the requirement of showing that the individual poses a danger or is a flight risk. As David Cole had explained to the Senate Judiciary Committee in 2010, the foreign national can be "locked up even after he has been granted relief from removal, which is akin to saying that the government can keep a prisoner behind bars even after the governor has granted him a pardon."[40]

The detention authority specified in the act was not used until Trump's time in office. In 2017, however, an individual convicted of material support of terrorism for an act committed prior to 9/11, but not alleged to be associated with 9/11, was put in preventive detention by Attorney General William Barr after the expiration of his prison sentence. Adham Hassoun, born in Lebanon to Palestinian parents, moved in his late twenties in 1989 to the United States, where he had married and raised a family. Hassoun was charged and tried because of his outspoken support in the 1990s of ethnic minorities defending themselves in conflicts abroad. He finished serving his fifteen-year sentence, only to be the first person detained under the detention provision of the Patriot Act. Hassoun was held without charge in this preventive detention for two and a half years. Finally, with the American Civil Liberties Union (ACLU) pushing litigation in the courts, a deal was arranged and Hassoun was resettled to Rwanda.[41] But the Trump administration's intention to use the Patriot Act as broadly as possible was apparent.

The immigration provisions tucked into the Patriot Act also gained the Trump administration's attention, and as we will see, helped along one of the first and ultimately signature policies of the administration— southern border controls. The allowance for vague application of the law would prove dispositive in using increased authorities passed in the name of the war on terror as law enforcement measures to aid anti-immigrant policies. The Patriot Act thus turned out to be what Senator Feingold had feared—a "bait and switch."[42]

By the time Trump took office, the Patriot Act was deeply embedded in the policies that would come to define his presidency at home, and had neither been resolved nor sufficiently countered. The act allowed for expansive authorities against those deemed to be terrorists and it laid the groundwork for the use of the Department of Justice to detain terrorists and immigrants. But powerful as it was, its breadth and scope paled when compared to the Homeland Security Act.

3

Homeland

I think it is a fine opportunity for confusion, for waste, for overlap, for
duplication, and quite frankly, for a splendid amount of delay.

CONGRESSMAN JOHN DINGELL, JULY 17, 2002

PRESIDENT GEORGE W. BUSH had announced the Patriot Act one day
after the passage of the Authorization for the Use of Military Force
(AUMF). One day later, he delivered a speech to a joint session of
Congress and to the nation—his first since the attacks of 9/11.[1] In it, he
christened a seminal term defining the war on terror: "homeland" and
its cousin, "homeland security."

On October 8, the president followed up with an executive order
announcing plans to establish an Office of Homeland Security in the
White House and a Homeland Security Council.[2] The homeland security advisor would take a seat alongside the national security advisor at
the White House. A year later, a full-fledged Department of Homeland
Security (DHS) was created within the executive branch.

While the AUMF provided expansive military authorities, and the
Patriot Act expansive law enforcement and intelligence authorities, now
another bill outlined authorities for a brand-new entity—a department
devoted entirely to domestic security. Riding piggyback on the tried-
and-true success of vague words, imprecise terms, and unrestrained
definitions, the executive was able to move further in the direction of

imprecision, blurring institutional responsibilities, legal authorities, and professional expertise, and finding a secure resting place inside the culture of a newly purposed government.

"Homeland"

Once again, language opened the door to a totally new vista. In 2001, "homeland" was a word with little resonance in American governance, policy, or law. In the late 1990s, the Pentagon had raised the specter of future threats to the "homeland," and included nuclear weapons, terrorism, and information warfare.[3] But as a *New York Times* article pointed out, the term had been virtually nonexistent until 9/11, and when used, it carried with it a disconcerting historical resonance.[4] Even as lawmakers expressed their outrage on the day following the attacks, some were wary of endorsing the word "homeland."

Though it had biblical roots, the term, like Ground Zero, echoed the era of World War II. For many, it conjured up the lethal xenophobia of Nazi Germany. Hitler and Goebbels had unveiled the expression at the infamous Nuremberg Rally announcing the Nazi party, calling for racial purity and the supremacy and exclusiveness of German blood in the homeland. The word quickly became synonymous with the Nazi agenda of ethnic cleansing. Some pointed out these troubling historical overtones as the term gained traction post 9/11. As Peggy Noonan, the conservative columnist and former advisor to President Reagan, put it, the term "grates on a lot of people, understandably. *Homeland* isn't really an American word . . . it has a vaguely Teutonic ring—*ve must help ze Fuehrer protect ze Homeland!*" Noonan considered the word plainly "Nazi-resonating."[5] The political blogger Mickey Kaus, later a Trump supporter, called it "un-American," "creepy," and . . . "uncomfortably Teutonic-sounding."[6]

The discomfort was shared by some in Congress. Senator Russell Feingold remembers the "squeamishness" over the word with its resonance to Adolf Hitler and the Vaterland. In addition to its Nazi overtones, it seemed misplaced given America's character as a land of immigrants. "Homeland is what's over there, where we came from." It was the old country.[7] But the lawmakers equally disliked the alternatives (such as "interior police").

Like Ground Zero and patriot, homeland, once used, was here to stay. And, when it came to the drafting and passage of the act that created the first new department since the establishment of the Department of Defense and the National Security Council in 1947, the AUMF and the Patriot Act seemed like rehearsals in the embrace of vagueness as well as in the reliance on secrecy. In the new department, yet another subtle tool would emerge—bureaucratic porousness. Following from the imprecision of language, with bureaucratic porousness the authorities and boundaries between agencies were merged rather than kept distinct, professional expertise was assigned rather than earned, and overall missions were diverted to new goals that obscured specific departmental responsibilities.

As with the AUMF and the Patriot Act, so for the Department of Homeland Security—the intentional vagueness was codified in institutional confusion at a structural level.

Originally, President Bush had rejected the notion of a separate department. He was content with the reorganization within the White House that had taken place in October 2001, when the Homeland Security Council was created alongside an Office of Homeland Security headed by the former Pennsylvania governor Tom Ridge. Bush felt secure in Ridge's ability to handle the mission of prevention and risk assessment from that perch. But others disagreed, concerned that the White House appointment did not give Ridge the clout he needed to bring together the numerous agencies and interests involved in protecting the homeland. For months, the president batted away the idea of creating a new department, resisting pressure from advisors and Congress alike.[8]

But then the critics' predictions came true. Ridge attempted to create an interagency process for coordinating the various departments, offices, and agencies responsible for cross-border activities. The attacks of 9/11, as the 9/11 Commission Report would later conclude, had resulted in part from a lack of coordination and communication among agencies. Most consequentially, the CIA had failed to inform the FBI of individuals residing in the United States who were suspected of ties to al Qaeda. Ridge's goal, among others, was to enhance interagency coordination by consolidating the Immigration and Naturalization Services, the Customs Service, and the Coast Guard along with some new departments important to the task, such as the Transportation Security Agency that had been created in the immediate aftermath of 9/11. Ridge failed, however, to win approval and buy-in from the individual entities with whom he was trying to coordinate. The failure dampened Bush's resistance to the department.

The Department of Homeland Security

On June 6, 2002, President Bush, addressing his concern for minimizing any vulnerabilities in homeland defense, addressed the nation and announced the creation of a full-fledged Department of Homeland Security, a much-expanded version of the Office of Homeland Security that had been established in the White House eight months earlier. The new department, in essence, would serve as a massive ministry of the interior, attentive to the many issues pertaining to emergency preparedness and response, as well as to border control. The president promised that the new cabinet department would coordinate what he estimated to be "as many as a hundred different government agencies" with "some responsibility for homeland security" and thereby "increase [the government's] focus and effectiveness" when it came to "securing the homeland of America, and protecting the American people." The president pointed to an overriding problem that the creation of the new department would solve, one that could serve as a measure of its success. In the current structure, the president said with clear disapproval, "No one has final accountability."[9]

The president's announcement of a planned new department surprised everyone: the plans for this new agency had germinated in secret. Everyone who attended the meetings in the Presidential Emergency Operations Center where the plans were being drafted—a roster that began with Ridge and three other White House officials and grew to include approximately a dozen members, including Vice President Dick Cheney and his chief of staff, Scooter Libby, presidential advisor Karl

Rove, White House chief of staff Andrew Card, White House counsel Alberto R. Gonzales, national security advisor Condoleezza Rice, and deputy national security advisor Stephen J. Hadley—was sworn to secrecy.[10] Papers were collected after meetings; nothing was left behind. In fact, as a letter from Congressmen Henry Waxman and David Obey written days later said, "the plan was put together with so much secrecy that '[n]o Cabinet secretary was directly consulted about a plan that would strip 170,000 employees and $37 billion in funding from existing departments.'"[11] Essentially, the idea behind the plan was to address the kind of stovepiping among agencies that could lead to a breakdown in adequate security measures. If 9/11 had, among other things, been a problem of interagency cooperation, and if Ridge had failed to effect coordination from his post within the White House, then a megadepartment, hosting a wide range of domestic security activities, was the perceived solution.

The White House proposal, and the draft bill that followed, recommended that one entire agency—the Federal Emergency Management Agency (FEMA)—and twenty-seven departments and offices be moved into a newly created department whose purpose would be to protect the homeland.[12] With a cabinet-level secretary at the helm, the new department would cover four areas of national security: information analysis and infrastructure protection; chemical, biological, radiological, and nuclear countermeasures; border transportation and security; and emergency preparedness and response. The departments from which the offices would be taken were spread across government and included the General Services Administration, the Departments of Justice, Commerce, Energy, Agriculture, Treasury, Transportation, Defense, and Health and Human Services. All told, twenty-two distinct entities would eventually be moved.

Debates in Congress over the proposed bill were heated. As with the AUMF and the Patriot Act, legislators homed in on the dangers inherent in the lack of clarity throughout the bill. Representative Dingell found the president's proposal a "fine opportunity for confusion, for waste, for overlap, for duplication, and quite frankly for a splendid amount of delay." "Being exquisitely precise," Dingell offered, was key to preventing these pitfalls.[13] He predicted "enormous confusion and mess." In their letter to Ridge, Congressmen Waxman and Obey argued against the proposal, envisioning it as "an entirely new bureaucracy" with "more than the number of Deputy, Under, and Assistant Secretaries at the Department of Health and Human Services which administers a budget about ten times the proposed budget of the new Department of Homeland Security." The envisioned DHS, they said frankly, was both unwieldy in size and not viable in practice. They called instead for merely expanding the White House office occupied by Ridge.[14]

There was also confusion over how the new department would interface with others across government. Of particular concern was the inclusion of part of the visa process inside the department; how that would be coordinated with the State Department, which was not slated to have any offices moved under DHS, was left unresolved. The role of the attorney general in coordinating with DHS activities was mentioned one hundred times in substantive ways in the act as it passed, an acknowledgment, among other things, that the new DHS would have the largest number of law enforcement positions of any department in the country.[15]

But despite doubts and protestations, momentum for the vast reorganization won the day. The spirit of vagueness that had characterized the AUMF and the Patriot Act was now poised to spread to an institutional level, and to combine with a bureaucratic imprecision that would impair oversight and defy accountability.

The lack of clarity and the reliance upon secrecy were not the only echoes of the earlier post–9/11 legislative efforts. Despite its tremendous complexity and the number of territorial sensitivities and jurisdictional lines impacted by it, the Homeland Security Act, announced by President Bush in June and considered until August 1 when Congress broke for the summer, passed into law on November 25, after a total of only four months' deliberation.

The reason for the rushed pace was political. In the midterm elections, set for November 5, the Senate faced a fierce contest. The Democrats faced losing their slim majority. While in off-year elections, the party other than that of the incumbent usually wins the most seats, 9/11 had changed the calculus. The passage of the Homeland Security Act was seen as potentially ensuring Republican gains in the Senate. As Senator Feingold explained it, the Republicans' mindset was "Aha! we're going to take this tragedy [of 9/11] and we're going to get our majority back in 2002." And in fact they did.[16] For the first time since the start of the Depression, two years into the presidency of FDR, the president's party held onto its majority in both the House and the Senate.

With the establishment of the Department of Homeland Security in January 2003, imprecision became institutional in scale, with overlapping authorities, unclear responsibilities, confused lines of command, and a mixture of agendas. Its agenda included not just terrorism per se, but other forms of criminal activity as well.

Immigration

In December 2004, two years after the passage of the Homeland Security Act, two think tanks in Washington—the Heritage Foundation and the more centrist Center for Strategic and International Studies (CSIS)—presented the results of their joint task force to address vulnerabilities in the new department: the CSIS/Heritage report "Rethinking the Department of Homeland Security."[17] The report identified the three mission areas of the antiterrorism agency as border security, critical infrastructure, and intelligence analysis, and delved into the bureaucratic structure that had been devised for these missions. The report judged DHS to be rife with fragmentation and confusion. According to the task force, a lack of coordination, overlapping responsibilities, and muddled chains of command had rendered the department inefficient and at times dysfunctional.

Notably, although the report began with a lengthy statement about the purpose of the Homeland Security Act as countering terrorism, one focus that stood out was on the tangle of authorities and strategy at the borders. Border security was a chief vulnerability on 9/11, but in the following decade, southern border security issues tied to potential criminal activity and illegal immigrant status took on increasing focus. And in the area of border and immigration policy, the dysfunctionality of

DHS was unparalleled. Under the auspices of Customs and Border Protection (CBP) and Immigration and Customs Enforcement (ICE), DHS took the mandate premised upon the attacks of 9/11 and, in addition to policies aimed at international entry at the airports and ports, enhanced its southern border policies.

The new DHS created structures that attempted—unsuccessfully—to divide activities and authorities at the border from those inside the country, with CBP and ICE, respectively. The CSIS/Heritage report shed light on the absence of clarity in border and immigration bureaucracy and policy, noting in particular the confused and overlapping responsibilities of ICE and CBP; the indistinct mission of the Transportation Security Administration (TSA); and the mixture of goals when it came to policy implementation. The "split of responsibilities between ICE and CBP" seemed to have been done without a "compelling reason." Also of concern was "the unclear mission of the TSA." Commonly associated with "baggage screeners at airports," the TSA's responsibility for "security in all modes of transportation" had confused things at the border, creating friction with other DHS agencies, notably CBP and the Coast Guard, whose primary focus was the border, for example, when it came to "securing the movement of cargo into the United States." Overall, the report found, "the organization is weighed down with bureaucratic lawyers, is rife with turf warfare, and lacks a structure for strategic thinking and policymaking."[18]

Of particular concern to the task force was the lack of channels for communication between the federal department and local and state entities that would suffer in responding to a terrorist attack, or for that matter, a natural disaster. A DHS inspector general report issued the next year would reiterate the concerns about bureaucratic and "mission confusion" that plagued the agency. The report, conducted to answer the question of whether CBP and ICE should be combined, recommended "merging the two organizations," the CBP and ICE, into one entity.[19]

Even before the CSIS/Heritage report came out, Secretary Ridge resigned following the reelection of President Bush in 2004. In early February 2005, Michael Chertoff left a federal judgeship to replace

Ridge as head of DHS. On September 11, 2001, Chertoff had been serving as a top Department of Justice official in charge of terrorism investigations. He had also coauthored the Bush administration's draft of the Patriot Act. He focused on rethinking and reorganizing the department as his chief mission.

But before Secretary Chertoff was able to make any major changes at the border or elsewhere, the Department of Homeland Security faced its first major test, and failed, exactly along the lines its critics had predicted.

Hurricane Katrina

In August 2005, a category five hurricane hit the southeastern United States. The major levee protecting the city of New Orleans, Louisiana, broke during the storm, and thousands found their houses underwater. While many tried to leave by bus or car, the aging Superdome became a refugee camp for thirty thousand citizens of the city, who huddled together under a leaky ceiling, with little sanitation and a general sense of chaos. The devastation was so great that national security advisor Condoleezza Rice reflected, "It reminded me just a little of the days in the aftermath of 9/11.[20]

As a Government Accountability Office (GAO) report on the Coast Guard's relatively successful activities during Katrina summed up the devastation, "Hurricane Katrina was clearly a catastrophe and arguably the most devastating natural disaster in United States history." The details, according to the report, were these: "More than 1,300 people lost their lives; damage stretched over a 90,000 square mile area; more than a million people were driven from their homes; buildings, bridges, roads, and power and communications infrastructure were destroyed or severely damaged; and millions of gallons of oil were spilled into the environment. We may never fully know the financial cost of Hurricane Katrina, but one projection has put it at more than $200 billion."[21]

In the days and months that followed, experts would try to nail down what had gone wrong. The ultimate conclusion was that the response was as disastrous as the hurricane. The former DHS secretary Tom

Ridge, who had left earlier in the year, called it "a bureaucratic disaster," and "a disastrous instance of turf warfare that resulted in many civilian casualties."[22] His diagnosis had everything to do with the messy structure of DHS. He pointed out that FEMA, the lead government agency for responding to natural disasters, had never quite felt at home inside DHS; the two agencies embodied, in Ridge's words, a "clash of cultures." FEMA head Michael Brown, on whom much of the blame for the casualties and chaos was directed in the immediate aftermath of the disaster, saw DHS as an "impediment to his work." This lack of bureaucratic integration and the confusion to which it led hampered effective communication during Katrina. Brown initially bypassed Secretary Chertoff and DHS and contacted the White House, breaking a chain of command that would have led to a more rapid response from DHS. In addition, Ridge pointed out, the interagency team that had been created in the early days of DHS was not assembled as it should have been in the days leading up to the expected hurricane.

A 2006 inspector general (IG) report on what went wrong with FEMA enumerated a wide range of vulnerabilities. The report noted inadequate planning, insufficient command, and poor communications with the citizens of New Orleans and with higher-ups in Washington. But the confused mission of DHS was also considered a factor. "Finally, the integration of FEMA, all hazards preparedness, and disaster response and recovery capabilities within DHS requires additional attention. After the terrorist attacks of September 11, 2001, DHS' prevention and preparedness for terrorism have overshadowed that for natural hazards, both in perception and in application."[23] The creation of DHS had diminished FEMA's efficiency.

In the more than two-hundred-page report, the DHS IG concurred with the other diagnoses. The Katrina disaster resulted from a confluence of circumstances including neglect, poor preparedness, and inadequate leadership. Secretary Chertoff would later cast much of the blame on city residents and politicians who refused, despite warnings, to reinforce the levee that was needed to protect against a hurricane. But the bottom line was that the confusion of authorities was paramount. Mayor Ray Nagin had refused to let the Coast Guard respond as quickly as it would have liked and FEMA director Michael Brown had failed to deliver food and medical supplies, to deploy rescue teams, and to manage the response in any comprehensive way. Under much criticism, Brown resigned shortly after the disaster.[24]

The DHS IG report issued thirty-eight recommendations intended to prevent a repetition of the government's disastrous response.[25] The forensic debrief read like a reiteration of congressional caveats on the floors of the House and Senate from the days of DHS's creation, now apparent in the wake of Hurricane Katrina. The recommendations from the IG's report were pointed, and spoke directly to the lack of clarity that legislators had warned was baked into the reorganization. More than a quarter of the recommendations addressed the issue of vagueness and imprecision that had undergirded the formation of the department. Specifically, the recommendations begged for more clearly defined roles and responsibilities, lamented the "lack of coordination," and blamed "duplication of efforts" among the various agencies in DHS, most notably, between FEMA and DHS leadership.

The soul-searching that came after the disaster of Katrina led to calls for major proposals for change in regard to FEMA, even for its removal from DHS, a proposal Chertoff rebuffed. In his assessment of the DHS's first five years, Chertoff concluded that "FEMA remains an integral part of the overall mission of DHS and can pursue its own mission far better under the DHS umbrella than alone."[26] Similarly, he rejected the notion of combining ICE and CBP that many had proposed in an effort to ease the confusion of authorities and responsibilities.

Trump

DHS was a troublemaker's dream, a playground for anyone who wanted to confuse authorities, blur legal distinctions, undermine customary procedures, and escape accountability in the morass of shared and indistinct responsibilities. The bureaucratic porousness that the subtle tools of imprecision and secrecy had enabled defined the institution that would become central to the presidency of Donald Trump's subversion of American democracy—the Department of Homeland Security.

Separately and combined, these subtle tools had led to a serious disruption of norms, a disregard for custom and tradition, and a tendency toward exceptions in laws and processes. True, presidents, legislatures, and bureaucracies had succumbed to wrongful tendencies in the past, as in Watergate, Iran–Contra, and Vietnam, but the post–9/11 era ushered in a set of unprecedented institutional changes, each of them crafted with the subtle tools. The AUMF digressed from the norms positing a potential limit to the battlefield and criteria for the end of hostilities. The Patriot Act knowingly pushed aside the norms of law as a restraint on untethered practices by law enforcement. The Department of Homeland Security cast aside the distinctions between agencies that honored clear authorities, a limited scope of activities, and an unambiguous hierarchy. The use of the subtle tools was rarely subject to accountability, making their continued and enhanced use all the more attractive, and leading, as we will see, to further abandonment of norms both trivial and fundamental.

Sensing the power of the tools—imprecision and the degradation of language, the disdain for transparency, and a green light for bureaucratic imprecision and disarray—and their collective ability to strengthen the fourth tool, the disruption of norms, the forty-fifth president gathered them up and wielded them without restraint. In doing so he transformed the presidency, the larger executive branch, and the culture of governance in America. Under Trump, the subtle tools, increasingly used in combination with one another, would become weapons, aimed directly at the heart of American democracy.

4

President Trump and the Subtle Tools

The President is the Executive.

WILLIAM BARR, JANUARY 16, 2019

"FROM THIS DAY FORWARD," the forty-fifth president notified the nation on Inauguration Day, January 20, 2017, "a new vision will govern our land."[1] In his inaugural speech, Donald Trump promised to lift the country out of "American carnage" and to make "America first" again. Trump's presidency did in fact promote a "new vision"—but the tools he employed to realize that vision were not new. As much as his goals and policies would stand in opposition to those of Obama and even of George W. Bush, as much as he would defy tradition in terms of law, policy, and process, the framework for his actions was not novel. Its elements were rooted deep inside the transformations that had been forged by the war on terror and its subtle tools. Trump would exploit the new realities created by these tools, repurposing what had once been exceptions to law and policy in the name of the war on terror for a full-out attack on the institutions of governance inside the country. In addition, Trump instinctively understood that when used in combination, the three tools of imprecise language, bureaucratic porousness, and secrecy constituted and enabled the fourth tool, one that would define Trump's presidency: the disruption of norms.

The continuity in policy from the post–9/11 period to Trump was often obscured by the unusual theatrics of the president and his administration, and the many ways in which he broke the presidential mold. He was not only the oldest person to assume the presidency but also the first to come to office with neither government nor military experience. Trump reveled in this, telling audiences that he would be the one to finally rescue the country from "a small group in our nation's capital" that has "reaped the rewards of government while the people have borne the cost."[2]

Yet in important ways, the differences in policy and leadership were a matter of scale, not of kind. At the outset of his presidency, Trump—often informally—blurred distinctions among the branches of government, trampled existing law, and experimented with the limits of secrecy. And when Attorney General William Barr took office midway through Trump's term, the subtle tools that helped guide the president at the outset were converted into weapons designed to diminish transparency, transgress standing law, and overturn the checks and balances of government in transformative ways.

The Administration

Trump began his presidency by paying overt homage to the war on terror. His first appointments went to military officers who had led American troops in the Iraq War. On Inauguration Day, U.S. Marine general James Mattis was sworn in as secretary of defense, and U.S. Marine general John Kelly as secretary of homeland security. General Mattis had commanded forces in the Persian Gulf, Afghanistan, and Iraq, leading United States Central Command from 2010 to 2013. General Kelly served in Iraq, and then as combatant commander of United States Southern Command, which included oversight of the detention facility at Guantanamo Bay. Trump also appointed Michael Flynn as his national security advisor; Lieutenant General Flynn had served in Iraq and Afghanistan in counterterrorism and counterinsurgency operations for the army, later assuming several top positions in military intelligence, including as deputy director of national intelligence and then as director of the Defense Intelligence Agency for Obama, a post from which he had been pushed out in 2014. Less than a month after his appointment to the Trump administration in January 2017, Flynn was forced out for lying to Vice President Mike Pence about the contents of his phone call with the Russian ambassador to Washington. He was replaced by another high-profile war on terror veteran, General H. R. McMaster, who had served in both Afghanistan and Iraq.

These appointments carried the legacy of the war on terror into many parts of the new government, including foreign affairs, national security, homeland security, and most importantly, in July 2017, the White House, when John Kelly moved from the Department of Homeland Security to become chief of staff to the president. In so doing, he became the first high-ranking military officer to serve as chief of staff to the president in four decades.[3]

Trump's appointments encompassed not just those involved in the military legacy of the war on terror but also those involved in crafting its unsavory and illegal policies. To head the Office of Legal Counsel (OLC) at the Department of Justice (DOJ), Trump chose Stephen Engel, who had served in the office during the Bush administration and had defended detention policies in the war on terror as deputy assistant attorney general. In July 2007, he signed off on an opinion "conclud[ing] that so-called 'enhanced interrogation techniques' were legal under domestic and international law." These techniques included "sleep deprivation for up to 96 hours . . . depriving detainees of the ability to use toilet facilities, and forcing them to wear diapers; and various uses of force." The opinion had determined that "such techniques did not constitute 'cruel, inhuman or degrading treatment,' inflict 'serious mental pain or suffering,' or 'shock the conscience.'"[4]

Engel's January 2017 nomination was met with resistance, including by Senator John McCain, a survivor of torture himself, and Dianne Feinstein, who had overseen the Senate's investigation into the CIA's use of torture. Nevertheless, by the fall, the Senate would confirm Engel's appointment.

In June, Trump nominated another individual tainted by the policy on torture—Steven Bradbury—to be general counsel at the Department of Transportation. Bradbury, acting head of the OLC at the time, had revisited the John Yoo torture memos. In 2002, Yoo had written memos legalizing the use of "enhanced interrogation techniques" during interrogations of war on terror detainees in U.S. custody. Bradbury's predecessor at OLC, Jack Goldsmith, had withdrawn the authority of the memos. In 2005, Bradbury issued several new memos that reconsidered the legality of the techniques. Though arguing on different legal terms and offering some constraints, Bradbury nonetheless still approved of the use of thirteen enhanced interrogation techniques, including waterboarding. As with Engel, Bradbury's nomination was opposed by Senator John McCain and by numerous human rights groups. As Senator Tammy Duckworth, who had served in the Iraq War, said during the confirmation hearing, Bradbury's evident "willingness to aid and abet torture" and to evade the law and the constitution to do so was a nonstarter for her.[5]

This was not the first time Bradbury had stirred opposition; as Senator Duckworth recounted, when Bradbury was nominated to be the OLC's assistant attorney general in 2005, the opposition was so intense that the Senate majority leader Harry Reid had offered to trade approvals for eighty-four pending nominations in exchange for the withdrawal of Bradbury's one nomination. His nomination was put on hold, and he remained in the position as acting assistant attorney general until the end of Bush's term in 2009.[6] Now Bradbury faced confirmation in a new era, under a new president, for a new job. This time, he was confirmed. In 2019, he would become acting deputy secretary of the Transportation Department.

Even more closely involved in the creation and implementation of the torture policy was Gina Haspel, who was named deputy director of the CIA under Mike Pompeo. Haspel had been pivotal in carrying out the torture policies of the Bush administration during the early years of the war on terror. As the Senate Select Intelligence Committee Report would document, Haspel traveled to a CIA black site in Thailand to personally observe the use of "enhanced interrogation techniques" against alleged leaders of al Qaeda.[7] These techniques were intended to destroy the egos and thereby wear down the resistance of the captives through the relentless application of brutality including beatings, waterboarding, and being hung from the walls by their arms. In May 2018, Haspel would rise to the position of CIA director when Trump appointed Pompeo secretary of state in April 2018.

The inclusion of officers from the battlefields of Afghanistan and Iraq as well as those who had been involved with the worst deviations from law during the Bush era provided a bridge from the war on terror period to the Trump era. That many politicians, experts, and policymakers came to consider the Iraq War to be the worst mistake in U.S. history mattered not as became apparent as Trump—who had campaigned on his opposition to the Iraq War and Bush's support for it—rolled out his cabinet. Not only did these first appointments serve as a reminder that there had been no accountability for the lawbreaking, lies, and deviations from traditional moral and legal norms that had defined the war on terror—they also signaled that the incoming administration saw no reason to disavow the policies and departures from law that had come before, choosing to reward rather than penalize many of those who had carried out the war and its policies.

Once the appointments of cabinet members and others who had managed the war on terror era were in place, the Trump administration used them to establish new rules that would later be extended into wholly unrelated areas. The representatives of the war on terror thus provided the gateway for expanding the reach of the subtle tools to include bypassing norms in order to carve out exceptions to the law.

The first cabinet appointment—of General James Mattis to secretary of defense—relied on the imprimatur of the war on terror to garner an exception to the letter of the law. The 1947 National Security Act, which created the Department of Defense (DOD), mandated that the office be occupied by a civilian. The purpose of the provision was to maintain the time-honored principle of civilian control of the military even as the military structure of governance was fundamentally reorganized.[8] In addition to protecting against both military control of the civilian government and what some legislators had worried might be an over-zealous proclivity toward war, the law recognized that the responsibilities of the secretary of defense included oversight of civilian employees, a role for which a sufficient interval of time as a civilian would prove beneficial. The law thus prohibited a recently retired military officer from occupying the post, mandating at least ten years from retirement to appointment. In 2008, the time required after retirement was reduced to seven years as a compromise made to those who wanted to eradicate the requirement entirely, arguing that the absence of a draft had fundamentally changed the civilian-military relationship and that such a gap between the two spheres was no longer necessary.

It was only the second time that a waiver had been requested. The first time had been nearly seventy years earlier and it had been granted in a manner that expressly sought to limit further exceptions to the rule. President Truman had appointed George Marshall, chief of staff of the army during World War II, to the position of secretary of defense. Both houses of Congress were required to agree to the waiver and both had granted Truman's request for one, but in so doing had put in place extremely strong warnings against any repetition of the exception. The Marshall waiver included a passage declaring that the waiver "not be construed as approval . . . of continuing appointment of military men to the office of Secretary of Defense in the future," adding for emphasis that "after General Marshall leaves the office . . . no additional appointments of military men to that office shall be approved."[9]

General Mattis, however, had been retired for less than four years; his appointment would require a waiver from Congress. Some who opposed granting the waiver did so not in opposition to Mattis per se but in an effort to keep law and policy from being disrupted by presidential say-so; further friction came from the transition team's refusal to let Mattis testify before the House Armed Services Committee in advance of the vote, seemingly based on little but a desire to show disrespect for Congress. Many, even those who voted against him, saw Mattis as a possible agent of restraint for a president they worried might make rash decisions when it came to the use of the military. As Senator Richard Blumenthal of Connecticut mused, "Your appreciation for the costs of war in blood, treasure and lives and the impact on veterans afterwards will enable you to have a check on rash and potentially ill-considered use of military force."[10] Nonetheless, Blumenthal and fellow Connecticut Democratic senator Chris Murphy, along with several others, voted against the waiver. Ultimately, though, it passed, with a 268–151 vote in the House and an 81–17 vote in the Senate.

The Trump exception ignored the admonition that had accompanied Marshall's appointment, and instead included merely a watered-down version of that warning. "This section applies only to the first person appointed as Secretary of Defense . . . and to no other person." Unlike the language accompanying Marshall's waiver, the wording in Mattis's waiver did not name Mattis directly, nor did it tie the exception to Mattis exclusively, thus leaving open the possibility of its use for another nominee if the request for Mattis failed to go through.[11] (With the door opened in this way, Biden would nominate General Lloyd Austin for secretary of defense. Austin had been retired for only four years, instead of the seven years required by law, but he too would receive the waiver from Congress and be confirmed in the post of secretary of defense— thus institutionalizing an exception and jettisoning a fundamental norm that was tied to the post.)

The Mattis waiver was significant not only because it broke with norms but also because it did so by relying upon the reputation of a war on terror commander whose service led to the vote in his favor. And as it turned out, Trump would use this success as a first step in violating norms more broadly. With Mattis's exception achieved, Trump proceeded to ask for further exceptions to the appointments process.

For starters, the president wanted to appoint his son-in-law Jared Kushner as a senior White House advisor. As with the Mattis appointment, the appointment of Kushner was forbidden by law, namely, the 1967 Anti-Nepotism Statute. Since the country's founding, presidents had been known to appoint family members to positions in their administrations—but in 1967 the practice was made illegal. The law (nicknamed the Bobby Kennedy law due to his appointment as attorney general during his brother John F. Kennedy's administration) stated that a public official may not "appoint, employ, promote, advance, or advocate" the appointment to "an agency in which he is serving or over which he is in control . . . any individual who is a relative of the public official."[12] Fueled by animosity between President Lyndon Johnson and Robert Kennedy, its passage resulted from serious concerns over the financial or political advantages that could be realized from such positions, or the dangers of inexperience. The law had blocked appointments even into the Obama administration, preventing Obama's half-sister from joining the White House Fellowship Commission and his brother-in-law from a commission on physical fitness.[13]

The Mattis appointment, reliant on the war on terror, was a first step in legitimizing departures from norms that for decades had informed and regulated the process of filling important executive branch positions. As subsequent norm-flouting by the Trump administration would show, the use of war on terror symbolism as a means to achieving exceptions outside of that war would become a pattern of the Trump years. In the case of the Kushner appointment, yet another legacy of the war on terror came to the aid of Trump's attempt to bypass the law—namely, the Department of Justice's Office of Legal Counsel.

The OLC inside the DOJ is charged, as the law professor and former OLC lawyer Annie Owens explains, with "providing legal advice to the President and executive branch agencies."[14] The OLC has the authority to issue decisions on the law, but as the war on terror played out, it had become more of a rubber stamp for what the president wanted than an issuer of opinions independent of those political objectives. The OLC has served repeatedly as a vehicle for the subtle tool of secrecy, issuing secret memos during the Bush presidency that authorized indefinite detention at Guantanamo and championed enhanced presidential powers in the name of national security. Most notably, the Office of Legal Counsel had redefined torture as legal, giving it a new name ("enhanced interrogation techniques") but approving with graphic descriptions the sanctioned techniques for hitting detainees, putting them in stress positions, and waterboarding (renamed "water dousing" by Bradbury).

Obama too relied on the OLC in his case to claim executive privilege in response to the congressional investigation over "Fast and Furious," a DOJ operation that allowed illegal gun sales as part of an attempt to identify Mexican drug cartels. Obama also used OLC memos to justify—in part via opinions not publicly released at the time—his drone program generally as well as its decision to target an American citizen in Yemen.

Building on that legacy, the OLC dutifully came in on Trump's behalf, extending an exception to standing practice for Kushner as it had for Mattis via a January 20, 2017, memo nullifying the anti-nepotism ban.[15] The memo reasoned that the Office of the President was not an executive agency, and therefore, despite the history of compliance with the ban on family members from positions controlled by the president, the prohibition did not apply in the case of President Trump. The president, the memo stated, had "*total discretion in the employment*, removal, and compensation... *of all employees in the White House Office.*"

It was a brazen act, reversing decisions made over the course of four prior presidencies, and thus echoed not just the Mattis exception to the Anti-Nepotism Statute but also the transformative use of the OLC in the war on terror to enhance the powers of the presidency.

From this moment forward, the OLC became an essential element in Trump's determination to use the subtle tools in newly powerful ways. Trump's OLC issued opinions on secrecy, opining as Owens explains, that "executive branch agencies are not legally obligated to provide information in response to requests from ranking members of congressional committees."[16] While Bush's OLC had assumed secrecy in matters related to national security and laid the groundwork for its authority in determining the contours of law, Trump's OLC essentially claimed even more defiantly its own—and the executive branch's—authority over that of Congress. In addition to promoting secrecy, this stance thus further obscured the bureaucratic roles and governmental responsibilities of the executive and legislative branches of government, disrupting the traditional processes that promoted the separation and balance of power within the federal government.

Trump not only leveraged the OLC to escape legal restrictions on the appointment-making process but also undermined the procedures

attached to appointments. By law, certain appointments in an administration require Senate confirmation. But Trump repeatedly avoided
presenting candidates for Senate confirmation by making acting appointments, or delaying in appointments overall, thereby evading the
vetting process and, moreover, making subsequent changes in appointments easier. The Trump administration further side-stepped filling
positions requiring Senate confirmation by, as NPR reported, leaving
"key jobs vacant at a given agency, while delegating the authority of
those positions down to subordinates who do not need to be confirmed
or even nominated for the job."[17] At the beginning of 2020, which would
be Trump's last year in office, 24 percent of key positions requiring
Senate confirmation had no nominee in place.[18]

The habit of relying on acting appointees extended beyond positions
requiring Senate confirmation, highlighting yet another dimension of
Trump's strategy in appointments—a disregard for independent professional judgment and a determination to surround himself with loyalists.
According to a Brookings Institution report, the administration over the
course of its four years would experience turnover in 91 percent of the
positions held by senior-level advisors, those below the level of cabinet
officer. Of fifty-nine positions, 39 percent had seen more than one change
of appointment during those four years. This "record-setting" pattern of
musical chairs encouraged a bureaucratic incoherence that would become a signature trait of Trump's administration—which as we shall see,
became apparent through a wide range of domestic and international
policy directives.[19] Trump was straightforward about the appeal of the
strategy, admitting on CBS's *Face the Nation*, "It gives me more flexibility."[20] But for Trump, flexibility would often mean abandoning long-held
norms—as with his stunning decision to remove the head of the FBI,
one of the most well-protected positions in government.

Firing Comey

The position of FBI director comes with a ten-year term limit, put in
place after the death of J. Edgar Hoover who held the position for forty-
eight years. Hoover had exercised his role as the commander of a

personal fiefdom, immune from interference; during his reign over the bureau, he used the powers of law enforcement to persecute political enemies, from those he deemed to be communists to Black activists and those who opposed the Vietnam War. A decade-long appointment, the reasoning held, would limit the time any individual director could hold the office and accumulate the powers Hoover had, but it would also minimize political interference by outlasting the allowable two terms of any presidency.[21]

Insulating the director from the changes in administration promoted the independence of the FBI from the White House and had evolved into a long-standing and fiercely protected norm. The expectation over-all is that the Department of Justice should remain free of politics.[22]

The DOJ's independence had been tested during the Watergate scan-dal of the Nixon years. Nixon's White House had attempted to interfere with law enforcement's investigation of an attempt by Nixon's reelection committee to break into Democratic National Headquarters. On Satur-day, October 20, 1973, Nixon ordered Attorney General Elliot Richard-son to fire the special prosecutor who had been appointed to investigate the matter, but Richardson refused, and resigned his position, and the deputy attorney general resigned as well, rather than comply with the order. Finally, the solicitor general, Robert Bork, complied—but a re-placement special prosecutor ruled that the dismissal had been illegal. As the plans for the burglary and the cover-up came to light, Nixon, facing impeachment charges, was forced to resign, and many of his sub-ordinates were convicted and sentenced to prison.

The Saturday Night Massacre, as it was called, set an explicit norm for future attorneys general. As the law professor and OLC alumnus Jack Goldsmith writes, "every presidency since Watergate has embraced policies for preserving DOJ and FBI independence from the President in certain law enforcement and intelligence matters."[23] As the Brennan Center for Justice has pointed out, under Presidents Ford and Carter, "the White House, Justice Department, and others adopted formal and informal practices that aimed to ensure arm's-length dealings—in pub-lic and in private—between senior political officials and career law en-forcement personnel."[24]

Still, the value placed on independence, as many scholars have pointed out, has come less from the law than from norms. As Goldsmith put it, "the most important guarantees of DOJ/FBI [independence] come not from the Constitution or statutes, but from norms and practices that since Watergate have emerged within the Executive branch."[25] Career civil servants and department officials alike have set a tone in which the conventions of independence have taken precedence.

Only once since the Watergate scandal had a president fired the bureau's director. In July 1993, Bill Clinton had dismissed William Sessions, who had been accused of mishandling government funds. But when it came to the next FBI director, Louis Freeh, who conducted investigations into matters personal to Clinton, the latter had refrained from interfering. For years, Freeh and Clinton remained at loggerheads as Freeh pursued investigations into Clinton's personal life, including the Whitewater scandal over Bill and Hillary Clinton's business dealings, and Clinton's affairs with Gennifer Flowers and Monica Lewinsky. But still, Clinton did not fire Freeh. While no law explicitly prevented him from doing so, there were strong norms—and the memory of the fallout of the Saturday Night Massacre—to dissuade him.

In 2013, Barack Obama appointed James Comey to the position of FBI director. Comey had served in the administration of George W. Bush as the deputy attorney general for John Ashcroft and had earned a reputation for standing up for principle. In one famous instance in March 2004, Comey had intervened in a dramatic hospital scene while Ashcroft was sick with pancreatitis and recovering from surgery for gall bladder removal. As Barton Gellman reported, White House counsel Alberto Gonzales was trying to get Ashcroft, who was full of painkillers, to sign a renewal for a warrantless eavesdropping program that the Department of Justice had warned exceeded lawful authorities. Comey, who was acting attorney general during Ashcroft's illness, prevailed, preventing Gonzales from getting Ashcroft's signature.[26]

Yet a decade later, while serving as FBI director, Comey's judgment would be roundly questioned over a decision he made at a critical point during the 2016 presidential election campaign between Hillary Clinton and Donald Trump. In violation of a Department of Justice policy prohibiting employees from interfering with elections—or even giving the appearance of doing so—Comey took it upon himself two weeks before election day to send a letter to Congress informing them of his intent to reopen an investigation into the emails of Democratic candidate Clinton. Many believed that Clinton's chances in the election were greatly harmed by Comey's letter. As a 2018 inspector general (IG) report on FBI activities in advance of the election would conclude, in "depart[ing] from policy/practice," Comey "made a serious error of judgment."[27]

When Trump was elected, Comey faced another test of political independence as he prepared to serve under a president who seemed to value loyalty above all. On January 6, 2017, in a private briefing for the president elect at Trump Tower in New York City, Comey had perhaps inadvertently signaled a willingness to breach the divide between the FBI and the White House when he informed Trump that some "salacious and unverified" material had come up in the bureau's investigation into Russian efforts to interfere with the 2016 election and potential collusion toward that end with the Trump campaign.[28] In part, Comey informed the Senate Select Committee on Intelligence in June 2017 in a hearing on possible Russian interference in the 2016 election, he had conveyed the information to the president in order to "blunt" any effort "to compromise an incoming President." At the Trump Tower meeting, Comey assured the president-elect that "we were not investigating him personally."[29]

A week after the inauguration, President Trump invited Comey to dinner at the White House, again for a private conversation, during which he expressed his expectation that Comey would serve as his ally in the investigation. Comey attempted to disabuse the president of the idea that the Department of Justice would be a willing ally in the president's endeavors, and declared that he was "not on anybody's side politically and could not be counted on in the traditional political sense." The president stated bluntly, "I need loyalty, I expect loyalty."[30]

Comey remembered trying to explain that any such bureaucratic porousness was ill-advised. In his prepared statement for the June 2017 Senate hearing he recounted his exchange with the president about "why it was so important that the FBI and the Department of Justice be independent of the White House"—namely, to maintain "public trust in institutions and their work," a trust that "blurring those boundaries" could harm. According to Comey, Trump had ignored Comey's caveats about compromising institutional integrity and independence. Trump had gone so far as to ask Comey if he would drop the investigation into the former National Security Agency (NSA) director, Michael Flynn, who had lied to Vice President Mike Pence about his contacts with Russians during the transition period. "I hope you can see your way clear to letting this go," Trump told Comey.[31]

In March 2017, the president made it clear yet again that he would not honor the institutional boundary Comey had tried to set. He called the FBI director to complain about the "cloud" hanging over him in the Russia investigation, hoping Comey could provide some relief. Comey was not the only one he went to with this request; the president also continually asked his attorney general Jeff Sessions, his campaign manager Corey Lewandowski, and his White House counsel Don McGahn to intervene in the bureau's investigation. Sessions had recused himself from overseeing the Russia investigation and the potential involvement of the Trump campaign, stating, "I should not be involved in investigating a campaign I had a role in," as the grounds for his refusal.[32] Repeatedly, Trump asked Sessions to "un-recuse" himself, trampling the principled divide each time.

On May 9, Trump fired Comey. He alleged that Comey "wasn't doing a good job" and attributed his decision in particular to Comey's handling of Hillary Clinton's use of a private email server. Trump said he had done so upon the "clear recommendations" of Jeff Sessions and the deputy attorney general Rod Rosenstein—an assertion that was later declared inaccurate by the acting FBI director, Andrew McCabe. Once again, Trump had bypassed the procedural safeguards for making decisions of consequence. Days later, in an interview with NBC's Lester Holt, Trump admitted that "this Russia thing" had been on his mind at the time he made the decision.[33]

With the firing of Comey, and Trump's impatience with the notion of the Department of Justice as an independent entity, the president further signaled a willingness to defy norms when it came to respecting the boundaries between the Department of Justice and the White House. Meanwhile, as he cast about for allies in his overt departures from law and policy, Trump looked to another of the subtle tools—secrecy—to help him along the way.

Secrecy

The war on terror had broken new ground in terms of secrecy. Not only had the Department of Justice lawyers penned memos legalizing torture, but top officials at the CIA had secretly implemented a torture program and then gotten rid of the evidence, destroying videotapes of the interrogation sessions in which the so-called enhanced interrogation techniques were used. Similarly, Stellar Wind, the warrantless surveillance program secretly put in place after 9/11 and authorized by the OLC, had given law enforcement unprecedented access to the communications of potentially all Americans.

President Obama had come into office expressing his intention to reverse the secrecy that had defined the war on terror and that had taken it down unprincipled and unlawful roads. On his first day as president, he had issued a Presidential Memorandum titled, "Transparency and Open Government." "My administration is committed," the order read, "to creating an unprecedented level of openness in Government." He pledged to "disclose information rapidly in forms that the public can readily find and use."[34] It was an honorable intention, but one that ultimately fell short of what he had promised, and was at times contradicted by his administration's actions.[35] When it came to counterterrorism, for example, Obama approached the question of whether or not to declassify "documents related to the CIA's Bush-era waterboarding and rendition programs"—that is, in response to Freedom of Information Act (FOIA) requests—by splitting the difference. As he explained in his 2020 memoir, *A Promised Land*, "Yes to legal memos justifying such practices, since both the memos and the programs themselves were already widely known; no to photos of the practices themselves, which the Pentagon and State Department feared might trigger international outrage and put our troops or diplomats in greater danger." Obama balanced the public's need for information with the fear of providing it to terrorists, recalling that his "legal teams and national security staff wrestled daily" with "how to meet our obligations for transparency without tipping off *New York Times*–reading terrorists."[36]

Obama classified fewer documents than had any president in recent history, and vastly below the huge numbers racked up by George W. Bush. He curtailed the use of signing statements, and made Freedom of Information Act requests for OLC memos more readily available.[37] In December 2009, he issued an executive order on "Classified National Security Information," intended to promote transparency by tightening the parameters for classifying documents and expanding those for declassification.[38] Toward that end, Obama created a National Declassification Center, housed at the National Archives.

But despite his efforts on behalf of transparency, Obama nonetheless often availed himself of the subtle tool of secrecy—particularly when it came to the war on terror. At the end of 2014, Dianne Feinstein, the chair of the Senate Select Committee on Intelligence, released the findings of a six-year investigation that delved deeply into the details of the CIA's enhanced interrogation program, which had been set up in the years after the 9/11 attacks to interrogate "high-value detainees" using a series of techniques amounting to torture but determined to be legal by the Department of Justice's Office of Legal Counsel. While Feinstein was "pleased" to release the 525-page executive summary, the CIA—which had interfered directly with the report by infiltrating the Senate committee's computers—opposed any release of the full 6,700-page report. Obama supported the decision to keep the full report from public view at the time of its release. In 2009, even before he took the inaugural oath, Obama had told ABC's George Stephanopoulos that he had "a belief that we need to look forward as opposed to looking backwards." "Part of my job," he explained, "is to make sure that for example at the CIA, you've got extraordinarily talented people who are working very hard to keep Americans safe. I don't want them to suddenly feel like they've got to spend all their time looking over their shoulders and lawyering."[39] In this way, secrecy not only amplified the abandonment of norms regarding the use of torture but also signaled that such misconduct would, in remaining secret, go unpunished.

Once the leadership of the Senate flipped in 2015, the new chair of the Senate Select Committee on Intelligence, Richard Burr, sought to further barricade information about the sins of torture. Burr recalled the copies of the report, with the intention of destroying them and preventing any future release. Obama countered by adding the report to his presidential records. While this would prevent its complete erasure, it would also keep it restricted and classified for at least another twelve years—nearly three decades after the events themselves had occurred.[40]

When Trump took office, the culture of secrecy premised upon the threats posed by the war on terror had been curtailed but not entirely reversed. Obama had made some significant steps forward when it came to transparency. As Jameel Jaffer, founding director of the Knight First Amendment Institute, summed it up, President Obama deserved "credit for releasing White House visitor logs, for reversing Attorney General John Ashcroft's presumption against disclosure, for reforming the Justice Department's rules relating to media subpoenas, and for releasing the Justice Department memos authorizing torture."[41] Another example came from Steven Aftergood, director of the Federation of American Scientists Project on Government Secrecy, who pointed out that the Obama administration declassified information on the size of the U.S. nuclear weapons arsenal "for the first time ever," and likewise was "the first ever to publish the amount of the intelligence budget request for the following year." In line with this commitment to transparency, Obama "achieved the lowest number of 'original classification decisions' (or newly-generated secrets) that had ever been reported by the Information Security Oversight Office," a number that continued to drop during his last years in office.[42]

Nonetheless, when it came to certain matters—such as the refusal to release the full report on torture compiled by the Senate Select Committee on Intelligence—the Obama administration, as Jaffer has pointed out, "was more notable for the extraordinary lengths it went to control disclosures and manage public opinion about its decisions and polices."

Jaffer was referring in part to the withholding of OLC memos surrounding the targeted killing program in the Middle East and beyond, as well as to the prosecution of "more whistleblowers and leakers than all previous administrations combined."[43]

Before leaving office, as if acknowledging his failure to create "an unprecedented level of openness," Obama took further action.[44] In June 2016 he signed the FOIA Improvement Act, which aimed to create rules to enforce the "presumption of disclosure" in responding to Freedom of Information Act requests.[45] Over his eight years in office, his administration granted a higher percentage of FOIA requests than Bush had over several areas—but when it came to FOIA requests concerning the OLC, denials occurred at a slightly higher rate than during Bush's presidency. FOIA requests for Immigration and Customs Enforcement (ICE) documents were also frequently subject to exemptions, with denials in this space jumping to 43 percent in 2013, well over twice Bush's rate of denial at its highest point.[46]

In other words, while Obama had made some headway in improving transparency, he did not dismantle the architecture of secrecy, leaving mechanisms for secrecy in place and available for exploitation by a president not as committed to open government. Trump reached for the subtle tool of secrecy in its many forms, brandishing it publicly against a wide array of perceived threats.

From the earliest days of his presidency, Trump made clear his interest in reversing direction from the intentions Obama had expressed. He preferred to withhold information as a matter of course, and sometimes to prevent a record from even being created. Once again, the Mattis confirmation proved a harbinger of things to come when, during the waiver hearings, the Trump transition team had refused to let the four-star general appear, as scheduled, to answer questions before the House Armed Services Committee. This would become a frequent tactic in its defiant noncompliance with ordinary process or the provision of information.[47]

Withholding information became a pattern that persisted with increasing frequency, intensity, and success throughout Trump's term in office, particularly when it came to congressional access to executive department information. While the Bush administration had written secret memos justifying torture and warrantless mass surveillance in defiance of domestic and international law, had classified documents with alacrity, and had shielded information that would likely have mandated investigations of officials, Trump introduced an even wider array of strategies intended to keep information under wraps, including withholding documents and testimony, abrogating reporting requirements, and even forbidding the creation of the documentary record. John Bolton revealed an instance of this in his 2020 memoir, in the context of a private meeting between the Russian president Vladimir Putin and Trump that took place during Bolton's term as national security advisor.[48] The discussion ranged, apparently, from Syria to the issue of election meddling—but since Trump ordered his interpreter not to take any notes during the meeting, she had to debrief officials from memory after the fact. Similarly, Trump was known to berate high officials such as national security advisor H. R. McMaster and White House counsel Don McGahn for taking notes.[49] Furthermore, he repeatedly blocked officials from testifying on a wide variety of issues, including nuclear safety inspections, planned missile defense tests, and climate change.[50]

The administration's insistence on withholding information also took the form of preventing access to documents. For example, when Trump's second nominee to the Supreme Court, Brett Kavanaugh, faced his Senate confirmation hearing in September 2018, the White House refused to provide the documents the Senate had requested from Kavanaugh's years working in the George H. W. Bush White House. As the journalist David Rohde reported, "the White House refused access to more than a hundred thousand pages" from Kavanaugh's time in the Bush administration. "Blank sheets of paper arrived on Capitol Hill stamped 'Constitutional privilege,' a category that members of Congress said they had never heard of before."[51]

Similarly, reporting requirements built into congressional oversight functions were repeatedly ignored or curtailed. The administration blocked DOD reporting on defense spending and nuclear weapons facilities inspections, and the Pentagon stopped publishing its yearly report on the effectiveness of each of its weapons systems, a reporting routine that it had followed since 1980.[52] When the COVID crisis hit, the administration's default move was to keep the alarming information secret, in line with its pattern of hiding information. The pattern was set early and grew in size and scope throughout Trump's term in office.

The subtle tools—secrecy, imprecise language, bureaucratic porousness, and the disruption of norms—were constant features during the first two years of the Trump presidency. But when William Barr came to the administration in 2019, they took on new life.

Throughout the war on terror, the subtle tools had strengthened the powers of the presidency and the executive branch, eroded the separation of powers between branches of government, and shielded people from accountability even when they broke the law. Barr took this strategy to greater levels in his two years as President Trump's attorney general. For Barr, of particular interest was the bureaucratic porousness that Comey had rejected in the form of the blurred boundary between the White House and the DOJ. Barr saw this not as an impediment or danger; instead, he saw degrading the distinctiveness of bureaucratic authorities as a useful tool for a theory of governance that had motivated him throughout his career.

Barr's DOJ

William Barr, who had worked as an intelligence analyst at the CIA while attending George Washington University Law School, had later served in the Department of Justice, first as the head of the Office of Legal Counsel in 1989 and then, from 1990 to 1992, as attorney general for George H. W. Bush. One lesson he took away from his time as attorney general, he would later recall, was that the Department of Justice should be subservient to the White House. "I have come to feel," Barr told interviewers for an oral history project nearly two decades before joining the Trump administration, "that political supervision of the Department is very important. . . . Someone ultimately has to answer to the political process."[53] According to Barr, the attorney general needed to answer that call. "I felt while I was there the utmost deference to the

[Justice] Department as the enforcer of the laws and the developer of policy. I thought that was good."[54]

After leaving the George H. W. Bush administration, Barr served as general counsel of the telecommunications company GTE and of its successor after a merger, Verizon, until 2008, after which he worked in private practice. From the sidelines, Barr watched as Special Prosecutor Robert Mueller investigated Russian meddling in the 2016 election. As part of the investigation, Mueller looked into potential collusion between Trump associates and Russia. Angered at the investigation, President Trump's firing of FBI director Jim Comey in May 2017 led to a focus on possible obstruction of justice by the president. By June 2018, Mueller had indicted dozens of Trump associates while continuing his investigation into possible obstruction, even considering interviewing the president. Remaining true to his beliefs about the intersection between politics and the Department of Justice, Barr decided to provide some unsolicited guidance. In a June 8, 2018, letter to the deputy attorney general and the head of the Office of Legal Counsel Steven Engel, Barr offered the Trump administration advice about how to protect the president from the Mueller investigation. In his nineteen-page letter, which Barr distributed broadly to lawyers and others attached to the White House, he weighed in specifically on his belief in the sweepingly expansive authorities of the president and his conviction that there need be no daylight between the White House and the Department of Justice. "Mueller should not be permitted to demand that the president submit to interrogation about alleged obstruction," he wrote. If allowed, the interrogation "would do lasting damage to the Presidency and to the administration of law within the Executive branch"—in other words, within the Department of Justice. As Barr went on to explain, Mueller's theory of obstruction "would have potentially disastrous implications, not just for the Presidency, but for the Executive branch as a whole and for the Department [of Justice] in particular."[55]

Barr's interpretative principle for this assertion stemmed from the unitary executive theory of government that had motivated the architects of the war on terror. In his acceptance of broad presidential authority, the Barr letter echoed the memos John Yoo had written from 2001 to 2003 to justify severe departures from existing law, including indefinite detention, torture, and the president's limitless power to prosecute the war on terror, and in so doing push aside constitutional protections and international covenants. Like Yoo, Barr saw the president as having largely untethered powers. Yoo had reasoned repeatedly that in the context of war, the president as commander in chief had "the fullest range of power . . . belonging to the military commander" and therefore "complete discretion" in exercising that power."[56] Yet while Yoo had focused on powers conveyed by wartime circumstances and in relation to the international context, Barr now claimed those powers as pertaining to presidential activity at home.

According to Barr, the president had the power to make final decisions across the executive branch, including for the Department of Justice. "[The President] alone *is* the Executive branch. As such, he is the sole repository of *all Executive powers* conferred by the Constitution. Thus, the full measure of law enforcement authority is placed in the President's hands, and no limit is placed on the kinds of cases subject to his control and supervision." Barr also made it clear that "the Constitution vests *all Federal law enforcement power*, and hence prosecutorial discretion, in the President." For these reasons, the president had the absolute authority to—for instance—fire Comey. Emphasizing the finality of the president's decision-making power, Barr considered "the President's discretion in these areas" to be "absolute" and his decisions "non-reviewable."[57]

Mueller's investigation, he warned, would have "grave consequences" for the functioning of the government. If allowed to continue, it would "do lasting damage to the Presidency" and not just for the presidency "but for the Executive branch as a whole and for the Department in particular." Barr's letter was a final realization of the claim to presidential power that had come of age in the war on terror, with the underlying rationale based not on external threats but on the theory that a functional government required the granting of vast powers to the president. Barr's theory thus veered far afield of the holding that a balance of powers among the independent branches of the government was the healthiest, and most constitutionally validated, form of American democracy.

In the eyes of many, the Barr letter was a job application for attorney general.[58] The audition was successful. In February 2019, he was confirmed to the position—ready, in the words of the *New Yorker* writer David Rohde, to become Trump's "Sword and Shield."[59]

Barr immediately championed a tight-knit relationship between the Department of Justice and the White House. Whereas Congress and post-Nixon administrations had for decades been careful to acknowledge the separation of law enforcement from politics, Barr saw the department's role as not to restrain but to enable presidential powers. A month after he was sworn in as attorney general, ahead of the public release of Mueller's findings, Barr issued another impactful missive—this one a misleading four-page summary of Mueller's report that was intended to get out in front of the headlines and preempt Mueller. Barr wrote that the special counsel "did not draw a conclusion—one way or the other—as to whether the examined conduct constituted obstruction." Barr twisted this to conclude that the report had revealed "no actions" of "obstructive conduct," and no signs of "corrupt intent," and thus confirmed that there was insufficient evidence to prove obstruction."[60]

Mueller had reached no such conclusion, and had in fact suggested the opposite. "While this report does not conclude that the President committed a crime, it also does not exonerate him," Mueller wrote. Mueller suggested instead that Congress could proceed with its own investigation, as it was not similarly restricted. "The conclusion that Congress may apply the obstruction laws to the president's corrupt exercise of the powers of office," Mueller wrote, "accords with our constitutional system of checks and balances and the principle that no person is above the law."[61]

Rather than base his decision not to indict Trump on findings of innocence, Mueller referred to standing policy inside the DOJ. The restraints he referred to came neither from Congress nor from judicial rulings but from recommendations made in memos that had been issued by lawyers at the Office of Legal Counsel. In 1973 and again in 2000, memos had argued against the indictment of a sitting president on the grounds that "the indictment and criminal prosecution of a sitting President would unduly interfere with the ability of the executive branch to perform its constitutionally assigned duties, and would thus violate the constitutional separation of powers." Mueller deferred to this prevailing opinion, which he took as a hard and fast rule, and in so doing, tossed the ball from the Department of Justice to Congress.[62]

Stepping into the confusion that Mueller had wrought, Barr saw the chance to further obfuscate the report's conclusion. It was, he claimed, not Congress but the DOJ that would and should decide if and how to proceed in the wake of Mueller's report. "The Special Counsel's decision to describe the facts of his obstruction investigation without reaching any legal conclusions leaves it to the Attorney General to determine whether the conduct described in the report constitutes a crime."[63] It was up to Barr, in other words, to make the final assessment as to whether or not there was wrongdoing.

Barr was not just bypassing a norm that dictated distance between politics and the White House—he was resetting it. In hijacking the Mueller investigation, Barr adopted a tone of defiance and interference that would last through the remaining two years of the Trump presidency. He, perhaps more than anyone else in the administration, fortified the image of the president as all-powerful and tore away at the separation of powers theory of government in favor of the unitary executive.

Despite Barr's assertion, Congress considered taking steps toward impeachment, with House Judiciary Committee chairman Jerrold Nadler aiming to pick up where the Mueller investigation had left off. Nadler focused on the allegations around the administration's obstruction of justice regarding the investigation. In response, the administration took the pattern of withholding information from Congress to a new level of defiance.

For instance, as part of the inquiry, Nadler issued a subpoena for former White House counsel Don McGahn, who had been interviewed for thirty hours in the Mueller investigation. Yet White House counsel Pat Cipollone forbade McGahn's testimony, claiming executive privilege, insisting that "the records remain subject to the control of the White House for all purposes" and "legally protected from disclosure under long-standing constitutional principles."[64] Cipollone cited a secret OLC memo, dated May 20, 2019, which focused on McGahn and insisted that White House appointees were "absolutely immune" from having to give the testimony on the grounds that preparing to testify would impede the functioning of the White House.[65] Bureaucratic functioning now replaced national security in the context of the war on terror as a reason for deviations from existing law and policy. "The President cannot allow your constitutionally illegitimate proceedings to distract him and those in the Executive Branch from their work on behalf of the American people," Cipollone wrote, adding: "The President has a country to lead."[66] Nadler, refusing to take "No" for an answer, filed a motion in the DC circuit court. It would be November before a judge would rule in the case. Meanwhile, others, including several officials at the Department of Justice, former national security advisor John Bolton, and former deputy national security advisor Charles Kupperman refused to testify as well.

Despite Nadler's efforts to build a case of impeachment against the president, Speaker of the House Nancy Pelosi resisted the idea, concerned with political fallout for the Democrats and possible distraction from other legislative issues. A new allegation—and one that further illuminated the tight relationship between the White House and Barr's DOJ—changed her mind.

On August 12, a whistleblower complaint was sent to Michael Atkinson, the inspector general of the Intelligence Community. The complaint expressed "urgent concern"—the baseline standard for a whistleblower complaint—regarding "information from multiple U.S. Government officials" that the president of the United States had offered a "quid pro quo" deal to the Ukrainian president Volodymyr Zelensky. The complaint alleged that Trump threatened to withhold congressionally approved military aid to Ukraine in exchange for compromising information on Joe Biden and his son Hunter that could be used in the upcoming election campaign. The complaint further alleged that "Attorney General Barr appears to be involved as well."[67] In September, the whistleblower made his concerns public in a letter written to Senator Richard Burr and Congressman Adam Schiff.

With the whistleblower's allegations in hand, Congress looked to obtain evidence, again issuing subpoenas for top White House officials and others. But the OLC once more stepped in to shield members of the executive branch from testifying. In yet another secret memo, dated September 3, 2019, OLC head Steven Engel argued that the rules established for whistleblowing did not pertain to the complaint about the president's conversation with Ukrainian president Zelensky.[68]

According to the 1998 Intelligence Community Whistleblower Protection Act, only complaints of "urgent concern" are supposed to be sent to Congress. Engel argued that the contents of the phone call did not qualify as rising to the level of an "urgent concern" because, he reasoned, "the alleged conduct"—the conversation—"was not about 'the funding, administration, or operation of an intelligence activity under the authority of the Director of National Intelligence,'" but rather "arises out of a confidential diplomatic communication between the President and a foreign leader." Engel argued by extension that the conversation did not directly involve the intelligence community and therefore was not subject to a whistleblower complaint from someone in the intelligence community.[69]

But even as Engel's memo set out to nullify the contents of the whistleblower's letter, the contents had become public knowledge by early fall. Trump's predilection for secrecy seemed to have encountered an obstacle, made possible by the adherence to oversight norms. In September, Congress was sent a copy of the whistleblower's complaint, and the White House released a summary version of the phone call transcript. On December 4, impeachment hearings began in the House of Representatives, with Congressman Adam Schiff heading the inquiry. Schiff issued letters and subpoenas to former and current administration officials in the White House and across the executive agencies, seeking testimony about the Ukraine deal. Once again, many refused to testify. However, seventeen former and current officials testified either behind closed doors or in public, or both. And on December 13, the House voted to approve the two articles of impeachment.

On January 15, 2020, the articles were sent to the Senate for trial; on February 5, the Senate voted to acquit the president. During it all, Barr, who had been named in the whistleblower complaint, stayed relatively quiet.

Throughout the period of the impeachment hearings, legislators and the public debated the issue that had been hovering over all three branches of government with particular urgency since 9/11; namely, how far could the president take an insistence on secrecy? During the Bush administration, the tragedy of 9/11 and the fears of another attack had enabled habits of secrecy to thrive inside the executive, mostly untested by the courts and Congress. In the Obama years, the edges of that policy were questioned and, once the policies of executive overreach had been exposed, were at times curtailed (as in the case of the Patriot Act's surveillance provisions).

Trump stumbled in his expectations of secrecy, but he did not fall. Ultimately, full transparency failed. The top officials in the cabinet who were called to testify at the House impeachment hearings refused to do so. Among them were Trump's personal lawyer Rudy Giuliani, Vice President Pence, Secretary of State Mike Pompeo, acting White House chief of staff Mick Mulvaney, and former national security advisor John Bolton. The White House strongly supported the obstructionist stance and succeeded in stonewalling Congress and keeping information from coming to light. Trump remained in office. Barr remained attorney general and Steven Engel remained head of OLC.

Meanwhile, Nadler's attempts to insist on transparency in the courts also ultimately proved unsuccessful. In November 2019, the DC district court had rejected the administration's claim to "absolute immunity" and compelled McGahn to testify. On appeal, the case lingered for yet a second year and in August 2020, an appeals court ruled against Congress's power to enforce the subpoena, claiming that Congress did not have the authority to ask the court for a subpoena against an executive official. The decision, as reporters Josh Gerstein and Kyle Cheney wrote, "gutted the House's historically broad subpoena power."[70] In October 2020, with weeks to go before the election, the full DC circuit decided to rehear the case, setting the hearing for February 23, 2021, several months after the presidential election.[71]

The Trump administration had essentially won the battle, not only with McGahn but also over calls for transparency—aided at every step of the way by the Department of Justice, led by Attorney General William Barr. With the testimony of McGahn and the other administration officials put on hold, the mantle of secrecy and the close relationship between the president and the Department of Justice stood poised to remain in place even beyond Trump's last days in office.

Silencing the Inspectors General

As a part of its defiance of the rules against excessive secrecy, following Trump's first impeachment, his administration decided to make some structural changes, and once again to elide the borders between agencies and responsibilities. In addition to blocking witness testimony, withholding documents, and forbidding the creation of a written record, the Trump administration attempted to interfere with the formal mechanism governing executive branch transparency and accountability— namely, the appointment of the inspectors general who could file whistleblower complaints. Combining the expansive view of secrecy with the erosion of the DOJ's independence from the White House, Trump and his legal team went to work to silence yet another source of disclosure.

In 1978, Congress had passed the Inspector General Act in an effort to expand oversight of the executive branch. Beginning with twelve inspectors general housed inside the Department of Justice, it had grown by Trump's time in office to over seventy officials, the more senior of them appointed by the president and others appointed by agency heads. As the overseers of government accountability, they are tasked with reporting fraud, abuse, illegality, and other violations in the departments they each oversee. Their removal from office is rare. Obama replaced one, the inspector general for National and Community Service, an independent agency of the government. George Bush did not remove any, not even Department of Justice inspector general Glenn Fine whose report forced the resignation of one of Bush's closest allies in government, Alberto Gonzales, in the wake of allegations that Gonzales had mishandled classified information related to the NSA's war on terror wiretapping program.[72]

In the course of six weeks from April to May 2020, Trump dismissed five inspectors general from their responsibilities as internal watchdogs for agencies across the executive branch, including for the intelligence community, transportation, defense, health and human services, and the state department.[73] Absent the IGs, the conduct of those departments—and in particular the waste and mismanagement that IGs were appointed to prevent—could more easily proceed without discovery or correction.

Among the casualties of Trump's IG firings was the intelligence community inspector general, Michael Atkinson, to whom the whistleblower complaint had been sent and who was fired for calling attention to it. Barr went on Fox News and heatedly defended the president's firing of Atkinson. He "did the right thing," Barr stated.[74]

The removal of inspectors general sent a message to IGs generally that exposing incriminating information could be cause for dismissal; furthermore, in compromising the oversight mechanism of the executive, it was essentially a means of making secrecy the new norm. For a few months, the five IG positions remained vacant. In the fall, on the eve of the election, the president finally nominated inspectors general for the Department of Transportation and the Intelligence Community, but neither was confirmed before the presidential election. Meanwhile, no new names were submitted for replacement IGs for Health and Human Services, State, or Defense.[75] As with the prevention of the McGahn testimony, the IG contest successfully shut off the public's access to information for the remainder of the Trump presidency.

The removal of IGs further shrouded the activities of the executive in secrecy. In so doing, it spoke directly to the early aims of the subtle tools as employed in the war on terror—an enhancement of the powers of the president, an erosion of the separation of powers principle, and an escape from accountability for those who did the president's bidding. As John Yoo had dutifully justified whatever it was the White House wanted to do in the name of keeping the country safe, now Steven Engel pledged to protect the president and those in the executive branch from any scrutiny from Congress or the courts. Under Trump, the absence of accountability that had marked the war on terror in the name of national security was now claimed government-wide. As Obama had said in the presidential memorandum issued at the outset of his presidency, "Transparency promotes accountability."[76] Its absence, the general embrace of secrecy exemplified by the IG firings suggested, was preferable to his successor.

Taking cues from his predecessors, Trump had used the tools of the war on terror for his own purposes, increasingly detached from the context of the war on terror. With these tools at his disposal, and surrounded by individuals who knew how to use them and who understood what powers they commanded, especially when used in combination, Trump applied them to the major policy decisions of his presidency—beginning with matters of immigration.[77]

5

The Muslim Ban

To accept it here is to accept that the President can take an iron
wrecking ball to the [immigration] statute. . . . That can't be the law of
the United States.

NEAL KATYAL, APRIL 25, 2018

ANNOUNCING HIS CANDIDACY at Trump Tower in June 2015 Trump
took the opportunity to invoke fears of "Islamic terrorism." "How are
they going to beat ISIS?" he asked about his fellow candidates. "I don't
think it's gonna happen." As he got into matters of policy, Trump complained that "Islamic terrorism is eating up the Middle East." That day,
he couched the threat in business terms. "They've become rich, I'm in
competition with them."

As his candidacy progressed, he turned his attention away from business concerns and the Middle East region to the threat Islamic terrorism
posed to the safety and security of Americans. Trump insisted repeatedly and explicitly that Muslims constituted a dangerous enemy. He
told audiences around the country: "You have people coming out of
Mosques with hatred and death in their eyes." "We are at war with radical Islam." "Islam hates us." If made president, he promised to counter
the enemy with full force. He envisioned a "total and complete shutdown of Muslims entering the United States," saying he would suspend
immigration from "places like Syria and Libya." He pledged further to

create an "ideological certification to make sure that those we are admitting to our country share our values and love our people."[1]

Islamophobia had raged in the days and years following 9/11; fanning the flames of the fear of Muslims was one of Trump's first acts as president. As he had used the war on terror generally to initiate deviations from policies across the executive branch, so now he would first use the war on terror to create a framework for reducing immigration to the country and then apply it to immigration policy writ large.

The Muslim Ban

On January 27, 2017, the White House issued Executive Order 13769, "Protecting the Nation from Foreign Terrorist Entry into the United States."[2] Embracing the tone of the war on terror, the executive order (EO) signaled that foreign terrorism remained a significant threat to the nation. It brought to a complete halt entry from seven countries—Iraq, Iran, Syria, Sudan, Somalia, Libya, and Yemen, all predominantly Muslim—and suspended immigration entirely from the named countries for 90 days while a review of the policies for those countries was pending. It also banned all refugees from the listed countries for 120 days and from Syria indefinitely. The travel ban was immediately labeled the "Muslim ban," a term initially bestowed on the policy by Trump himself.

Referencing the September 11 attacks several times, the executive order cast blame on Trump's Republican predecessors for their "failure" to prevent 9/11. "State Department policy," the EO argued, had failed to keep the 9/11 hijackers from entering the country. It had "prevented consular officers from properly scrutinizing the visa applications of several of the 19 foreign nationals who went on to murder nearly 3,000 Americans." The country "had continued to suffer," the order declared, as policy failed "to stop attacks by foreign nationals who were admitted to the United States." The executive order was set to ensure that this would not happen again.

Trump's ban intended to enhance the subtle tools that had underlain Bush's approach, beginning with imprecision in language as a means of creating policies applied broadly and arbitrarily. The ban was aimed at entire countries, rather than at individuals or groups. It thus followed a pattern that had characterized earlier counterterrorism efforts—even those efforts that were condemned for violating the First Amendment, the Fourth Amendment, and the due process rights of affected targets of the policy. For instance, the New York Police Department (NYPD), which had conducted surveillance of Muslims at the community level, had settled a suit with New Jersey Muslims for choosing targets based on race and religion, rather than individual suspicion of guilt. The NYPD pledged to reform its activities in light of the suit.

Trump, unconcerned with the track record of prior policies that embraced quantity and breadth over quality and precision, took the strategy into immigration policy with aggressive conviction. Though unprecedented in its breadth, Trump's travel ban was built on the foundation of post–9/11 fears as a basis for remedies applied over a vast policy, political, and legal landscape.

His travel ban was not the first attempt to wed the strategy of breadth to immigration policy. A year after 9/11, Attorney General John Ashcroft had implemented the National Security Entry-Exit Registration System (NSEERS). Broad to the point of indiscriminate, the program tracked "virtually all of the 35 million foreign visitors who come to the United States annually."[3] Ashcroft's goal was to share the collected data with law enforcement agencies nationwide. "We will place their photographs, fingerprints, and information in the National Crime Information Center (or NCIC) system" and make it available to "the nation's 650,000 police" who "check this system regularly in the course of traffic stops and routine encounters."

The scope of NSEERS constituted a stark departure from Fourth Amendment protections against warrantless search and surveillance, and revealed just how willing law enforcement officials, legislators, and the public at large were to abandon constitutional principles when it came to Muslims and suspected terrorists in the aftermath of the September 11 attacks. Designed to track national security risks, the program ultimately collected information not just on those suspected of criminal and terrorist activity, but on mere visa violators as well. It was another threshold moment, an example of bait and switch, erasing the distinction between criminal and civil violations, expanding the application of law enforcement and criminal investigations in the name of national security, and ushering in a tactic that would later find a home in immigration policies more widely—including at the southern border.

Obama brought NSEERS to a halt in 2011—but largely because his advisors deemed the program "obsolete," not because it was unlawful or unconstitutional, despite its vast breadth and scope. According to one Department of Homeland Security (DHS) official, NSEERS "no longer provided an increase in security in light of DHS's evolving assessment of the threat posed to the United States by international terrorism."[4] The Obama team relied on other, more advanced data tools for collecting, analyzing, and sharing information, emphasizing precision and individualized screening. In 2015, Obama signed the Visa Waiver Program Improvement and Terrorist Travel Prevention Act, which put additional restrictions on visa applications from individuals from countries deemed to pose a "terrorist threat" to the United States.[5] Iran, Iraq, Sudan, and Syria were listed initially. Yemen, Somalia, and Libya were added. The idea was to exercise more attention in scrutinizing individuals seeking visas to ensure that they did not have terrorist pasts. Worried that Trump might try to revive NSEERS and its expansive reach, Obama formally ended the program in 2016.[6]

The limits Obama tried to impose turned out to be in no way binding upon Trump. Straightaway, Trump exceeded even the staggeringly vast scope of the NSEERS registration system, rejecting the Obama policy of more careful, individual vetting of individuals and replacing it with a broader ban.

Immediately, the scope of the "Muslim ban" led to chaos and confusion, in part because the White House failed to follow the normal processes for vetting and planning for the executive order. DHS, the main agency responsible for implementing the order, was "barely consulted," according to Peter Bergen, who has written extensively about the early years of the Trump presidency. "Even John Kelly," secretary of homeland security at the beginning of the presidency, "had almost no time to review it," Bergen notes. Other top national security officials were also excluded from the decision-making process, including those at the Department of Justice (DOJ). The president signed the executive order before the planned White House conference call with officials to discuss it. Secretary Mattis, General Joseph Dunford, chair of the Joint Chiefs of Staff, and the yet to be confirmed secretary of state Rex Tillerson, all professed to be blindsided by the substance of the order. Congress was not consulted either. "GOP lawmakers said their offices had no hand in drafting the order and no briefings from the White House on how it would work," Bergen recounts.[7]

In bypassing the norms of decision making, the administration failed to give the Transportation Security Administration (TSA), airport employees, border security guards, and others charged with implementing these policies time to prepare for the changes. At airports and other entry points, TSA officials and border security guards had no plans for dealing with those who were caught in transit as the executive order came down. Half a million passengers were suddenly affected by the decree—including students, green card and visa holders, and children with noncitizen parents.[8] Abroad, U.S. representatives scurried to make sense of the new policy.

The executive order was premised on the assumption that Islamist terrorism still posed an existential threat to the homeland. In fact, there had been no deadly terrorist attacks by foreign organizations within the United States since 9/11, and the number of terrorism-related Department of Justice investigations and prosecutions in the United States in 2016 suggested that the lure of Islamic terrorist groups in the homeland was at its lowest since 9/11. Without the usual vetting and decision-making process, facts that would have contradicted the viability and need for the policy likely went unspoken. And so, with no basis in reality, the executive order stoked the fears of another terrorist attack and revived the fears based on religion and ethnicity.

Given its broad scope, its defiance of legal norms, and the chaos its hasty announcement caused, the travel ban instantly triggered legal challenges. Public opposition to the ban, led largely by the American Civil Liberties Union (ACLU), swelled immediately as thousands

gathered at airports to protest the policy in the wake of the ban's announcement. Lawyers gathered at airports to intervene between passengers and authorities, offering help to people whose status had been
changed midair and were now landing in a country that had banned
them. Advocacy groups began filing lawsuits to try to prevent instant
deportations. By nightfall on the day following the ban, federal judges
in New York and Virginia had issued rulings blocking the ban. Washington, Hawaii, Maryland, California, and Oregon followed with their
own suits.

Lawsuits

Lawyers specifically challenged the use of the subtle tools, focusing in
their arguments on the imprecision of the ban and the vast application
this imprecision had unleashed, as well as its bypassing normal channels
of executive decision making, and its disruption of a number of state
and local interests and functions. By March 30, 2017, an amicus brief
filed by attorneys general in sixteen states set out the legal bases for the
challenges.[9] The state attorneys general contested the ban on the
grounds of its overly broad discrimination as well as its unlawful interference in state affairs. They argued that the ban would cause harm to
universities, public health staffing, and state economies due to the loss
of taxes. Outside of courtrooms, national security officials and the Iraqi
government assailed the ban's inclusion of Iraq—a country in which the
United States had supposedly been helping build democracy at the cost
of much blood and treasure for fourteen years.

Influenced by these and other objections, the administration issued
a revised executive order on March 6. The new version removed Iraq
from the list of banned countries and exempted certain visa and green
card holders from the ban. Nonetheless, the suits and protests continued while for the most part, despite a few lower court interventions, the
ban would stay in effect as the cases made their way through the appeals
process. In September 2017, the administration produced yet another
version of the ban, a proclamation, whose authority did not differ essentially from that of an executive order. The new proclamation actually

expanded the number of targeted countries, banned travel to the United States for most nationals from seven countries, including six Muslim countries—Chad, Iran, Libya, Somalia, Syria, and Yemen—as well as from North Korea and imposing new restrictions on immigration from Venezuela and Iraq.[10] The proclamation did provide some carve-outs, laying out the possibility of case-by-case waivers for students, families of lawful permanent residents, those in need of medical care, U.S. government employees, and those traveling for work related to international organizations.[11] But the embrace of breadth over precision persisted.

Each iteration of the ban had led to several lawsuits filed on behalf of those who sought entry to the country. Immediately, suits claiming the orders were unlawful began to be filed against the first and second versions in New York, Virginia, Hawaii, Maryland, and in Seattle, Washington, and included requests for halting the ban. Several judges honored these requests, including with a decision in the Eastern District of Virginia where, in mid-February, Judge Leonie Brinkema banned the order for violating the U.S. Constitution's First Amendment Establishment Clause prohibiting discrimination. When the third proclamation was issued, suits were again filed in Maryland and Hawaii, reiterating the request for an injunction on the policy, despite its amendments.

Faced with these continued legal actions, the government was moved to violate long-standing restraints on interfering with lower court decisions. The DOJ rapidly countered the injunctions that had been issued in the lower courts, at times not waiting for them to go through the normal judicial process, and asked the Supreme Court to remove injunctions against the travel ban. The Supreme Court, while it allowed the ban to hold in some instances, proved sympathetic to the government's requests. As national security law expert Stephen Vladeck has pointed out, the court issued a record-breaking number of stays over the travel ban litigation, ordering six stays at the request of the Department of Justice. Compared to those requested during the Bush and Obama years, it was an exceptional number. According to Vladeck, over the course of George Bush's eight years in office, five such stays had been issued in total. Obama's DOJ sought three stays in its eight years in office. Trump's DOJ requests for six stays in the matter of the travel ban were among a remarkable total of twenty-one stays in Trump's first thirty-two months in office.[12]

The violation of norms was apparent not just in the number of stays requested for the travel ban but also in the impatience of the Department of Justice when it came to the third version of the travel ban, the proclamation. In that case, Solicitor General Noel Francisco did not even wait for a circuit court's decision, the customary process for cases that reach the high court. Instead, as soon as the district court issued the injunction in an attempt to halt the ban nationwide, Francisco went straight to the Supreme Court where he was granted the stay he sought. As the case reached the date of Supreme Court argument, the ban held in place.

More than a year after the issuance of the first travel ban, the Supreme Court listened to the arguments in the case of *Trump v. Hawaii*, which brought to the fore the subtle tool of imprecision and overbreadth and its close-knit relationship to racism.

Trump v. Hawaii

Standing before the Supreme Court justices in April 2018, Neal Katyal argued against the ban. The forty-eight-year-old Katyal was an experienced litigator, having argued before the court more than thirty times, both as deputy solicitor general and acting solicitor general for Obama, and as a lawyer representing parties against the government. Among other cases, he had argued against the Bush administration in the high-profile war on terror case *Hamdan v. Rumsfeld*,[13] a successful challenge to the Guantanamo military commissions. And when he was deputy solicitor general under Obama, Solicitor General Elena Kagan had argued another war on terror case—*Holder v. Humanitarian Law Project* (*HLP*). The case had put the subtle tool of imprecision and its consequences under direct legal scrutiny.

Holder v. HLP exemplified the Supreme Court's tolerance for breadth when it came to cases involving terrorism. The plaintiff, Humanitarian Law Project, a U.S.-based human rights organization, had brought suit to challenge the vagueness and breadth of the laws pertaining to terrorism prosecutions. In particular, lawyers were challenging the Patriot Act's addition of "expert advice and assistance" to the definition of the crime of material support to terrorists, alongside financing terrorism, procuring weapons, providing personnel, and strategizing to commit acts of terror. Termed the "Material Support Statute" (later amended as part of the Intelligence Reform and Terrorism Prevention Act of 2004 [IRTPA]), it was the statute used most commonly to prosecute terrorism suspects in federal court. HLP lawyers argued that the statute was "unconstitutionally vague" and violated First Amendment civil liberties' protections of freedom of speech.

The case revolved around whether or not HLP could lawfully offer advice and assistance to two designated terrorist groups: the Kurdistan Workers' Party and the Liberation Tigers of Tamil Eelam. HLP acknowledged that it was providing services and training to the groups but contended that those activities did not support terrorism but, on the contrary, provided "training in the use of humanitarian and international law for the peaceful resolution of disputes" thereby "*reducing* resort to violence." HLP lawyers contended that the broad applications of antiterrorism law resulted in the "blanket criminalization of pure political speech that seeks to further only lawful, nonviolent activities."[14]

In 2010, Solicitor General Elena Kagan had argued the case for the government. Congress, she wrote, considered the provision of personnel, training, and other services to have "harmful consequences for American interests," and blamed the plaintiffs for "second-guess[ing] that judgment," adding that "this Court should not." Voicing an argument that had colored terrorism-related litigation since 9/11, the government explained that "because this case involves sensitive national security and foreign affairs interests," a "heightened degree of deference to Congress and the Executive Branch is warranted."[15]

The Supreme Court, in a unanimous decision written by Chief Justice John Roberts, accepted the government's argument. In so doing, it supported an expanded definition of the use of material support, essentially holding that, by definition, any services provided to terrorist groups constituted support for terrorism and should therefore be prohibited. Relying on comments expressed in congressional debate and on State

Department affidavits, the court agreed with the DOJ that the intent of the law and the reality of the security risks mandated acceptance of the State Department assertion that "all contributions to foreign terrorist organizations further their terrorism." Roberts wrote, therefore, that "to serve the Government's interest in preventing terrorism, it was necessary to prohibit providing material support in the form of training, expert advice, personnel, and services to foreign terrorist groups, even if the supporters meant to promote only the groups' nonviolent ends."[16]

In addition to accepting the expansive application of the law, the court underscored the need to give deference to Congress and the executive when it came to national security in conjunction with foreign policy. Explaining their belief that "national security and foreign policy concerns arise in connection with efforts to confront evolving threats in an area where information can be difficult to obtain and the impact of certain conduct difficult to assess," the court said it could not judge assertions about threats to national security, and so left these judgments to the executive.[17]

The HLP decision, issued midway through Obama's first term in office, was a crushing defeat for those who had hoped that the injustices of the post–9/11 years, meted out in the name of national security, would retreat under Obama. On the contrary, the case reinforced the subtle tool of imprecision and allowed its broad applications of policy and law, setting a foundation for the Muslim ban case that would be argued eight years later.

In 2018, Katyal, arguing *Trump v. Hawaii* before the Supreme Court, attempted to convince the court to reverse the stance it had taken in *Holder v. HLP*.[18] In the intervening years, fears of terrorism had grown to include the threat of ISIS (the Islamic State of Iraq and Syria), at first in Iraq and then throughout Arab and Muslim countries. Like *Holder v. HLP*, the Muslim ban case pitted heightened national security concerns against constitutional rights advocates. Arguing against the ban, which had taken the imprecision and breadth of *Holder v. HLP* to unprecedented levels, Katyal rebuked the administration on three points in particular. He contended first, that the ban was in its imprecision and scope "broad and sweeping"; second, that the president had assumed powers that negated the will of Congress, which was authorized by the Immigration and Naturalization Act to set immigration policy; and third, that the ban constituted a form of religious discrimination.

Katyal rose to the occasion to reset the parameters in the court's handling of national security. He first challenged the legitimacy of such a wide, imprecise, and indiscriminate ban, referencing the long history of wartime restrictions on immigration that had previously allowed for case-by-case considerations of groups and individuals suspected of posing a threat. The wide scope of a "flat nationality ban," Katyal argued, abrogated existing norms. There were "fine-grained reticulated" vetting procedures already in place that were precise and fact-based rather than broad and unspecific, Katyal told the court, and thus precluded the need for the ban.[19] Katyal further contended that the ban violated the First Amendment's Establishment Clause, which protected the freedom to exercise one's religion. Essential to the plaintiff's argument was the suggestion that the anti-Muslim policies and attitudes that Trump had relied upon throughout the campaign shone through the ban itself. The Islamophobic legacy of the war on terror was now being weaponized in a new way.

At the Supreme Court argument, Solicitor General Noel Francisco rebutted Katyal's claims by reverting to war on terror language, laws, and justifications. Francisco insisted that the countries in question provided insufficient information and that security demanded the blanket ban. He made no statement about any new policies or breaches in the informational flow, but, following the application of vastness rather than precision, defended the total ban as necessary given an overall distrust of information as reliable.

Katyal's second issue was also central to the liberty versus security debate in the war on terror and one that had found support in the court's *Holder v. HLP* decision—namely, the persistent deference to the president on the matter of the ban, which Katyal argued violated the intent of the law and undermined the separation of powers principle of government, in particular the powers granted Congress under Article I of the Constitution. The Supreme Court argument in the Muslim ban case revolved in part around two sections of Title 8 of the U.S. Code, which codifies federal immigration law: Section 1152, which forbids discrimination in the issuance of visas, and Section 1182, which defines "aliens who are inadmissable." (Both had first been enacted in 1952, and amended numerous times, notably in 1965 and in the case of Section 1182, in the Patriot Act of 2001.)[20] Katyal urged the court to remember that "Congress is in the driver's seat when it comes to immigration, and that this executive order transgresses the limits that every President has done with this proclamation power since 1918." While deference to the president on national security matters had defined the war on terror policies, the sweeping and unilateral nature of the travel ban had empowered the president to misappropriate the law, and in essence "take an iron wrecking ball to the statute and pick and choose things that he doesn't want for purposes of our immigration code."

The government's argument insisted that the deference due to the president after 9/11 was still due to the president now, and the law allowed for that. After all, Francisco told the court, it was up to the executive to determine the "whole vetting system." He elaborated, "It's up to the executive branch to set it up. It's up to the executive branch to maintain it. It's up to the executive branch to constantly improve it."

On the third point of argument, the allegations of religious discrimination, Francisco considered it best to stay away from debate. Rather than deny or even discuss Trump's statements of bias against Muslims, which were made in public and frequently, Francisco merely claimed that Trump's statements about Muslims on the campaign trail were those of a private citizen and thus were irrelevant to the discussion at hand. Anything said before taking the oath of office was not applicable to the case at hand, the solicitor general asserted.

The upshot of all three points of discussion was to debate the legitimacy of presidential power given the national security threats allegedly posed to the country by Muslims. A reiteration of the debates that had populated the national security sphere since 9/11, it was a stark reminder that the legal and policy tensions of the war on terror persisted into the Trump era, and were brought into the open by the Muslim ban.

In support of the plaintiffs, an amicus brief shed additional light on the ways in which the government's arguments defending the Muslim ban relied essentially upon the subtle tools. Submitted by Harold Koh, the State Department legal advisor during the Obama presidency, and signed by fifty-one former national security officials and Senator Richard Lugar, who had served as chairman of the Senate Foreign Relations Committee under Bush and as ranking member under Obama, the brief argued that the interruption of procedural norms had led to the unlawful policy. Had the executive orders gone through the proper governmental processes and been properly vetted, the amicus brief argued, they would have taken a different, less expansive form. None of the three versions of the Muslim ban, the authors argued, "emerge from meaningful Executive Branch judgment and deliberation." Rather, as the changes made in the revised versions of the ban revealed, "the Executive's national security and foreign policy experts played no role at all" in the drafting of the bans. The amicus brief saw this "overbroad suspension of travel," and the avoidance of norms, as posing a national security risk. In sum, the ban "not only failed to advance our national security or foreign policy interests, but is seriously damaging those interests."[21] The bypassing of procedural norms had been the gateway to the expansive imprecision of the ban, a combination of the subtle tools that would come to define the Trump immigration policy going forward.

The Opinion

The majority of the justices were not convinced by Katyal's arguments. In a 5–4 decision, issued in June 2018, Chief Justice John Roberts, joined by Justices Alito, Thomas, Kennedy, and Gorsuch, ruled that the proclamation constituted a lawful exercise of the president's statutory authority and did not violate the Establishment Clause. Their reasoning had everything to do with the subtle tools. Focusing on the language of the proclamation, rather than on its application, the court found the ban was not overly broad. Writing for the majority, Roberts did not agree with the argument that the ban was overly broad, repeatedly referencing the *Holder v. Humanitarian Law Project* decision that he himself had written eight years earlier.[22]

Roberts based the court's acceptance of the expansive policy, and its rejection of the policy as discriminatory, on the very premise that so much war on terror legislation had aimed at—namely, enhanced presidential powers in the name of national security. Now that power was extended clearly to the immigration realm in a way that gave untethered power to the president. "The President has lawfully exercised the broad discretion granted to him under §1182(f) to suspend the entry of aliens into the United States," he wrote. Further, the court held that the ban was not discriminatory, stating that "common sense and historical practice confirm as much," and noting that the law in question "has never been treated as a constraint on the criteria for admissibility in §1182. . . . The Proclamation is expressly premised on legitimate purposes: preventing entry of nationals who cannot be adequately vetted and inducing other nations to improve their practices. The text says nothing about religion."

Roberts dismissed Katyal's reminder that Congress had a constitutional role in this matter. The Immigration and Naturalization Act, Roberts wrote, "exudes deference to the President in every clause" and grants "the President broad discretion to suspend the entry of aliens into the United States."

Roberts explicitly connected the subtle tool of imprecision to the expansiveness of presidential powers, and to the fact that the court did not have the expertise to counter the judgments of the president on such a substantial matter. Court deference to national security interests as expressed in *Holder v. HLP* was to be expected. "Plaintiffs and the dissent . . . suggest that the policy is overbroad and does little to serve national security interests. But we cannot substitute our own assessment for the Executive's predictive judgments on such matters, all of which are 'delicate, complex and involve large elements of prophecy.'" The courts simply were not equipped to challenge the president on national security matters. Citing the *Holder v. HLP* decision, as he would do throughout his opinion, Roberts concluded that "when it comes to collecting evidence and drawing inferences on questions of national security, 'the lack of competence on the part of the courts is marked.'"

The forever war that had been launched by the passage of the 2001 Authorization for the Use of Military Force had cast a long shadow. If congressional authority and judicial process were meant to constitute a check on presidential powers that overstepped constitutional and statutory provisions, Roberts was acknowledging that when it came to the war on terror, that check did not exist. Even in 2018, with a president who was claiming victory against ISIS and continued to express his intention to wind down the deployment of troops in Syria, Afghanistan, and Iraq, the court refused to counter arguments made on the basis of national security claims. Roberts's opinion made it clear that the imprint of the war on terror had embedded itself deeply, if not irrevocably, on the nation, on the principle of checks and balances, and on the ultimate authority of the president over not only Congress but the court itself.[23]

The court's further legitimization of broad and unspecific applications of the law set in place two premises that would have an impact on presidential actions during Trump's time in office. First, it signaled a green light when it came to presidential decisions about the war on terror abroad. As we shall see, the president would invoke his commander-in-chief Article II powers in the decision to kill the Iranian general Qasem Soleimani in 2020. And more immediately, it propelled forward a conversation about expansive executive authorities in the domestic area. As the Muslim ban case involved immigration law and policy, arguing that security was a valid basis for exclusion on a grand scale, so the Trump administration from its earliest days had been assuming that posture in its southern border policies.

In the Muslim ban decision, the Supreme Court injected new power into the tools forged during the war on terror, bringing them into the present as well as closer to the domestic sphere. The "wrecking ball" image that Katyal had invoked to describe Trump's vast claims to authority and his disregard for standing law and policy was playing out even as the case made its way through the courts. The ground was now set for the executive branch to exclude immigrants from the country in virulent and unprecedented ways. The national security claims that had characterized twenty-first-century executive power in matters abroad would now come home to roost.

6

Crisis at the Border

There are only two end games: You either lock them up or you shoot them, one or the other. Basically, it's either a Justice end game, or it's a national security end game.

WILLIAM BARR, APRIL 5, 2001

"FOR TOO LONG YOUR AGENTS haven't been allowed to properly do their jobs," the just inaugurated president told a room full of Department of Homeland Security (DHS) employees gathered together to welcome their president and their new secretary. "But that's all about to change."[1]

With these remarks, Trump launched an era of restrictive immigration that used the subtle tools to ratchet up detentions, deportations, and prosecutions of undocumented immigrants and those with immigration violations. Imprecision in language gave way early in his administration to a staggeringly broad application of removal efforts. The violations of norms and the neglect of law led to policies of immense cruelty, while bureaucratic meddling gave expanded powers to officials who substituted their own rules for those codified by law.

Going forward, Trump promised the assembled agents, the law enforcement capacities of DHS would be expanded. But he was not talking about the terrorist threat that the Department of Homeland Security was created to counter. Nor was he talking about cyber threats or the other five areas of concern outlined by the outgoing Homeland Security secretary in his exit memo, prepared as part of the Obama team's efforts to aid the incoming administration's transition.[2] He was talking about law enforcement at the southern border.

Heartened by Trump's campaign promises to get more aggressive at the border, the union of Immigration and Customs Enforcement (ICE) employees had endorsed his candidacy—the first such endorsement since the creation of DHS in 2003. The Customs and Border Protection (CBP) union had endorsed Trump as well. He's finally "taking the hand-cuffs off," said Thomas Homan, an Obama-era immigration official. Homan would be Trump's initial choice as acting director of ICE, a position which would see a series of appointees during Trump's term, all serving as acting directors. Homan's "handcuffs" comment referenced what he considered to be the lax immigration enforcement of the Obama administration. "ICE is open for business," he remarked.[3] Anticipating what it would mean for business, private contractors for immigration detention facilities had donated $500,000 for the inauguration.

"We are in the middle of a crisis at the southern border," the new president said. To address this, he promised to hire thousands more officers, to end programs and policies that enabled immigrants to stay beyond their visas, and to demand retribution for families who suffered from the criminal acts of those who entered the United States across the southern border.

As Trump spoke, John Kelly—confirmed and sworn in earlier that day as the new DHS secretary—stood by his side. Kelly applauded as Trump outlined the task that lay ahead for the department. He shared the concern about the dangers posed by those coming across the border with Mexico, and he was determined to ratchet up law enforcement efforts as a countermeasure. "The American people voted in this election to stop terrorism, take back sovereignty at our borders," Kelly said during the confirmation process. He put the southern border at the top of his list of concerns. "In my view," Kelly wrote in response to questions posed by the Senate Committee on Homeland Security and Governmental Affairs, "the number one threat to the nation is that we do not have control of our borders."[4]

As with the Muslim ban, discrimination based on race, ethnicity, and nationality marked the southern border agenda. On the campaign trail, Trump had frequently disparaged those who crossed the border into the United States. "When Mexico sends its people, they're not sending their best," he said in the speech announcing his candidacy. "They're sending people that have lots of problems, and they're bringing those problems with us [*sic*]. They're bringing drugs. They're bringing crime. They're rapists." Almost as an afterthought: "And some, I assume, are good people."[5] He was not only concerned about crime, but also feared, "They're killing us economically." During his DHS speech on the day of Kelly's swearing in, Trump reiterated his biases. "The day is over when they can stay in our country and wreak havoc."

The embrace of discrimination, broadly accepted in the war on terror and now turned southward, had been a crucial factor in Trump's choice of Kelly. The latter had caught Trump's attention for being, in the president's eyes, "not somebody politically correct." Trump had framed this quality as essential when he approached his new secretary of defense General James Mattis to seek nominations for the position—and Kelly embraced the characterization, pledging to take strong and expansive measures at the border and to "put a stop to political correctness that for too long has dictated our approach to national security."[6] He's a "hardass," one Republican congressman assured his colleagues.[7]

Bringing a war-hardened general to the southern border suggested that this was America's new battlefield. In substance as well as image, Kelly delivered on the expectation, recommending the use of military technology and "force multipliers" at the border, such as "an appropriate mix of tactical infrastructure; mobile and fixed technology, including radar and cameras; and manned and unmanned aerial vehicles." As incoming DHS secretary, Kelly was committed to eradicating illegal immigration, telling CNN's Wolf Blitzer, "I would do almost anything to deter the people from Central America to getting on this very, very dangerous network that brings them up through Mexico into the United States."[8]

To help Kelly realize this ambition, Trump issued two executive orders aimed at strengthening DHS's powers at the southern border.

Both orders signified that DHS would treat interactions at the border as an encounter with an enemy rather than a standoff with the thousands of individuals in crisis in Latin America. Avoiding any internal disagreements, neither of the orders were legally or administratively vetted. Such attentiveness to procedure, Trump's chief of staff Reince Priebus and his national security advisor Michael Flynn decided, was more trouble than it was worth.[9] Together, these measures would take border security and enforcement into a chilling new phase.

The Southern Border before Trump

Trump's administration was not the first to focus on strengthening law enforcement to counter illegal immigration. Even before 9/11, from the presidency of Bill Clinton onward, immigration challenges had provoked increasingly harsh and expansive measures at the southern border. In 1996, Clinton had initiated a pivot toward deportation with the passage of the Illegal Immigration Reform and Immigrant Responsibility Act, or IIRIRA, which expanded the offenses that could lead to deportation and diminished rights for immigrants prior to their deportation.[10] The result was the wholesale deportability of many immigrants whose previous existence in the United States had been authorized. Because these policies were applied retrospectively, it also meant that many immigrants who had earlier resolved criminal cases with guilty pleas had unknowingly signed their own deportation warrants.

After 9/11, new policies brought IIRIRA's criminal provisions into partnership with counterterrorism strategies—and also increased the budget for security at the border.[11] Under the Patriot Act, border funds grew by $300 million, and laws passed in 2004, 2006, and 2010 directed "funds to the Border Patrol for equipment, aircraft, agents, immigration investigators, and detention centers," as well as "to purchase new cameras, satellites, and un-manned drones for use in border enforcement." Funding to the Border Patrol was increased by $244 million as an emergency supplement in the 2010 Southwest Border Security Act. All told, between 9/11 and the final year of the Obama presidency, the CBP budget increased by more than 100 percent, climbing from $5.9 billion to

$13.6 billion. The ICE budget doubled as well.[12] Between 2003, when DHS was created, and 2008, the final year of Bush's presidency, the number of border agents expanded from 10,000 to 17,000.[13]

As with other policies he inherited, Obama endeavored to provide precision when it came to immigration law and policy. To begin with, his administration attempted to distinguish between three groups: recent arrivals, immigrants already in the United States who had a criminal record, and those in the United States but without criminal records. The difference in enforcement actions toward each group was pronounced.

Obama's policies toward recent arrivals were, with some important exceptions, harsher than Bush's. In office at a time when border crossings were higher than they would be during the Obama years, Bush preferred returns rather than formal removals. Yet Bush's aggressive internal policies set the stage for early Obama efforts. The Obama administration, in an attempt to deter migrants at the border, prioritized deportation hearings and accelerated deportation timelines.[14] His policies backed away from voluntary returns—often referred to simply as returns—and moved to formal deportation hearings and removals. In 2014, new procedures were put in place for expedited hearings—and thus potentially expedited removals—for unaccompanied minors and families with children through a policy known as the "rocket docket."[15] Between 2014 and 2016, about 40,000 cases were closed by "rocket docket" courts, and in reportedly 70 percent of them, the migrant families did not have legal representation.[16] It was an aggressive policy applied with a broad stroke, substituting breadth where precision had been promised, a tactic reminiscent of the war on terror's law enforcement efforts toward Muslims. Like its war on terror predecessors, the policy privileged a vast application of law enforcement efforts to groups in decisions inattentive to the specifics of individual cases.

But when it came to undocumented immigrants inside the country who did not have a criminal record, Obama often preferred a path to stability and inclusion.[17] Overall, interior removals—that is, of anyone other than those apprehended by Border Protection at airports or other points of entry or at interior traffic or transportation points—declined sharply under Obama.[18] In addition, the Obama administration ended enforcement operations at work sites. And in 2011, ICE was instructed not to make arrests for immigration violations in "sensitive locations," including schools, churches, hospitals, funerals, weddings, and at marches, rallies, and parades. In 2014, Obama ended a policy that his administration had initially extended from the Bush era: the Secure Communities policy, which allowed the Department of Justice (DOJ) to share information with ICE on undocumented immigrants as a prelude to aggressive enforcement efforts. He replaced it with the Priority Enforcement Program (PEP), a multilevel set of legal distinctions and remedies that distinguished between individuals who were a national security or public safety threat, those who had multiple misdemeanors or unlawful entry charges, and those who had been formally ordered removed. Each level authorized its own remedy with priority given to addressing those deemed to be the most dangerous.[19]

At the end of his second term, Obama took a particularly hard stance toward immigrants who were serving time in prison. In 2016, his administration initiated a policy that enabled the DOJ's Bureau of Prisons to transfer prisoners subject to deportation into immigration custody toward the end of their sentences, even in defiance of local authorities who wanted to keep the prisoners in their own custody. The decision was part of a larger battle between state and federal authorities, as so-called sanctuary cities like New York, Chicago, San Diego, and Miami attempted to protect immigrants from deportation by refusing to cooperate with the federal government's tough removal policies. Sanctuary cities and states barred or put restrictions on cooperation between local law enforcement and the federal government. Obama stood behind ICE's preference for issuing detainers as a way of bringing individuals into federal custody, despite the preference of local authorities to set their own policies for cooperation with federal immigration authorities. It was a form of bureaucratic porousness—of encouraging an overlap of authorities, in this case the federal agency over the state or local government—that propelled the subtle tool forward.[20]

One signature advance in immigration policy that occurred during the Obama term stemmed from frustrated earlier efforts to pass the

Development, Relief, and Education for Immigrant Minors (DREAM) Act, a piece of legislation that had been working its way through Congress since 2001 and that was reintroduced in 2009. The bill provided a path to legal status and potential citizenship for certain undocumented youths. But in 2010, the bill failed in the Senate. In response, in 2012 Obama issued an executive order to create the Deferred Action for Childhood Arrivals (DACA) program, also known as the Dreamers program. DACA protected undocumented youths from expulsion and allowed them access to education and employment in the United States. Absent the deferred action protections, this group would otherwise have fallen back, as journalist Jonathan Blitzer described it, into "fully undocumented status, vulnerable to arrest and deportation at any moment."[21]

Obama attempted to widen opportunities for undocumented immigrants further in 2014, with an executive order that expanded DACA eligibility and brought in (through a new program called Deferred Action for Parents of Americans, or DAPA) protections for parents of U.S. citizens and lawful permanent residents. Twenty-six states challenged the order and in June 2016 the case reached the Supreme Court. In a 4–4 vote—a tie made possible by the death of Justice Antonin Scalia who had yet to be replaced—the lower court decision blocking the program stayed in place. Obama called the decision "heartbreaking."[22]

Obama left office with a mixed record overall on immigration policy. He earned the name "Deporter in Chief" for his aggressive deportation stance, but according to the Migration Policy Institute, overall there were "fewer removals and returns under the Obama administration than by his two predecessors, George W. Bush and Bill Clinton." Obama deported more than five million immigrants while in office; George Bush had deported nearly twice as many, and Clinton even more than that, his deportation numbers reaching over twelve million.[23] Obama's administration also tried to restrict the use of some of the subtle tools, giving some clarity to broadly applied laws and thereby curtailing some of the more expansive law enforcement efforts of existing immigration policy. And his administration attempted to put in place safeguards in the sharing of information between the localities and the federal government. But, overall, his policy reinforced many of the harsh measures of his predecessor and even created some new roadblocks, such as the "rocket dockets," which sped up deportations and consequentially led to many removals without hearings.[24]

As he had promised on the campaign trail, in his first days in office, Trump attempted to reverse any ameliorative and inclusive policies by reaching hungrily for the subtle tools.

The First Executive Order

On his fifth day in office, and two days before issuing the Muslim travel ban executive order, Donald Trump signed two executive orders addressing immigration policy on the southern border. The first focused on the border itself. The second addressed policies aimed at the interior of the country. Both were intended to turn back any elements of the Obama policy that had diminished the breadth of application and tried to introduce distinctions within an otherwise blanket policy of enforcement inside and outside of the country.

The first executive order expanded the grounds for expulsion at the border. Titled "Border Security and Immigration Enforcement Improvements," it called for the construction of a "physical wall along the southern border"—a prominent campaign promise of Trump's—and outlined the administration's aggressive and expansive strategy for countering the "clear and present danger to the interests of the United States" that illegal immigration posed. It ordered an increased number of border guards by five thousand agents, as well as an increase in asylum officers to determine who among those crossing the border was doing so illegally.[25] The order aimed "to prevent illegal immigration, drug and human trafficking, and acts of terrorism." The reference to terrorism harkened back to an unfounded fear in the post–9/11 days that terrorists were entering the country at the southern border. As NBC's Julia Ainsley would later report, although Trump administration officials claimed that "CBP stopped nearly 4,000 known suspected terrorist from crossing the border in fiscal year 2018," CBP figures presented to Congress showed, by contrast, that the agency had "encountered only six immigrants at ports of entry on the U.S.-Mexico border in the first half of fiscal year 2018 whose names were on a federal government list of known or suspected terrorists."[26]

The order called for an expansion of the detention system, instructing agents "to immediately construct, operate, control, or establish contracts to construct, operate, or control facilities to detain aliens at or near the land border with Mexico." The executive order further emphasized the need to "end the abuse of parole and asylum provisions" that enabled undocumented immigrants to stay in the country. The message was clear. DHS was pivoting with full force from the terrorism agenda to an all-out war against undocumented immigrants and those with immigration violations no matter how minor.

In an additional attempt to ramp up law enforcement at the border, the border security order tasked the government with ending "Catch and Release," a reference to a custom relied on by Bush and Obama in which immigrants were released into the country while they awaited their immigration hearings. Trump would later call the practice a "ridiculous" loophole exploited by immigrants. The executive order called instead for "detention of aliens" pending the hearings, meaning that the numbers who would be in immigration detention would most likely skyrocket.

Relying on the subtle tool of imprecision in its vague language, the order was vast (and discriminatory) in application and relied on tough law enforcement measures to carry it out. As the order explained, "We cannot faithfully execute the immigration laws of the United States if we exempt classes or categories of removable aliens from potential enforcement." It was a generalized threat, with nebulous details; those susceptible to removal were expanded to include the "category of aliens subject to expedited removal to the extent the DHS Secretary determines is appropriate."[27] Rather than using criminality as a means of focusing resources for deportation, the executive orders authorized the prioritization of all undocumented immigrants in the country— estimated at eleven million people—for deportation.

The border security executive order also broadened the pool of border agents, authorizing local officers or employees to "perform the functions of immigration officers in relation to the investigation, apprehension, or detention of aliens in the United States," and to do so quickly. The border security order called for the department to "immediately construct" detention facilities and to "immediately assign" asylum officers and immigration judges to immigration detention centers.

This rapid deployment depended upon the tool of bureaucratic porousness at work—it assumed one type of officer could readily be exchanged for another, disregarding the need for special training and the professional expertise of border guards. A November 2018 DHS Inspector General's report on training needs for the hiring of the fifteen thousand border patrol agents highlighted this problem, noting that "uncertain funding commitments and overextended throughput capacity" threatened to "lead to a degradation of training and standards." If the situation continued, the report warned, the newly trained guards would be "less prepared," which ran the risk of "potentially impeding mission achievability and increasing safety risk to themselves, other law enforcement officers, and anyone within their enforcement authority."[28]

The Second Executive Order

Trump's second executive order, "Enhancing Public Safety in the Interior of the United States," even more drastically revoked the Obama-era policies. Signed on January 25, 2017, it focused on those already in the United States rather than those crossing the border, with the stated intent to counter the dangers posed by "tens of thousands of removable aliens" who were living in the country.[29] The order blamed the immigrants' "home countries" for refusing to repatriate them and contended that "many of these aliens are criminals who have served time in our Federal, State, and local jails." Portraying the group as enemies, the Public Safety Order concluded their very presence in the country was "contrary to the national interest."

Further rolling back Obama-era reforms, the public safety order ended outright the Priority Enforcement Program and its policy of differentiating among dangers posed by distinct categories of immigration violators. The executive order also threatened to punish state and local entities that acted as sanctuary cities for undocumented aliens. The order stated that such cities were "not eligible to receive Federal grants, except as deemed necessary for law enforcement purposes by the Attorney General or the Secretary."

Both orders empowered expansive authorities, blurred legal distinctions, and relied heavily on a form of bureaucratic porousness that defined the Trump years—the close-knit relationship between DHS and the Department of Justice. Trump's first attorney general, Jeff Sessions, came to the office from a career in which racism and antipathy to immigration had played a part. In 1986, Sessions had been nominated for a federal judgeship, but due to his history of racial intolerance, his nomination was not confirmed, only the second time in U.S. history that the Senate had made such a refusal.

During his time in the Senate, Sessions became known for his anti-immigration affiliations and opinions.[30] This stance had led to his connection with Stephen Bannon, Trump's close ally and campaign advisor. Bannon had brought Sessions onto Breitbart's Sirius FM show and given him a platform for anti-immigrant sentiments. Andrew Breitbart had started the far-right-wing media company in 2005; when Breitbart died in 2012, Bannon took it over and shaped it into a highly trafficked white supremacist site that stood self-consciously in opposition to political correctness. Sessions fit into the ideology of Bannon's Breitbart. Sessions informed Breitbart audiences, as the journalist Emily Bazelon has reported, of his admiration for the stringent, Chinese exclusion policy of the early twentieth century and the parsimonious quotas placed on Italians, Jews, Eastern Europeans, Africans, and Middle Easterners in that period. As he told Breitbart listeners, Sessions considered the quota system to be "good for America."[31]

The Orders Take Effect

The impact of the executive orders was immediate and brutal. Between the two orders, 15,000 new positions opened up, 5,000 for guards and 10,000 for immigration officers. Raids in eleven states in February 2017 led to the placement in custody of more than 600 undocumented immigrants. By late February, Secretary Kelly had put a new policy in place that allowed ICE agents to arrest immigrants for immigration violations, "freeing them from the Obama-era rules that prevented agents from arresting immigrants whose only violation was their immigration status."[32]

The order spurred immediate policy changes. At DHS, the new head of the US Office of Immigration and Citizenship, Lee Francis Cissna, scrubbed the words "nation of immigrants" from the agency's mission statement.[33] And in June 2017, DHS secretary John Kelly formally rescinded Obama's 2014 DAPA directive.[34] In April 2018 Attorney General Sessions announced a full-blown "zero-tolerance" policy at the border, which aimed to prosecute anyone found to be crossing the border illegally. Sessions outlined the enhanced aggressive measures that the new policy would entail. DHS, he said, would now "take on as many of those cases as humanly possible until we get to 100 percent" for prosecution. Prior to this, individuals who crossed the border illegally would be released and told to appear for a hearing at a given time, unless they were accused of a criminal offense such as trafficking in weapons or child smuggling, in which case they could be detained. Illegal entry was otherwise considered a civil violation, punishable by a fine, or possibly removal proceedings. Now, the very act of crossing the border was grounds for criminal detention, charge, and conviction.[35] Prosecutors began to "criminally charge any adult who crossed the border unlawfully in the El Paso sector, which spans from New Mexico to West Texas."[36]

Sessions, summing up the policy, repeated almost verbatim the warnings his Bush-era predecessor had voiced in the context of the war on terror. "If you cross the border unlawfully, then we will prosecute you—it's that simple."[37] He was echoing John Ashcroft's warning to noncitizens right after 9/11: "Let the terrorists among us be warned," he had said, "if you overstay your visa even by one day, we will arrest you. If you violate a local law, you will be put in jail and kept in custody as long as possible." Sessions was intent on spreading the aggressive stance against noncitizens well beyond terrorists and criminals, to those with visa violations.[38] According to the American Immigration Council, as a result of the zero-tolerance order, "the number of federal criminal prosecutions for illegal (or "improper") entry and illegal reentry skyrocketed from 53,614 in FY 2017 to 106,312 in FY 2019—an increase of 98 percent."[39]

As well as initiating a major uptick in prosecutions, the zero-tolerance policy represented a major legal transformation. Whereas Obama had tried to focus on criminal activities as grounds for expulsion, in the new DOJ's understanding, to be undocumented was to be subject automatically to criminal rather than civil penalties. With this hugely expanded definition of crime, the public safety order had concluded that "tens of thousands of removable aliens" needed to be apprehended and repatriated to their home countries. And in fact, within a year, it had led to thousands of family separations at the border.[40]

To put a fine point on its no tolerance policy, on September 5, 2017, Trump ordered an end to DACA, revoking Obama's 2012 executive order.

The legacy of the war on terror was patently clear in all aspects of the southern border executive orders. These were the very tools of the 9/11 toolbox. There was the bureaucratic creep evidenced in using DHS for purposes well beyond terrorism, coupled with the reliance on vague and imprecise language to broaden the pool of those subjected to the most onerous application of the law. Together they allowed a discriminatory system to thrive.

Going forward, additional tools would expand the scope and cruelty of immigration law and policy even further. Just as DOJ, beginning in the wake of September 11, had bypassed legal and procedural norms in the name of national security to create new rules for detention and torture, now the department became the gateway for bypassing norms at the southern border. So profound was Sessions's domination of the immigration process that he was, in the words of the journalist Franklin Foer, "the de facto secretary of homeland security."[41]

Starting on October 1, 2017, immigration judges, whose oversight lay with the attorney general, were ordered to prosecute seven hundred cases a day, at times forcing dozens of cases to be heard at one time. The mandated number of cases meant that little serious consideration of any case could take place. Sessions's directive was so egregious that the immigration judges' union pushed back, claiming it violated due process.[42] Once again, the Department of Justice was utilized for breadth and quantity of enforcement over individualized consideration and the application of the law on a case-by-case basis, which took a backseat to the security aims claimed by the administration.

To ensure his iron grip on the expansive immigration policy, Sessions relied heavily on his solicitor general. In that position, Noel Francisco had successfully led the charge and on numerous occasions had interfered with decisions in lower courts regarding the Muslim ban lawsuits. Now Sessions directed him to interfere with the lower courts again, calling repeatedly for certiorari before judgment—that is, asking the Supreme Court to hear the case before it had made its way through the normal appellate process—in cases involving DACA.[43]

As another means of upending norms, Sessions employed an expansive use of the attorney general's "certification power."[44] As the top administrator for the immigration courts, the attorney general (AG) has the power to take a case away from an appellate immigration court and issue his own binding rulings on the interpretation of the law. He also has the power to appoint the judges and to supervise their activities. The power enables the AG to intervene directly with judges' decisions and thus with precedent and norms, and arrogates to the executive branch the meaning of the law itself, a firm break with bureaucratic integrity and authority.[45] Prior to the Trump administration, the power had been used sparingly during recent Democratic presidencies. Under Obama it was used four times in eight years; under Clinton, three times. By contrast, George W. Bush's attorneys general had used the power in sixteen cases over eight years. Now Sessions, in only two years in office, had used it eight times; Barr would use it an additional four times in his two years as AG.

Sessions's first use of the "certification power" was in a case known as *Matter of A-B-* that claimed most immigrants fleeing domestic and gang violence did not qualify for asylum.[46] Sessions's use of the power eliminated the ability of judges to administratively close cases, a technique they had customarily used to temporarily remove a case from an active docket—which, in addition to allowing judges to prioritize other cases, gave the migrant a chance to find other forms of relief, for example, to make an asylum claim if they had not already done so. As with the ending of PEP, Sessions's elimination of the practice removed distinctions among cases—a reversal from Obama's efforts to distinguish between the kinds of cases in the system.[47] With these new methods in place, Sessions's DOJ intensified apprehensions, detentions, and removals, which rose 30 percent from 2016 to 2017.[48] As a 2018 ICE report summarized, enforcement was up across the board in administrative and criminal arrests, interior removals, and detentions.[49]

Nowhere did the changes in immigration under Trump appear more harsh than toward children. While the foundations for detention and expulsion were put in place during the spring and summer of 2017, by the fall Trump was ready to put the final nail in the coffin of Obama's policies.

Children

In Sessions's ever expansive anti-immigrant policies, not only were children not protected, they were singled out for punishment and treated as pawns in the administration's strategies for implementing immigration policy. Ending DACA punished the children of undocumented immigrants inside the country, and due to Session's "zero-tolerance" directive, in which he insisted that "100 percent of those crossing the border be charged with a crime," children in the company of adults were placed in Health and Human Services (HHS) detention when their parents were detained. Kelly had promised to "do almost anything" to strengthen the border. Now, the ground was being laid for conditions of detentions and legal procedures, that—like Guantanamo, which Kelly had supervisory authority for prior to joining the Trump administration—would constitute cruelty, physical deprivation, and harm, in deviation from standard due process and international law protections.

For children, as for the adults, the changes in policy began with changes in language. For noncitizen adults the term "criminal alien" had been expanded to include those who previously were subject only to civil penalties. Now for children, the term "unaccompanied" was manipulated to include not just children who arrived in the country without an adult but also those separated from adults by virtue of government actions taken at the border. As they were intended to do, the changes introduced more aggressive and punitive enforcement tactics. Once again, the definition, and therefore the rules, were changed.[50]

The number of "unaccompanied children" skyrocketed, and government detention centers and privately run shelters were now flooded with children. Under Obama, families with children who crossed the border were usually detained together in a handful of family detention centers. Under Trump's zero-tolerance policy, parents and children were detained separately by DHS, with the children eventually transferred to Health and Human Services' Office of Refugee Resettlement (ORR), which was tasked with finding them a place with a qualified sponsor.

Separating children from their parents was not merely a consequence of the larger policy aims. It was a goal in and of itself, and one Trump had openly discussed as early as the first weeks of his administration. In his remarks at DHS on the day the executive orders were released, Trump expressed indignation toward those who complained about the family separations that had occurred on Obama's watch, despite the express decision by the Obama administration not to create a family separation policy. "Let's talk about how enforcing immigration laws can separate illegal immigrant families,"[51] Trump said with a mocking tone, conveying his annoyance at what he saw as misplaced compassion. The real families being hurt, the president insisted, were not the families of immigrants but American families harmed by the criminal behavior of undocumented immigrants. "The families they don't talk about are the families of Americans. Forever separated from the people they love. They don't talk about that. Ever." Trump was adamant about rethinking family separations in the context of administering immigration policy. "As your president, I have no higher duty than to protect the lives of the American people. First, these families lost a loved ones [sic]. Then they endured a system that ignored them all at the same time constantly rewarding those who broke the law. For these families it's been one injustice after another. That all turns around beginning today."[52]

True to the spirit of Trump's words and those of his executive orders, in February 2017 officials at ICE and CBP discussed implementing a family separation policy with officials at the Office of Refugee Resettlement (ORR), the agency at Health and Human Services that would be tasked with sheltering the separated children.[53] In March, DHS secretary John Kelly announced publicly that the government was thinking about family separations at the border; he later reversed himself, but Attorney General Sessions stayed true to the mission. In April, when Sessions issued his memo instructing prosecutors along the southern border to prioritize the prosecution of undocumented immigrants, family separations were the immediate result.[54] As pointed out in a draft Inspector General report that circulated in October 2020 (and that would be released officially in January 2021), the goal articulated by the administration was that removing parents from their children "would have a substantial deterrent effect" on others trying to cross the border.[55]

Previously, grounds for family separations were reasons of safety or illness. For Trump officials, the purpose was to send a message: don't come here. As one border patrol official at the time explained, "it is the hope that this separation will act as a deterrent to parents bringing their children into the harsh circumstances that are present when trying to enter the United States illegally."[56]

The expanded category of unaccompanied children and the conclusion that poor conditions would help serve as a deterrent led to a growing population of children being herded in large numbers into cage-like, open-air facilities. Deprived of beds, crowded together head to foot, the children slept in the open air on concrete slabs with aluminum blankets to protect against cold. Food and water were scarce. Medical attention and showers were nonexistent. Babies were left in soiled diapers. Children, unable to use the bathroom, dirtied themselves. Sounds of sobbing and cries for missing parents filled the air.[57]

A court resolution known as the Flores settlement agreement had been in place since 1997 as the authority regarding standards for the detention and release of unaccompanied minors.[58] The settlement mandated that children be kept in sanitary conditions with food, water, medical assistance, and contact with family members, yet it was completely violated by the new policy. It also required that the government release the children within three to five days, a condition extended in 2015 to 20 days in cases of "emergency" or "influx."[59] Reportedly, when addressing a meeting in the White House situation room on violations of the Flores agreement, "Sessions made a radical suggestion," journalists Julie Hirschfeld Davis and Michael D. Shear recounted. Speaking to a group assembled in the White House Situation Room, Sessions had said, "They should simply ignore Flores and start holding families for longer periods of time. Let the judge come after us."[60] It was an indication of the wider disrespect for children in custody—uttered defiantly by the nation's chief law enforcement officer—that defined the immigration policies of the Trump era overall.

At first, knowing full well that it was operating outside the norms, the administration tried to operate in secret. Journalists were kept at bay, as were lawyers who flocked to the detention centers offering their services to those detained.[61] Doctors, too, were kept away as were members of Congress.[62] Senator Jeff Merkley, Democrat of Oregon, arrived at a detention center in Texas only to be turned away by police who were called in by the detention center's supervisor.[63] Importantly, the secrecy included more than just hiding facts on the grounds from outside observers. In an effort to elude accountability for the mounting numbers of detained children, the detention centers stopped keeping lists of them. When they did try to track them, for instance, by tagging the children with numbers, the overlapping agencies involved assigned different numbers. For both reasons, confusion reigned as a result of yet another form of bureaucratic porousness, the result of which was an inability ultimately to reunite the children with their parents. When Trump left office, over six hundred children would remain unreunited with their parents.

The evolution of secrecy into a ban on creating records thus extended to the treatment of children in immigration custody as it had extended to so many other areas of the Trump administration. As with the heinous and illegal treatment of those in detention in the war on terror, the secret soon came out, as journalists obtained tapes of weeping children and published pictures of little bodies crowded together on the ground, exposed to rain, sun, and wind. By July of 2018, an estimated 2,300 families had been separated. In the Senate, Dianne Feinstein introduced a bill called the Keep Families Together Act, which was intended to prohibit DHS, DOJ, or HHS from separating parents and children at the border. Congressman Jerry Nadler introduced a version of the bill in the House. Both died in committee, would be proposed again in early 2019, only to fail in committee again. Also in July 2018, eleven Democratic senators sent a letter to DHS and HHS demanding weekly updates on the status of the children.[64] Presaging the future, the letter warned, "We are concerned that even as the Administration works to reunify families, it continues to deport adults and family members who had children taken from them—reducing their chances of reunification even further." Even the First Lady weighed in, through her spokesperson: "The First Lady hates to see children separated from their families. . . . She believes we need to be a country that follows all laws, but also a country that governs with heart."[65]

Under public pressure, in June 2018 Trump relented and signed an executive order ending the policy of family separation but said nothing about reunification. And in fact, the reunions, in light of the sloppiness and intentional hiding of facts, proved in hundreds of cases to be impossible.[66] Bureaucratic confusion, including limited sharing of information among the relevant agencies, had resulted in intensifying confusion while each agency blamed the other for the loss of records, names, and the like.[67] DHS blamed HHS and ORR. ORR blamed the DOJ. Bureaucratic porousness both created the problem and ensured that no one agency could be held accountable.

In January 2021, days before the inauguration of President Joe Biden, the DHS Office of the Inspector General (OIG) issued a report on Sessions's leadership at DOJ over the zero-tolerance policy, describing the vast application of the policy and the determination to separate families that drove it. The report focused on "in particular, the Office of the Attorney General," and its leadership in the family separation policy. It elaborated on the agenda that followed Sessions's conviction that "we need to take away children," and the dutiful efforts of Deputy Attorney

General Rod Rosenstein to implement the policy, no matter how young the children were—extending it even to children under the age of five.

The policy epitomized how damaging the subtle tools could be. Its imprecise directives "came at the expense of careful and appropriate consideration of the impact of family unit prosecutions and child separations." As so many DOJ initiatives had been at the outset of the war on terror, the policy was excessively broad in its implementation of previously unthinkable cruelty. Rather than bypass norms, Sessions merely dispensed with them, failing to put procedures in place for how to deal with the children, what criteria to apply to their treatment, and how to ensure the possibility of reunification. Without this, and with the poor coordination between DOJ, DHS, and HHS, the children were shamefully uncared for, physically and psychologically mistreated, and many were unable to be reunited with their parents.

The remedy, the OIG report concluded, was to forsake the subtle tools. The three recommendations for any future policies included clarity in the form of "coordinat[ing] directly with affected stakeholders," of norms in the form of "guidance and procedures," and of bureaucratic distinctiveness in the form of "formal interagency agreement" among the departments involved.[68] Though the report was not formally issued until the last days of Trump's tenure in office, the destruction that the subtle tools could cause when used in combination with one another was well-known, even before Sessions left office.

Enter Barr

During Jeff Sessions's tenure as attorney general, immigration policy had become as harsh as at any time in U.S. history. Toward this goal, the southern border executive orders and the child separation policy had weaponized the subtle tools in unprecedented and brutal ways. Imprecise language was used to broaden categories of immigration status to encompass their very opposites. Accompanied children were separated from their parents and thus turned into unaccompanied children, though the category was meant for those who arrived alone. Immigration violations were turned into criminal violations. Secrecy had been replaced by rank refusal to record facts such as identifiers for children. And bureaucratic porousness had been used to deflect blame and escape accountability.

As Barr came into office in February 2019, the aggressive nature of Trump's immigration policy became even more severe. Barr held onto the abandonment of norms that Sessions had exploited in terms of the degradation of legal categories and the policy of interfering with the course of immigration cases. Therefore, the numbers of deportations continued to rise. Under Sessions and Barr together, the numbers of those charged with "Improper Entry and Illegal Reentry" doubled.[69] Improper entry charges rose from 36,649 in 2017 to 68,740 in 2018 and 80,886 in 2019. Overall deportation numbers escalated 17 percent from the fall of Trump's first year in office to the fall of his second year, reaching 337,000 removals. In keeping with the trend toward secrecy and outright failure to maintain records, the numbers for 2019 were never released.[70]

In his confirmation hearing for the post of attorney general, Barr singled out immigration as a primary concern. "The immigration laws just have to be changed," he said. But as his oversight of immigration matters made clear, it was not legislation he sought. Rather, it was the authority to make immigration policy on his own.

As attorney general, Barr became chief judge of the DOJ's Board of Immigration Appeals—a role he relished. Wearing that hat, he bypassed procedural norms and legal determinations with regularity, overturning prior rulings and issuing his own sweeping and transformative decisions. In particular, Barr relied on the expansive use of the AG's "certification power," which Sessions had put in motion.[71] Making policy by decree and in ways that had binding authority for all similar cases, Barr issued a series of rulings that turned an already harsh system into one where cruelty and the denial of basic rights were guiding principles. He put his initial emphasis on increasing the numbers of migrants in detention. In April, he issued an order denying an asylum seeker the chance to post a bond. The ruling, in keeping with the authorities of the AG when it came to immigration courts, set a precedent for all of the immigration courts, enabling widespread application of bond denials in favor of detention.[72]

In July, Barr further demonstrated his determination to administer by decree rather than process when he overruled the Board of Immigration Appeals (BIA) in an asylum case known as *Matter of L-E-A*. The case involved a man whose life had been threatened by a drug cartel that wanted to sell drugs out of his father's grocery store. The man entered the United States and applied for asylum, saying that he had been targeted by the cartel "because of his membership in the particular social group composed of his father's family members, and he asserted a fear of persecution in the future on this basis."[73]

The immigration court judge rejected the son's asylum claim in the *Matter of L-E-A* on the grounds that the cartel had been interested in selling drugs, not in harming the son's family. The BIA also denied the asylum claim but remanded the case to the lower court to determine whether or not the son's membership in the family had led to his persecution. The law allowed for asylum claims "based on well-founded fear of persecution on account of race, religion, nationality, political opinion, or membership in a particular social group." The son claimed that his persecution was indeed based on his membership in a social group—his own family.

Barr stepped in and summarily reversed the decision of the BIA. His predecessor Matthew Whitaker had originally interfered with the case. Now Barr formally decreed that when it came to migrants, "almost every alien is a member of a family of some kind." Therefore, the nuclear family could not be considered a particular social group.

As an overview of the case in the *Harvard Law Review* explained, it was a sharp reversal of a customary finding that one's family did in fact constitute a social group. "The Attorney General's decision . . . represents a sharp break with . . . precedent, improperly dismissing decades of case law and contributing to continued efforts to erode the original definition of 'particular social group.'" Prior to this, families were consistently considered to constitute a particular social group.[74] Yet Barr decided that because the fear of persecution was based on the asylee's family, the man could not claim asylee status and was therefore subject to deportation.[75] Furthering his efforts to increase deportations, in

November, Barr lowered the bar even more, making low-level convictions cause for deportation.[76]

In his handling of immigration policy at the southern border, Barr took the abandonment of norms that Sessions had set in motion to a new nadir. In early 2001, reflecting on his first stint as attorney general a decade earlier, Barr had summed up his beliefs about migration policy, in this instance regarding Mexican migrants. "There are only two end games: You either lock them up or you shoot them, one or the other. Basically, it's either a Justice end game, or it's a national security end game."[77] As Barr took this philosophy to his role as Trump's attorney general, the image of the country as a nation of immigrants fell readily by the wayside.

With children as with adults, with migrants from the south as well as from around the world, the Trump administration's record on immigration under Sessions and Barr was as much about sharpening the subtle tools into multipurpose weapons as it was about reaping results. The use of imprecise language to confound legal categories such as noncriminal and criminal undocumented immigrants, and unaccompanied and accompanied children, harkened back to the use of imprecise language to obfuscate the difference between detainees and prisoners of war in the Bush era. Both were used to the same end—to deny the protections of standing law. Once again, the imprecision set the stage for an erosion of norms. At the hands of the executive department, and in particular the Department of Justice, the Trump administration had turned the tool of abandoning norms into outright attempts to use the Department of Justice as a "wrecking ball" not just against Muslims seeking to enter the country, but against immigrants from the south as well. Meanwhile secrecy, yet another of the subtle tools, had been turned into a weapon of information removal. Beyond just hiding facts, the government now decided to avoid creating a record at all. In addition, disruption of process had taken on new proportions in immigration policy as the attorney general aggressively nullified the role of the judges in immigration courts. And through it all, the government relied on a system in which bureaucratic porousness would allow the transfer of adults, and children, from one agency to another, without records, and without government accountability. The full box of subtle tools was applied to immigration with tragic consequences.

And even as these newly weaponized tools were used to forge disturbing realities on the home front, in areas distinct from the war on terror, they continued to remain important in the war on terror itself, applied by the Trump administration in newly expansive and weaponized ways.

7

The Deadly Strike

THE KILLING OF GENERAL SOLEIMANI

The 2001 AUMF does not authorize the President to use force against
every group that commits terrorist acts.

OBAMA FRAMEWORK, 2016

ON THE EVENING of January 2, 2020, President Trump signaled the
go-ahead for a strike to take place early the next morning. The target was
General Qasem Soleimani, a member of Iran's Islamic Revolutionary
Guard Corps and leader of its elite Quds Force, responsible for covert
and extramilitary activities outside of Iran. Soleimani had long been on
the list of top enemies of the United States and was considered to have
ordered numerous terrorist attacks carried out by Iran's proxy forces
throughout the Middle East. An estimated six hundred American service
members had reportedly been killed by attacks he ordered, largely via
the use of roadside bombs in Iraq.

At 1:00 a.m. local time in Iraq a U.S. MQ-9 Reaper drone shot two
Hellfire R9X missiles, hitting Soleimani's SUV as he drove away from
Baghdad International Airport.[1] The strike killed Soleimani and nine
others, including the commander of an Iran-backed Iraqi militia, Abu
Mahdi al-Muhandis.

It was a pivotal and dangerous moment for the United States. The worldwide response was immediate. United Nations secretary-general António Guterres was "deeply concerned" about the possibility of "another war in the Gulf," according to his spokesman. Many, along with the British foreign minister, Dominic Raab, acknowledged the danger that Soleimani posed and the destruction he had caused, but "urge[d] all parties to de-escalate." Democrats in Congress similarly pointed out that the strike was ill-advised. Presidential hopeful Joe Biden called the strike "a hugely escalatory move," akin to "toss[ing] a stick of dynamite into a tinderbox."[2]

Trump's administration had been honing the subtle tools since the beginning of his presidency. He had sharpened them for use domestically, in areas outside the war on terror—but he had also, as with the strike against Soleimani, further weaponized them in the context of the continuing war on terror. In the preparation and execution of the strike, imprecision in terms of the language and authorities expanded in new ways, and bypassing procedural norms and embracing secrecy enabled Trump to deflect opposition once the strike was done. The strike not only stood in outright defiance of domestic and international law, taking the country into dangerous and unprecedented territory; it emboldened the use of the subtle tools, both within and outside of the war on terror context.

Anti-Iran Sentiment

Iran had been cast in the role of enemy by Trump and his associates in the administration well before they came into office. For Trump and his two close foreign affairs advisors—John Bolton, his national security advisor, and Mike Pompeo, first his CIA director and then secretary of state—the country posed the twin threat of being a terrorist menace and a country in pursuit of weapons of mass destruction (WMD).

At the heart of their criticism was the JCPOA, the Joint Comprehensive Plan of Action that President Obama had signed in July 2015.[3] The JCPOA was the Obama administration's diplomatic attempt to find a way to impede Iran from developing nuclear weapons. Intensive negotiations under John Kerry as secretary of state had resulted in substantial concessions by the Iranians aimed at curbing their nuclear program and allowing inspections in return for sanctions relief amounting to billions of dollars. Also signed by China, France, Russia, the United Kingdom, Germany, and the European Union, the JCPOA was considered by experts and diplomats to be a tour de force by the Obama team. A letter from twenty-nine top scientists in support of the deal commended the president for his "innovative agreement," and its "much more stringent constraints than any previously negotiated non-proliferation agreements."[4]

However conducive to reducing the fear of nuclear weapons, the deal had opponents on both sides of the aisle.[5] Some expressed displeasure with the short time frame, predicting that Iran would begin to enrich uranium once the ten- to fifteen-year period of the deal expired.[6] Others did not trust the Iranians to be transparent with UN inspectors responsible for monitoring compliance with the deal. Further fuel for opponents came when Israeli prime minister Benjamin Netanyahu, in a speech before the U.S. Congress, associated Iran with terrorists and portrayed the deal as a precursor to war. "Don't be fooled," he said, "the battle between Iran and ISIS doesn't turn Iran into a friend of America."[7] Netanyahu's speech provided the treaty's opponents with additional justification to reject it.

Unable to garner Senate approval, Obama exercised presidential authority and entered the administration into the nuclear deal, not as a treaty but as an agreement, which, unlike a treaty, did not carry the force of law.[8]

On the campaign trail Trump repeatedly expressed outright disgust with the JCPOA, referring to the deal as "the highest level of incompetence."[9] In maligning the deal, he identified Iran as part of the threat of terrorism that the United States faced. "We have rewarded the world's leading state sponsor of terror with $150 billion and we received absolutely nothing in return," he lamented.[10] During the debate over the deal in Congress, Pompeo, then a third-term congressman from Kansas, had called the terms of the deal "a joke" and "a historic mistake" and underscored Iran as "the largest state sponsor of terror."[11] The accusation pivoted away from sixteen years of using the term "terror" to focus on al Qaeda, associated jihadist groups, and state sponsors such as Saudi Arabia and Iraq. Now, the term included Iran's role in terrorism and its use of proxy terror groups outside of al Qaeda and its affiliates. Throughout the first year of the Trump presidency, Trump's advisors refined the allegations of Iran's sponsorship of terrorism by focusing on attacks in Iraq conducted by Iranian proxies and authorized by Iranian officials.

In December 2017, Pompeo, acting in his capacity as Trump's first CIA director, brought attention to the threat in Iraq by focusing on Qasem Soleimani. In a speech delivered at the Reagan National Defense Forum, Pompeo informed the audience that he had sent a letter to General Soleimani warning the Iranian general against making any attacks on U.S. forces in Iraq, a plan that had been rumored to be in the works. An emissary reported back that Soleimani had refused to even open the letter, a sign that diplomacy was off the table.[12]

Farewell to the JCPOA

By May 2018, the rhetoric and the rationale for a major break with Iran were in place. On May 8, two weeks after Pompeo moved from the CIA to the State Department and one month after Bolton became national security advisor, President Trump called a press conference to announce that his administration was pulling out of the JCPOA, effective immediately.[13]

Providing little by way of detail, Trump leveled broad accusations about Iran's "malign behavior" in violation of the deal, saying that the agreement gave Iran a free pass to continue to enrich uranium and "over time, reach the brink of a nuclear breakout." In addition, he reiterated the emphasis on Iran as the "leading state sponsor of terror."[14] The allegations of terrorism combined with the threat of WMDs, in the context of American politics and foreign policy, were an alarming echo of those that were used to justify the Iraq War. The subtle tools of imprecision (the lack of a significant link between al Qaeda and Iraq) and secrecy (hiding facts that disputed assertions that Iraq had WMDs) had together led to the rationale for war with Iraq. Now Iran's involvement with terrorism and allegations—disputed by Iran and the International Atomic Energy Agency, the regulatory agency for nuclear weapons—of an illegal nuclear weapons program revived the pattern of the past.

Predictably, once Trump withdrew from the JCPOA, tensions with Iran began to escalate. Two weeks after the withdrawal from the treaty, and three weeks into his tenure as the new secretary of state, Pompeo fleshed out the terms of the United States' newly aggressive posture on Iran as part of a "maximum pressure" strategy designed to force negotiations for a new agreement by driving oil prices down and crippling the Iranian economy. Speaking before the conservative think tank the Heritage Foundation, Pompeo emphasized the administration's determination to tie the term "terrorism" to the administration's opposition to Iran. Pompeo issued twelve demands for the Iranians. If they complied with all twelve, then the sanctions would be lifted. The dozen demands included transparency in and cessation of Iran's nuclear and ballistic programs; the release of detained citizens from the United States and its allies; cessation of threats to Israel and the United Arab Emirates; and an end to support for terrorist organizations and interference in Iraq, Syria, and Yemen.[15]

Singled out in four of the twelve demands, the emphasis on Iran as a state sponsor of terrorism was pronounced. Once again, the use of the word "terrorism" blurred distinctions in ways that made the designation largely meaningless. Hezbollah, Hamas, the Taliban, the Houthis, and al Qaeda were named in Pompeo's demands as Iran's proxies and allies. The conflation of these groups brought a new level of imprecision to the conversation about terrorism. Overall, these groups were more dissimilar than similar. Representing distinct and antagonistic forms of Islam, as well as differing in size, relationship to state power, and aims, the elision of these groups included a powerful attempt to tie al Qaeda and the Taliban—the enemies identified in the wake of 9/11—to the threat of Iran. To give added power to his concerns about Iran and terrorism, Pompeo now did as Bush had done with Saddam Hussein and Iraq, accusing the Iranians of serving "as sanctuary for al-Qaida, as it has done since 9/11, and remain[ing] unwilling to bring to justice senior al-Qaida members residing in Tehran."[16] In classified briefings to Congress, Pompeo similarly emphasized the existence of connections between the Shia nation Iran and the Sunni terrorist group al Qaeda.[17] While members of the bin Laden family and other al Qaeda members had reportedly resided in Iran under house arrest in the decades after 9/11, and while there was some evidence that al Qaeda members in Iran helped with communications for the group and provided a mixture of sanctuary and surveillance for members of al Qaeda, the further suggestion that Iran was a collaborator, or an operational center for al Qaeda activities was at the time overstated. Their relationship was at best an uneasy one, at times an alliance of convenience, at times beset by suspicions and distrust.[18]

Pompeo had one person particularly in mind when he used the subtle tool of imprecise language to bolster the case for the use of force against Iran: Qasem Soleimani, whom he mentioned a total of nine times in his speech.

General Qasem Soleimani

Soleimani as well as the Quds Force were hardly household names outside of national security circles. But inside the halls of American strategic discussions, they occupied a prominent perch, and had done so well before Trump came into office. General Stanley McChrystal, the head of Joint Special Operations Command from 2003 to 2008 and then commander of U.S. and NATO forces from 2009 to 2010 in Afghanistan, saw Soleimani as "singularly dangerous," and his influence across the Middle East as appreciable.[19] In 2007, General David Petraeus, commanding general of the Multi-National Force in Iraq at the time, described Soleimani as a "truly evil figure," later seeing his death as "bigger than bin Laden."[20]

In 1979 at the age of twenty-two, Soleimani joined Iran's Revolutionary Guard Corps, inspired by the revolution in which the U.S.-supported Shah, Reza Pahlavi, was overthrown, and replaced by an Islamic Republic, headed by the Grand Ayatollah Ruhollah Khomeini. A child of the Iran–Iraq War that lasted from 1980 to 1988, Soleimani's "fervent nationalism," in McChrystal's estimation, grew out of the resistance to the U.S. presence in the Middle East and U.S support for Iraq during the Iran–Iraq War. Nearly two decades later, in 1998, Soleimani was named head of the Quds Force (Quds, in both Farsi and Arabic, is the word for

Jerusalem). The Jerusalem Force thus underscored the Muslim claim to the Holy City.

Under Soleimani's command, the Quds Force contributed to destabilization across the region, "tasked," according to the terrorism expert Ali Soufan, "with bolstering pro-Iranian regimes and militias abroad."[21] Soleimani's playbook aimed at transforming a wide array of institutional capacities into his proxies; according to a 2012 New Yorker article by the journalist Dexter Filkins, Soleimani "built the Quds Force into an organization with extraordinary reach, with branches focused on intelligence, finance, politics, sabotage, and special operations."[22] His widespread influence and his quiet, charismatic personality made him a beloved figure in Iran and throughout the region. Worldwide, he was commonly considered to be the second most powerful person in Iran, after Grand Ayatollah Ali Khamenei.

Despite a growing sense in the intervening years of the dangers posed by Soleimani, Americans had cooperated with him in their attempts to build a provisional government in Iraq. After 9/11, the powerful and strategically minded Soleimani had allied with the United States, at least initially, in the effort to defeat the Taliban. As Ryan Crocker, then deputy chief of the U.S. embassy in Kabul, recalled, Soleimani and the United States shared information in the early stages of the war in Afghanistan—for example, in locating an al Qaeda terrorist in Iran and turning him over to the Afghans. And the governing counsel that the United States set up had been vetted with Soleimani. "Maybe it's time to rethink our relationship with the Americans," Soleimani was reported as saying.[23]

But thereafter, the relationship was fraught with distrust and blame. "Soleimani alternated between bargaining with the Americans and killing them," according to Filkins.[24] Officials began blaming him directly for the slipping of the U.S. grip on Iraq and the increasing internal fragility of the country. As Ben Rhodes, Obama's deputy national security advisor, would later comment, rather than "examining our own support for Saddam Hussein, who used chemical weapons against Iran, or the fact that our subsequent removal of Saddam did more to empower Iran than anything else that has happened in the ME since 1979," the United

States blamed Iran and, increasingly, Soleimani, whom they put on the sanctions list several times.[25]

If there was any one person on whom to tag the rationale for expanding the war on terror, it was Soleimani. Alongside his efforts to destabilize Iraq, Soleimani's power base extended throughout the region and especially to Syria, where he supported the regime of Bashar al-Assad against U.S. allied forces. In the greater region, he worked alongside terrorist groups, including Hezbollah.

Attacking Soleimani, however, would constitute an unprecedented expansion of the war on terror, involving the leading general of a country, and blurring the distinction between counterterrorism and an attack on a nation-state. While the possibility of killing Soleimani had been raised during both the Bush and Obama administrations, it was decided—according to Elissa Slotkin, who had served as a CIA analyst for both the Bush and Obama administrations before entering politics in 2019 as a congresswoman from Michigan—that "the ultimate ends didn't justify the means."[26] The potential for violent retaliation was too high. As the journalist Chris Whipple has written, it would "draw a target on the back of every single US government official."[27]

The decision not to expand the war to a full-on confrontation with Iran reflected a measure of restraint in applying the authority of the Authorization for the Use of Military Force (AUMF), even inside Iraq where Soleimani often functioned. In 2007, General Stanley McChrystal, the head of Joint Special Operations Command at the time, had come close to Soleimani's location and, faced with the chance to kill him, had exercised restraint. Soleimani's caravan was heading toward Erbil but McChrystal reasoned that "to avoid a firefight, and the contentious politics that would follow, I decided that we should monitor the caravan, not strike immediately." As a result, McChrystal recounted, Soleimani "slipped away."[28] The intense U.S. opposition to the war in Iraq, according to retired army colonel Frank Sobchak, an editor of the army's report on the Iraq War, had an impact on Bush who "was not willing to risk the political capital and repercussions that could occur from expanding the war to that level." General Petraeus, who led the surge in Iraq from 2007 to 2011 said, days after the strike, "We'd never gone after him before."[29]

Alarm over the danger Soleimani posed to the United States grew after the discovery of a 2011 plot, attributed to Soleimani, to assassinate the Saudi ambassador to the United States at a public and popular venue in Washington, DC, Cafe Milano. The U.S. Treasury subsequently designated Soleimani a "specially designated national," attempting to restrict his travel and his ability to conduct financial transactions; the Quds Force had already been designated a terrorist organization under Bush in 2007.[30] But there was never any manhunt, according to Derek Chollet, assistant secretary of defense from 2012 to 2015. "To my knowledge there was never a decision of 'We've gotta go find this guy and get him.'"[31] The Obama administration reportedly feared that an attack on the general could lead to uncontrollable acts of violence against American troops and potentially war.[32] Even in a time of expansive application of the use of force on the grounds of an association with terrorism, the limits on attacking Soleimani remained in place.

Tensions Escalate

The Trump administration was not held back by these concerns. Reaching for the subtle tool of imprecise language as a key to increasingly expansive definitions, in April 2018, the United States designated the Islamic Revolutionary Guard Corps a foreign terrorist organization.[33] It was an unusual move—declaring the military arm of a foreign nation to be a terrorist organization. Prior to this, such designations had customarily been used for nonstate actors.[34] Iran responded in-kind, designating the United States a foreign terrorist organization. The war on terror had successfully been expanded, opening the door for the events to follow.

Beginning in the late spring of 2019, a series of naval encounters increased tensions between Iran and the United States. In June, explosions from limpet mines—explosive devices attached magnetically to ships— damaged two oil tankers in the Gulf of Oman, one Japanese, one

Norwegian.[35] The Trump administration immediately blamed Iran. One week later, the Iranians shot down a $220 million U.S. surveillance drone over the Strait of Hormuz. Top national security officials, including Pompeo and Bolton and CIA director Gina Haspel, recommended retaliation, but instead, the United States issued a series of sanctions against Iranian officials, including against Supreme Leader Khamenei and his office, against Soleimani, and against Foreign Minister Mohammad Javad Zarif.[36]

Raising the stakes, in the fall of 2019, Iran and its proxies launched at least a dozen strikes against bases with U.S. forces present, including attacks on two Saudi oil facilities on September 14. Predictably, the United States responded, deploying troops to locations throughout the Middle East, including Saudi Arabia and the United Arab Emirates, calling them "defensive in nature" saying it would primarily provide additional air and missile defense capabilities."[37]

Then, on December 27, a rocket attack in Iraq by an Iranian-backed militia killed an American contractor and wounded four U.S. service members. The United States responded two days later by attacking two Kata'ib Hezbollah camps in Iraq and Syria, causing more than two dozen deaths and wounding fifty-five. "We strongly responded and always will," Trump tweeted.[38] Inside Iraq, demonstrators gathered outside the U.S. embassy in Baghdad in protest against the U.S. air strikes that had killed twenty-four members of an Iranian-backed militia in Iraq. The protesters yelled, "Death to America," clashing with U.S. guards outside the embassy.[39]

Preparing for the Attack

Changes in top national security posts paved the way for the attack on Soleimani. In July 2019, General Mark Milley was confirmed to replace Joseph Dunford as head of the Joint Chiefs, and Pompeo's West Point classmate, Mark Esper, replaced General Mattis as secretary of defense.[40] In August, Joseph Maguire replaced Director of National Intelligence Dan Coats, who in January 2019—to Trump's dismay—had downplayed Iran's nuclear ambitions in his Worldwide Threat Assessment to Congress. "Iran is not currently undertaking the key nuclear weapons-development activities we judge necessary to produce a nuclear device."[41] Then, most consequentially, in September 2019 Robert O'Brien, a top hostage negotiator, replaced John Bolton as national security advisor.[42]

O'Brien, well-known for taking a strong, hard line against Iran, had written an entire book excoriating Obama's policy toward Iran. Accusing Obama of naively thinking that diplomacy and concessions would "earn goodwill and reciprocity," he criticized the former president's compromise-driven approach by which he claimed "the autocrats, tyrants and terrorists were emboldened." For O'Brien, the JCPOA was the modern equivalent of Neville Chamberlain's appeasement of the Nazis in 1938. To drive his point home, he tweaked the title Winston Churchill used in a book denouncing Chamberlain's approach—*While England Slept*—and made it his own: *While America Slept: Restoring American Leadership to a World in Crisis.* [43] As Churchill had seen Chamberlain's acquiescence as a "defeat without a war," so O'Brien considered Obama's nuclear deal with Iran to be just that—essentially a surrender.

The Obama Legacy

Amid the shuffling of personnel, the administration ignored several reforms that had been put in place at the end of Obama's term in an attempt to guard against future uses of the subtle tools, particularly those of secrecy and imprecise language. In December 2016, the Obama administration, as one of its final acts, produced the "Report on the Legal and Policy Frameworks Guiding the United States' Use of Military Force and Related National Security Operations." It was a detailed examination, meant to reflect the commitment to transparency that Obama had pledged in his early days in office, including five new documents that undergirded the administration's policies on the use of force. In setting out the legal and policy parameters of many aspects of the war on terror—from use of force, to targeted killings, to the detention and treatment of those who were captured—the Framework was intended to serve as an explanation of Obama's policies, to reflect the many complex discussions that had led to policy decisions, and to sum up for the incoming administration a template for considering the limitations of law and policy on the use of force.[44]

Three areas of discussion would come to bear directly on the decision to kill Soleimani. Two provided little by way of restraint: "imminence" and "assassination." Here, as in earlier memos, the Obama team defined "imminence" as something that did not require "specific evidence of where an attack will take place or of the precise nature of an attack," adding that the requirement of an imminent attack as a justification for the use of force did not prevent measures taken in self-defense. Rather than offering a more limited definition of the word "imminence," the Framework added a new element for consideration, namely, that the concept of imminence was changing "in light of the modern-day capabilities, techniques, and technological innovations of terrorist organizations."

Similarly, for "assassination," sophisticated semantics pulled the rug out from under lawful restraints. The Framework reiterated the Obama administration's conclusion that targeted strikes did not constitute assassinations and were therefore lawful. In 1976, President Gerald Ford had issued an executive order banning assassination. Since then, presidents had bypassed the ban by claiming "self-defense," as Reagan did in a failed attack in 1985 against the Lebanese cleric Mohammad Hussein Fadlallah, and as President Clinton did when contemplating an attack against Osama bin Laden in the 1990s. The Obama Framework reiterated the use of targeted killings as lawful and important. "Removing the senior leadership of terrorist groups against which the United States is engaged in hostilities—including those in charge of plotting attacks against the United States and its partners—is an important piece of the overall U.S. strategy for defeating these groups."

But when it came to "associated forces," the report offered some clear guidance limiting the use of the term to groups who were "co-belligerent with al Qaeda and the Taliban in hostilities" directed against the United States or coalition partners, not merely to those identified by ideological association. Nor, the Framework stated, did the AUMF "authorize the President to use force against every group that commits terrorist acts."

As much as the Obama Framework was about the content of decision making, it was also about procedure and good governance practices, and was thus attentive to the problems that lack of procedural norms could cause in the national security context. Throughout, the Framework touched on something that proved to be absent when it came to the decision to strike Soleimani—namely, the observance of in-depth consideration of each decision and each policy as they evolved. As it would throughout the report, the emphasis on determinations made "at the most senior levels" and only after "careful" evaluation, consideration, and fact-intensive reviews was considered to be essential. The Framework presciently and repeatedly emphasized the need to adhere to established procedures in order to ensure legitimacy and caution in the use of force. As Obama wrote in the Framework's preface, "I directed my team to work continually to refine, clarify, and strengthen the standards and processes pursuant to which the United States conducts its national security operations."

The report was accompanied by a presidential memorandum that called upon the next president's National Security Council staff to continue to prepare "on no less than an annual basis" an updated report to the Obama Framework, laying out in similar fashion the scope, breadth, and current interpretations of legal policies pertaining to the use of force, and to "arrange for the report to be released to the public." Congress agreed to the need for the updates and the 2018 National Defense Authorization Act called specifically for such a report to be delivered to the Congress by March 12, 2018. All told, the Obama Framework, while allowing for the expansive use of the terms "imminence" and "assassination," nevertheless drew newly precise lines when it came to the uses of the AUMF and the bureaucratic steps by which decisions of such consequence should be made.

Casting aside the regard for process and precision, the Trump administration ignored the procedural precision outlined in the Framework. They failed to produce the updated report within the first year—a refusal, as former senior director for counterterrorism at the National Security Council (NSC) under Obama Joshua Geltzer has pointed out, that enabled the administration to keep secret its legal reasoning behind the use of strikes in Syria, and to stay silent on whether the caveats of the Obama Framework—such as the expansion of the term "associated forces"—had been ignored or adhered to.[45] Rather than imprecision, there was simply a vacuum.

In October 2019, Trump's National Security Council—now authorized by Congress to do so—belatedly produced its own version of the Framework.[46] The Trump Framework—8 pages in length, compared to the 66-page Obama Framework, and with zero footnotes compared to the 259 footnotes in the Obama Framework—offered very little by way of analysis, or even policy goals. The message was one of disdain for details and for the task at hand. Frequently, it merely repeated passages from the Obama report. In its repetitive language and overall brevity, it conveyed the impression that publishing the report was regarded more as a nuisance than a task of any import.

When it came to the use of lethal drones in targeted killings, the Trump report was particularly brief. The Obama Framework had included an extensive section on the topic of targeted killings, reiterating the memos that had led to the policy of drone attacks, including the one authorizing the killing of U.S. citizen Anwar al-Awlaki. The Trump Framework reduced this "Targeting" section to a single paragraph, skipping gingerly over the matter of assassination and focusing on the effort to protect civilians, continuing "as a matter of policy, to apply heightened targeting standards that are more protective of civilians than are required under the law of armed conflict." The Trump Framework stayed silent on the legality of targeted killings even though the Obama administration had handed them a wide berth for conducting such activities.

By late fall 2019, the pieces—including the policy outline and the administration's support—were in place for the strike against Soleimani.

The Strike

When General Soleimani and his convoy were attacked early in the morning on January 3, 2020 in a convoy headed away from the Baghdad International Airport, he had just arrived from Syria. While few in the national security community disputed the danger Soleimani posed and the death and destruction he had caused, the path to the decision to kill him was laden with confusion over the aims and authorities underlying the act.[47]

In the decision to strike the general, Trump and his team cast to the wind custom and law, as well as the limits prescribed in the Obama Framework. If history and custom had been the guide, a full vetting in a closed setting with a wide panoply of other stakeholders participating in the national security conversation would have been present in person. Many former national security officials, including those who had served both Republican and Democratic presidents, determined that there had been an apparent absence of what Jonathan Stevenson, the former NSC director of political-military affairs for the Middle East and North Africa, called in an op-ed "proper interagency review." As "in the kind of robust interagency, national security decision-making process that the National Security Council (NSC) staff is supposed to supervise, such concerns would have been systematically raised, dissected and discussed, and a consensus reached to inform presidential action. No such process seems to have occurred here."[48] As John Brennan, former CIA director and President Obama's advisor on homeland security during his second term, remarked, "the lack of a rigorous interagency process would have been astounding for such an important decision."[49]

Michele Flournoy, under secretary of defense for Obama, noted just after the Soleimani strike that the neglect of standard decision-making procedures were common in the Trump administration. "[F]or a very long time now, that normal process has been nonexistent. The deputies rarely meet and the principals rarely meet. Very serious decisions are brought to the president without a whole lot of vetting and exploration of second- and third-order consequences."[50]

The setting for the decision, the events leading up to the decision, and the ultimate categorization of the event seemed to cast aside any and all best practices that the Obama Framework had recommended. Trump's Mar-a-Lago home in Florida was far from the experts, policy-makers, and access to information that such a momentous decision required. The physical distance from DC and the casual setting of a country club reinforced an underlying reality—the president was acting with little regard for the benefits, let alone the professionalism, of consultation. Congress had not authorized the attack, though House minority leader Kevin McCarthy and Senator Lindsey Graham were briefed, visiting Florida in the days leading up to the attack.[51] In addition, many of the professional voices that should have weighed in together were absent. It would have been important to have at the table those who best understood the delicate situation of Iraq, a predominantly Shia Muslim country, which since the U.S. invasion in 2003 had balanced its interests between pressures posed by the United States and Iran, the home of Shia Islam. Certainly, the heads of the intelligence agencies—particularly the director of national intelligence and the director of the CIA—would have been present. So, too, the voice of the ambassador to Iraq where the strike took place would have been important, along with recommendations from the secretary of energy, to address the impact it would have on the nuclear arms race generally and remaining signatories on the deal. The secretary of the Treasury would have been in attendance to address its impact on the sanctions regime. And the attorney general could help discuss legal parameters of the planned attack.

Detailing the norms that would customarily have been followed prior to a decision of such magnitude, three former national security officials penned an op-ed contrasting the norms that would customarily been followed with what seemed to them apparent in the Soleimani decision. "Instead of holding a tightly managed, inclusive debate in the Situation Room, Trump made one of the most dangerous choices of his presidency among a tiny group at Mar-a-Lago." The authors, who had collectively served twenty-five years in national security positions at the White House and in the Pentagon, described how such important decisions are "are supposed to be made." "Such decisive moments are usually preceded by hundreds of people spending countless hours in dingy government offices and conference rooms, building PowerPoint slides and questioning lawyers. These individuals create the parameters and permutations of what the decision-makers consider. They identify the possible options, vetting their likely operational, diplomatic, economic, and other effects. That work enables the commander-in-chief to make wrenching decisions about his military options wisely."[52]

The lack of norms in the decision making for the strike was, in the words of Jonathan Stevenson, a sign of "the abject dysfunction and deterioration of the national security process under Mr. Trump."[53] In a customary vetting process, the opinions, caveats, lawful parameters, and expectations voiced by each of these officials would in normal times have been crucial. But these were not normal times. The full National Security Council and its processes would have preceded the decision, with the deputies committee, the principles committee, and finally a meeting with the president in full command of the intelligence offerings of the government's top analysts and experts.

It's not that some of these individuals were not consulted—for example, AG Barr and CIA director Haspel later let it be known that they had weighed in on the decision. It's that the full complement of voices was not there in the room together to hash out the legal and political equities of a decision of such magnitude as would customarily be the case.[54] The subtle tool of ignoring process and protocol, and in so doing, enhancing the power of the president and his closest advisors to act unilaterally, was brandished here with a vigor that defied tradition in matters of great national consequence. The full-scale abandonment of procedural norms alongside the reliance on expansive interpretations of terms codified under law reflected yet again the zealous use of the subtle tools by the Trump administration. When the close hold on such decisions in the past had preceded acts of such import, the consequences could fall directly on the future of the presidency. Certainly, this was the case with Nixon's secret bombings and invasion of Cambodia, which led to the passage of the 1973 War Powers Resolution that puts stringent constraints on the president's making unilateral decisions about going to war.

The seemingly casual, insular, and neglectful method evidenced at Mar-a-Lago in January 2020 was not a unique instance of Trump upending process in matters of national security. The president was known to exclude top officials from meetings in which they would normally be involved as part of the Senate-confirmed responsibilities for their position. Similarly minimizing the importance of expertise, he added Steve Bannon—a media entrepreneur and 2016 campaign manager for Trump—to the prestigious and consequential Principals Committee of the National Security Council. Furthermore, he repeatedly marginalized his top intelligence official, Dan Coats, most remarkably when Coats learned in a live interview with NBC correspondent Andrea Mitchell during the 2018 Aspen Security Conference that the president had invited Putin to the White House without telling him. "Say that again?" Coats remarked, visibly stunned.[55]

If the wider group had been gathered for prolonged, intense, serial discussions, as protocol demanded, then caveats about the broad legal, geopolitical, and overall security concerns tied to such an extrajudicial killing would no doubt have arisen. Discussion would have focused on the limit of the AUMFs when it came to a strike like the one proposed. Relying on those authorities, officials would likely have noted, could broaden their scope in novel ways. Although the AUMFs for 2001 and 2002 had been interpreted by Bush and Obama to launch attacks on an increasingly broad set of targets, their application to an Iranian government official would represent an even further expansion. In particular, the 2001 AUMF, relied upon most heavily for geographical expansion, applied to nonstate actors, not high-ranking officials of a sovereign country.[56] As top U.S. generals from the theater of war explained it, for Iran, Soleimani served as the equivalent of the head of the CIA and the head of Joint Special Operations Command combined.[57] Therefore, the decision to attack, building upon the tendency of prior presidents to use the AUMF ever-expansively, recalled the original language of the AUMF, which authorized the president to "deter and preempt any related future acts of terrorism and aggression against the United States." Considered too broad an authority, even in the immediate days after 9/11, its intent had lived on, as the decision to target Soleimani illustrated.

Because these wide-ranging preparatory discussions did not take place, the dysfunction of the administration in the aftermath of the strike was also disorganized, bordering on incoherence. For starters, the top officials who brought the news to the American people could not agree on either the security rationale or the legal authorizations for the strike. The subtle tools of imprecision, bypassing process, and lack of transparency in providing the details of the decision thus came to the fore.

The Aftermath

In the immediate aftermath of the strike, the Trump team further wielded the subtle tools, again even more forcefully than their predecessors had. Having brazenly taken the concept of "imminence" to the targeting of a nation-state official, the distinction between state and nonstate actor seemed poised to vanish. As if to deflect any criticism on that point, Trump described Soleimani as a general and a terrorist, rather than acknowledging that he was part of the Iranian leadership. Speaking from Mar-a-Lago after the attack, Trump called Soleimani the "number one terrorist anywhere in the world," and explained that he was "plotting imminent and sinister attacks on American diplomats and military personnel," adding, "but we caught him in the act and terminated him." Trump also had another explanation, however. "He has been perpetrating acts of terror to destabilize the Middle East for 20 years."[58]

In subsequent days, the administration went back and forth on the explanation for the strike. Trump told Fox News's Laura Ingraham that Soleimani had been planning to attack four embassies, and provided details on one. "We will tell you that probably it was going to be the embassy in Baghdad."[59] It was imprecision masked as a national security secret. Secretary of State Pompeo informed the press that Soleimani had planned a "large-scale" attack against a range of U.S. facilities in the Middle East. As Trump had, Pompeo admitted not knowing the specifics of any such planned attack, only that an attack would occur and was considered to be imminent.[60] When pressed for specifics, Pompeo referred obliquely to the strike as being "in response to imminent threats to American lives." On CNN, he referred to Soleimani "actively plotting to take actions."[61] National Security Advisor O'Brien concurred. "We had very good intelligence that there was an imminent attack being planned.... I've seen the intelligence and it was it was incredibly strong intelligence."[62] Secretary of Defense Esper, who had at first confessed to no knowledge of an imminent attack, recanted and asserted that "Soleimani was in the act of planning attacks against Americans." It was an assertion without detail, specifics, or the presentation of credible evidence.

Almost immediately, the imprecise, generalized claims about the imminent threat against U.S. embassies was disputed by members of Congress and others who were determined to put restraints back in place on the unilateral use of force evidenced in the Soleimani strike. Democratic Senator Chris Van Hollen said it "just shows how they're making this up as they go."[63] Legally, the claims of imminence required some factual basis in order to comply with international law. To present the new argument, the president took to Twitter. The answer to "whether or not the future attack by terrorist Soleimani" was "'imminent' or not, & was my team in agreement. The answer to both is a strong YES." He concluded his tweet with "but it doesn't really matter because of his horrible past!" Under scrutiny for use of the term "imminent," President Trump and Secretary of State Pompeo began to redirect attention away from mere claims of imminence, emphasizing instead Soleimani's past acts against Americans.

The military leadership supported this emphasis on the killing as justifiable because of both imminence and retribution. Esper advocated for the long view:

> Qassem Soleimani was responsible for 20 years' worth of attacks on United States forces. He was also responsible for killing of civilians in other countries to include his own in Iran. He was responsible for the attacks leading up to the attack that killed the American on an air base and the siege of the embassy. And so there was complete agreement, based on what he had done and what he was planning to do, the broader attack that he was orchestrating in the region, that that would be bigger in scale and that would likely result in open hostilities, that this was a compelling target to take out.[64]

Mark Milley, chairman of the Joint Chiefs, emphasized imminence and knowledge of past deeds as justification for the attack, claiming the United States had "clear, unambiguous" intelligence that the top Iranian general, Soleimani, was planning a significant campaign of violence against the United States when it decided to strike him. He added that the risk of inaction exceeded the risk that killing him might dramatically escalate tensions with Tehran.[65]

Delving further into imprecision, the administration revisited its claims that Soleimani was a terrorist and insisted on emphasizing anew the connection between Iran and al Qaeda. Secretary of State Pompeo took to the conservative hustings. Speaking at Stanford's Hoover Institute, Pompeo first justified the killing by comparing Soleimani to the leader of al Qaeda on 9/11. "There is no terrorist except Usama bin Ladin [sic] who has more American blood on his hands than did Qasem Soleimani," "the mastermind" of attacks upon American troops and U.S. allies. His speech, titled "The Restoration of Deterrence: The Iranian Example,"[66] spelled out the ways in which the killing signified that "restoration of deterrence." Iran had pushed too far. It was time to show them what the consequences would be. "President Trump and those of us in his national security team are re-establishing deterrence—real deterrence—against the Islamic Republic. In strategic terms, deterrence simply means persuading the other party that the costs of a specific behavior exceed its benefits. It requires credibility; indeed, it depends on it. Your adversary must understand not only do you have the capacity to impose costs but that you are, in fact, willing to do so." The invocation of deterrence further confused the explanation for the strike, pivoting away from the claims of an imminent attack as the precipitating reason for killing Soleimani.

At the same time, the nation's top lawyer stepped into the arena of conflicting messages. Attorney General Bill Barr wanted to make it absolutely clear. The attack was "legitimate." Barr acknowledged that in fact the Department of Justice had been brought into the decision ahead of the killing of Soleimani, whom Barr claimed was "a legitimate military target." "This was a legitimate act of self-defense for us because it disrupted ongoing attacks," he said. "I believe that the president clearly had the authority to act as he did."[67]

When it came to the question of whether or not an imminent attack was being planned by Soleimani, Barr refused to get mired in the legal terminology. "The concept of imminence is something of a red herring," he said. With "attacks underway," Barr doubted the need for specific knowledge about attacks to come. "I don't think there is a requirement, frankly, of knowing the exact time and place of the next attack." Barr's statement was in accordance, as he noted, with the "position of the

Obama administration" with its broadened notion of imminence. One member of the press pointed to the fact that the Soleimani killing was the killing of a state official, not a nonstate actor. "Did you give any special consideration of the fact that he was a senior official of another government," the reporter asked, adding, "that he was a general of Iran?"[68]

Barr avoided the question and the legal quagmire it suggested, answering, "He was the head of a terrorist organization." He added, "Military targets are appropriate legitimate targets."[69]

The continued back and forth over the rationale behind the strikes circled around matters of constitutional, international, and statutory law. But the conclusion was never in doubt. National security officials knew well how to expand the terms of the war on terror framework in increasingly imprecise and expansive ways. Nevertheless, the Trump administration's response to the strike, and the lack of procedural, normative decision making leading up to it, exposed a disregard for even engaging the legal debate. Instead, in the aftermath of the strike, officials groped not for legal explanations but for talking points.

The determination to claim the authorities necessary to achieve their goals became apparent in comments made by Secretary of Defense Mark Esper to NPR. During an interview with the host of *All Things Considered*, Ari Shapiro, which aired on January 14, Esper, discussing retaliatory measures against Iran generally, referred both to the two AUMFs and the president's commander-in-chief powers as justifying any such future attacks. "Well, we feel we have sufficient authority now either under the commander-in-chief's Article 2 authorities or under the two authorizations to use military force, the so-called AUMFs, to do what we need to protect American interests, to defeat terrorism and to prosecute any operations that we need within those legal contexts."[70] But when NPR's Shapiro pushed Esper on legal authorities for attacking Iran itself, Esper admitted, "We do not have the authority right now to strike the country of Iran for actions taken by a proxy group."

After the taping, NPR received a call from Esper's press secretary, asking for a second taping, a chance "to clarify his answer pertaining to potential U.S. retaliation against Iranian proxy groups." Esper wanted to change his remarks about the lack of authority for a U.S. attack against

Iran. NPR agreed to give him the opportunity for clarification about his assertion, in Shapiro's words, "that the U.S. has authority to attack those militias in Iraq but not Iran and I understand you want to clarify that." "Right," Esper acknowledged, citing the 2002 AUMF authorities, and adding, "With regard to Iranian proxies I'd say this: First and foremost, we hold Iran responsible for its proxies and we retain the right to exercise self-defense and to take action where legally available and appropriate to hold those proxies accountable for their actions." Shapiro pushed further on attacking Iran directly. "Does that include on Iranian soil?" he asked. "We will take any and all legally available and appropriate actions to hold Iran accountable for the actions of its proxies." Making the significance of Esper's claims to the right to attack Iran crystal clear, Shapiro asked "Do you believe the U.S. has the legal authority to strike Iran for the actions of militias in Iraq?" "Yes, we do," Esper answered. This time he cited "the president's constitutional authority under the Constitution that many presidents have exercised for decades to protect America, to protect our people and to protect our forces."[71] The president, in sum, *did* have the authority to order an attack on Iran. When the interview ran, the addition was included as an addendum to the original interview.[72] The disregard for legal authorities that had led to the strike in the first place now colored the after-action explanation and the prospect of future potentially unilateral decisions by the president to attack Iran.

The Fallout

Despite worries that the strike could lead to war, Iran's retaliation was limited to rocket attacks on two American air bases—bases that were cleared out owing to Iran giving advance notice about the attacks to the Iraqi government.[73] Still, it was a risky and destructive move; while no one was killed, later accounts reported over one hundred injured in the form of traumatic brain injuries from the impact of the missiles. Foreign Minister Zarif used the language of international law to explain Iran's actions, saying that "Iran took and concluded proportionate measures in self-defense under Article 51 of UN Charter targeting base from which cowardly armed attack against our citizens and senior officials

were launched. We do not seek escalation or war, but will defend ourselves against any aggression."[74]

With Trump and the Iranians both talking tough, an attempt by Congress almost succeeded in pushing back against any further use of the
subtle tool of imprecision when it came to the interpretation of the law
as authorizing broad, unilateral behavior. On January 9, the House
passed an Iran War Powers Resolution prohibiting the president from
attacking Iran, referencing the 1973 War Powers Resolution restricting
the president from authorizing military attacks without congressional
authorization. The Senate followed suit on February 13, also authorizing
restraint on any use of force by the president against Iran. In May, the
president vetoed the resolution. The Senate was unable to muster the
two-thirds majority needed to overturn the veto. The attempt at restraint,
well-intentioned and sending a message, had ultimately not reined in the
president's potential future deployment of force against Iran.[75]

The move recognized the danger that an administration, armed with
the subtle tools, could pose. In the case of the strike against Soleimani,
Trump officials had used the subtle tool of imprecision as a gateway to
claiming expansive authorities in the use of force. Building on the broad
use of the terms of "imminence" and "assassination," on the ever-wider
application of the AUMFs, and adding in an egregious bypassing of the
procedural norms pertinent to national security, the Trump administration had taken the war on terror toolbox to a level that defied legal
norms and successfully resisted congressional restraint.

As the Obama Framework had articulated, the avoidance of specificity, clarity, and strict adherence to procedure and rules was essential to
pulling back on the expansive use of the subtle tools that had become
essential to U.S. foreign policy. But, as the strike against Soleimani
showed, those tools, once put into play, proved resilient.

With the assassination of Soleimani, Trump had taken the subtle tools
back to the context of their origins—the war on terror—and had transformed them into seemingly undeterrable weapons. Tethered neither by
the need to use lawfully accurate language, nor by the need to obey the
law, nor by the expectations of transparency, the killing of Soleimani set
the stage for a continually expansive use of the subtle tools in 2020.

8

The Black Lives Matter Protests

MILITARIZING THE HOME FRONT

When the looting starts, the shooting starts.

DONALD TRUMP, MAY 29, 2020

DHS was established for years like this.

CHAD WOLF, SEPTEMBER 9, 2020

ON THE EVENING of Monday, May 25, 2020, in the Powderhorn Park neighborhood of Minneapolis, Officer Derek Chauvin dug his knee deep into the neck of an unarmed, handcuffed Black man who was kneeling on the sidewalk, his head pressed against the pavement. Nine and a half minutes later, George Floyd was dead.

Floyd's murder at the hands of the police revitalized the Black Lives Matter protest movement that had originated in 2013 in response to the murder of Trayvon Martin. Now, in 2020, the country erupted in protests once again—first in Minneapolis, then in seventy-five other cities by week's end.[1] By the end of August, thousands of protests, large and small, had engulfed the nation.[2]

From the evening of the murder through the 2020 presidential election on November 3, as protesters gathered night after night, the administration's weaponization of the subtle tools reached a new level of ferocity and breadth, and in doing so, reached their limit for the first time since 9/11. Imprecise language and disregard for the boundaries between the Department of Justice (DOJ) and the Department of Homeland Security (DHS) allowed federal troops (deployed in defiance of the authorities legally pertaining to states) to target protesters—and in response, citizens, courts, and dissenters, many with government pedigrees, took a stand against vagueness, breadth, secrecy, and the bypassing of norms.

The War at Home

Three days after the murder, President Trump finally addressed it. "I feel very, very badly. That's a very shocking sight."[3] He said nothing about addressing police misbehavior or institutional racism. In the weeks to come, he would start reminding the press that "more White people" died at the hands of the police than Blacks, and would begin denigrating the demonstrators.[4]

Protests against the use of excessive police force began the next night in Minneapolis as hundreds of protesters amassed at the police precinct, leaving graffiti on cars as well as buildings, setting fires, and looting. The police responded with tear gas and rubber bullets. In cities across the country, similar protests and confrontations with police broke out. In New York City, clashes left protesters and the police wounded. Violence in Detroit, Chicago, and St. Louis led to injuries and three deaths. Reports of police using pepper spray and rubber bullets cropped up in Philadelphia and New York City. In Los Angeles, the 101 Freeway was blocked by protesters. By May 31, the National Guard had been deployed in more than two dozen states, and mayors in several cities had imposed curfews.[5]

On June 1, after five days of protests, Trump told the press assembled in the Rose Garden of the White House: "These are terrorists. These are terrorists," he repeated for effect, speaking of the protesters. "They're looking to do bad things to our country." Latching onto the vocabulary of the war on terror, Trump was also embracing the subtle tool of imprecision in language that had contorted the word "terrorist" to apply not only to insurgent groups abroad but to a wide swath of Muslims in the United States. Now, he appropriated it for protesters in the streets of America.

Facing the danger of "terrorists," Trump took the misplaced analogy one step further. He declared war against them at home as his predecessors had declared war against terrorists abroad. "I am dispatching thousands and thousands of heavily armed soldiers, military personnel and law enforcement officers to stop the rioting, looting, vandalism, assaults and the wanton destruction of property." Blurring the distinction between the military and law enforcement, Trump set in motion a muddying of authorities that would continue throughout many months of protests.

Earlier that day, the president had convened a call with the country's governors to talk about how to best respond to the protests.[6] "It's like we're talking about war," Trump said, "which it is a war in a certain sense, and we're going to end it fast." Secretary of Defense Mark Esper and Chairman of the Joint Chiefs of Staff Mark Milley joined him on the call, reinforcing Trump's message that the military was the appropriate counterforce for the protests—and Milley, Trump announced, would lead the government's response to the protests. A "fighter" and "a warrior," the president reminded his listeners, Milley, who had fought in Afghanistan and Iraq, could bring his skills to the American streets. Secretary of Defense Esper took the analogy to warfare further. "We need to dominate the battle space," Esper chimed in. This time the war would be waged not against Islamic terrorists, and not at the border, but against citizens in American cities.

Confounding the distinctions between law enforcement and military deployment even further, Attorney General Barr also joined on the call. The Department of Justice would stand at the forefront in this confrontation, expanding the role it had played in the war on terror into the protest movement. The attorney general immediately and forcefully established the link between the war on terror and the government's response to the protests. The Department of Justice, Barr explained, had tasked the Joint Terrorism Task Forces [JTTFs], a combination of FBI agents and local and state law enforcement distributed throughout the country, with identifying and arresting nonpeaceful protesters. "It's worked for domestic homegrown terrorists. And we're going to apply that model."

The aim of the president's discussion was to persuade the governors to call in the National Guard. While he had the authority to deploy them in DC, it was up to the governors, eleven of whom spoke on the call, to make the decision within the states, other than in exceptional circumstances. Trump chastised the governors for failing to have done so already; there were 350,000 National Guard troops available, but most states had only called in 200, and many had called in none. "You have to dominate." Trump exhorted. "If you don't dominate, you're wasting your time. They're going to run over you." The governors would, in other words, lose the war.

Minnesota governor Tim Walz, a Democrat from the state where the Floyd murder had occurred, rejected the nationwide call to war that the president was espousing on the phone, although Walz himself had called in the Minnesota National Guard days earlier after rioting, looting, and arson in Minneapolis had led to damage estimated at $82 million. Walz called in the first National Guard troops on May 28, deploying them incrementally over the next two days and activating a total of 5,025 by May 31. That same day, after Walz had already reached out to the Guard, the president tweeted out a threat to send in more National Guard units himself and reported that he had spoken to Walz about it. "Any difficulty," the president tweeted, irritated at Walz's independent actions regarding the Guard, "and we will assume control but, when the looting starts, the shooting starts."[7]

Walz had himself spent twenty-four years in the National Guard. He understood what assignments the Guard was normally tasked with. As Walz explained on the governors' call on June 1, the deployment of the National Guard had to be done cautiously and thoughtfully. You have to "make sure that it's not seen as an occupying force," he told the president. Instead, Walz recommended the use of local forces, composed of "their neighbors, schoolteachers, business owners."

Walz's use of local forces rather than a federalized National Guard was based not just on the potential destructiveness that militarization posed for communities but on the law itself. The Posse Comitatus Act passed in 1878 prevents the use of federal military troops on U.S. soil except in certain instances where the Constitution—theoretically for sudden emergencies or the protection of private property—or a statute has authorized it, as in the case of insurrection or domestic violence. A president could thus bypass this ban by invoking the Insurrection Act, which authorizes the president to deploy federal troops without congressional authorization at the request of a state government, or when an insurrection "impedes enforcement of federal law" or "obstructs the execution of state law so as to deprive persons within a given state of any constitutional right." It is not martial law, as constitutional civil liberties protections still apply. The law originated in 1807 under Thomas Jefferson and has been invoked twenty-two times by twelve presidents, most commonly to restore order during labor strikes and race riots. The last time it had been invoked was 1992 by George H. W. Bush in response to the Los Angeles race riots that followed the acquittal, by an all-white jury, of the policemen who had brutally beaten the Black man Rodney King. Even in establishing the Department of Homeland Security, the Congress had backed away from diluting the clear line dividing military forces from civilian space, instead, as a congressional research report summed it up, "reaffirming the continued importance and applicability of the Posse Comitatus Act."[8]

But Trump disagreed with Walz. This was war, and it was incumbent upon the governors to use the tactics of war. He was frustrated with the limits posed by the law. "I must say," Trump confessed to the governors, "I wish we had an occupying force." Trump praised the National Guard's use of paramilitary tactics in the face of the current protests. Recounting the aggressive behavior of the troops that had been sent into Minneapolis after Floyd's killing, he applauded the paramilitary aspects of the guards who were "wearing dark black uniforms. They got out and they got out and they were there in the thousands and they just walked right down the street, knocking them out with tear gas."

Outside the White House, the paramilitary behavior he championed would soon occur.

Protesters, many in their twenties and thirties, had gathered on the streets surrounding the White House and nearby Lafayette Square as

Trump gave his Rose Garden address. While the protest reportedly showed little by way of a serious threat, the numbers and varieties of law enforcement officials seemed to anticipate a battle scene. Officers from a broad array of agencies carried large body shields as well as face shields. Many sported grenadiers, some for launching tear gas, others for spewing out pepper balls.[9] Many carried wooden batons. The weaponized forces represented both law enforcement and the military, just as President Trump had promoted on his call with the governors. A Bureau of Prisons Special Operations Group (SOG)—trained to counter prison riots, not to deter youthful gatherings in a park—stood at the ready. Dozens of Park Police rode on horseback. Members of the Secret Service and the DC National Guard were there; over a thousand National Guard were deployed within the city as well.[10] They were joined by agents from the Drug Enforcement Administration, the FBI, the Bureau of Alcohol, Tobacco, Firearms and Explosives, and the Arlington County Police Department. Secretary Esper had put out a call to the states to send their National Guards as well, though many, including Virginia, Delaware, and New York refused to comply with the request. Troops from Tennessee, South Carolina, Utah, and West Virginia arrived, their units carrying in weapons and ammunition, consisting, according to the *New York Times*, of "thousands of rifle and pistol rounds" that were stored in the DC Armory.[11]

The president was scheduled to arrive at Lafayette Square at 7:00 p.m. that evening, after his Rose Garden speech. A newly ordered curfew announced by Mayor Muriel Bowser was set to begin at 7:00 p.m. as well; as such, the timing of the president's arrival seemed designed to maximize trouble and give the forces a chance to exercise their might. As the president's appearance drew nearer, tensions rose and law enforcement became increasingly aggressive. Video and firsthand reports show officers shoving, clubbing, and punching protesters in an attempt to disperse them from an expanding perimeter, as a directive issued late in the day from Attorney General Barr called for more and more area to be cleared.[12] Protesters threw eggs, candy bars, and water bottles, while law enforcement shot rubber bullets, launched pepper balls, and fired tear gas into the crowd.[13]

Just before 7:00 p.m., Trump began to walk from the Rose Garden toward the park. He was headed for St. John's Church, known as the Church of the Presidents, located across the street from Lafayette Square. Underscoring the militarized law and order message of the day, Trump was flanked by Chairman Milley, who was dressed in combat camouflage fatigues, by Secretary of Defense Mark Esper, and by Attorney General William Barr. As they walked, the police and guards intensified their attacks on protesters in the park and on the surrounding streets.[14]

Amid the turmoil, the president strolled 900 feet along Pennsylvania Avenue to the church, held up a bible, and then retraced his steps to the White House.[15] Within the next hour, 54 arrests were made. Over the course of a week of protests, 430 individuals were arrested, most of them for violating the four-day curfew. Of these, 80 were charged in DC Superior Court and six in federal court, most with felony rioting or burglary.[16] Meanwhile, as the acting chief of the U.S. Park Police later testified in Congress, objects thrown by protesters included "bricks, rocks, caustic liquids, water bottles, lit flares, fireworks, and 2 × 4 sections of wood." "These violent protestors," the acting chief reported, had "caused injuries to over 50 officers of the United States Park Police. Of those, 11 officers were transported to the hospital and three were ultimately admitted."[17]

Trump and Barr's staging of a militarized, weaponized response to the protests in DC brought national attention to the use of the subtle tools. Trump had blurred the distinctions between war and the home front, between the military and civilian spheres, and between the laws pertaining to war and the laws pertaining to the home front. It was linguistic imprecision (protesters as terrorists), bureaucratic porousness (an array of law enforcement bodies operating far outside their usual jurisdiction), and a violation of norms deployed in a coordinated manner that would define the administration's response to the protests.

But as it turned out, Trump's transformation of DC into a military zone had gone too far. He had taken the paired tools of overstepping norms and bureaucratic porousness one step further than the structures of government could bear. Several days later, Secretary Esper told reporters he had erred in accompanying Trump to the church, divulging that he had not known the purpose of the walk to the church—namely, that it was for a photo op—or about the plans of law enforcement to clear the park of protesters.[18] The following week, General Milley withdrew his support for the president's call for militarization as a response to the protests. He apologized for appearing alongside the president in Lafayette Square. "I should not have been there," he told graduates in a commencement speech taped for the National Defense University, acknowledging that he had created "a perception of the military involved in domestic politics."[19] Milley, it seemed, would not be heading the national response, as Trump had stated.

Milley and Esper had drawn a line in the sand when it came to bureaucratic porousness between the military and civilian spheres. These were the two highest officials inside the U.S. military, both presidentially appointed, and both disagreeing with the president. And they were not alone. Other colleagues in law enforcement were drawing their own lines in the sand, disputing the use of the subtle tools as their presence became increasingly overt.

The War on Terror versus Trump

On June 17, 2020, a bipartisan group, whom the *Washington Post* labeled "The G.O.P. Architects of the Post-9/11 Security Order," issued a statement, joining the chorus condemning the administration's response and expressing their opposition to "the use of the active military to patrol the streets of our cities in response to the ongoing protests."[20] The twenty-three signatories were members of the forty-person Homeland Security Experts Group, a nonpartisan group composed of national security officials and experts. Created in 2011 as the Aspen Homeland Security Group, its members met twice yearly to identify pressing national security issues and make recommendations to the secretary of homeland security and other relevant policymakers. The signatories to the letter decrying the use of military force on June 1 included the first two secretaries of homeland security, Tom Ridge and Michael Chertoff, as well as the man who would one day assume the position under

President Biden, former deputy secretary for homeland security Alejandro Mayorkas. Also included on the list of names was former CIA director and National Security Agency director Michael Hayden, former CIA and FBI director William Webster, and two former heads of the National Counterterrorism Center, Michael Leiter and Matt Olsen. Their signed statement served as a stinging rebuke from those most involved in the war on terror, a group that recognized well the tools at play, understood their power—and could no longer stay silent as these tools were turned on the American people.

In explaining their opposition to the use of the military to counter the protests, they bluntly rejected the manner in which the subtle tools had been used. A military response, they argued, confused the legal lines between "civilian and military authorities." Their statement implicitly referenced the Posse Comitatus Act, the country's long history of restraint in invoking the Insurrection Act, and the constitutional violations involved in the use of the military in a civilian context. "We reject a militarized response to protests to deny citizens their constitutional rights," they wrote, referring to the First Amendment right of assembly and free speech and the Fourth Amendment protections from unlawful search and seizure. "The mostly peaceful protests across the nation did not warrant such a response," they claimed, asserting "we believe our law enforcement and homeland security institutions are best situated both practically and legally to address these challenges."

While bureaucratic porousness and the violation of norms were of paramount concern, the tools of imprecision and secrecy had, according to the national security experts and officials, also contributed to the errors embodied in the deployment of the military in civilian space. "The blanket use of the label 'terrorists' to justify the use of para-military and military force is both factually wrong and legally unsupportable— contradicting core constitutional principles," they wrote. Moreover, when it came to police wrongdoing, they pointed as well to the perils of secrecy. "It is time," they concluded, "to adopt meaningful reforms on the use of force and accountability and transparency."

In tandem, the four tools of imprecision, secrecy, bureaucratic porousness, and norm violations were no longer being deployed with subtlety. Instead, they had been refashioned into outright weapons, used—as the letter highlighted—to attack those who opposed "the racism and injustice Black and other communities of color face in our country." Alongside the retreat of Milley and Esper from interference in the civilian space, former leading national figures were not willing to serve as allies to the president on the streets of American cities.

But Trump was not deterred. If the military would not take the lead in countering the protesters, if former national security officials from both sides of the aisle would abandon him, then he would look elsewhere. He turned to those who had proved loyal in bringing the tactics of national security in the name of the war on terror to his presidency—the Department of Justice and the Department of Homeland Security.

The Executive Order on Monuments

On June 26, 2020, President Trump issued an executive order (EO) that aimed to enable greater federal involvement in countering the ongoing protesters across the country. The "Executive Order on Protecting American Monuments, Memorials, and Statues and Combating Recent Criminal Violence" authorized withholding federal funding from local authorities who extended lawful protections to the protesters who attacked federal property.[21] The memo expanded the imprecise definition of the alleged vandals to include "rioters, arsonists, and left-wing extremists" who "explicitly identified themselves with ideologies—such as Marxism—that call for the destruction of the United States system of government." As many of the protests occurred around public monuments, for example, depicting leaders associated with the country's history of racism, and around courthouses and other buildings, the executive order could serve as an authority to address the protests nationwide.

Rather than military intervention, the executive order looked to the powers of the Department of Justice. It instructed the attorney general to "prioritize within the Department of Justice the investigation and prosecution" of "any person or any entity that destroys, damages, vandalizes, or desecrates a monument, memorial, or statue within the

United States or otherwise vandalizes government property" or "participates in efforts to incite violence or other illegal activity in connection with the riots and acts of vandalism," as well as "any person or any entity that damages, defaces, or destroys religious property." It encouraged bureaucratic porousness in requesting that DHS work alongside DOJ by providing "personnel to assist with the protection" of the monuments and other entities mentioned in the EO.

On July 1, to support implementation of the order, a new division was created inside DHS: the Protecting American Communities Task Force (PACT), whose purpose was to counter "civil unrest and property destruction." In addition, Customs and Border Protection (CBP)—the component of DHS that had been activated at the southern border—was deputized to help out in the cities. Various other offices of DHS were tasked with "providing support" to the Federal Protective Service, the uniformed security police division of DHS, including the Secret Service, Immigration and Customs Enforcement (ICE), and the Transportation Security Administration (TSA).

In addition to deploying forces around the country, DHS would extend the tactics that had won government approval during the war on terror, notably surveillance. An internal memo circulation by Public Affairs on CBP letterhead provided details on authorized law enforcement measures, including "information/intelligence sharing" that would occur between the Department of Justice, the Department of the Interior, and DHS and the presence of stand-by drones "to assist as needed."[22]

Armed with these new authorities, the administration launched a militarization of law enforcement that was unprecedented in American history. Acting effectively as the commander in chief in a war at home, Trump prepared to send troops out across the country, albeit in the guise of law enforcement. For his first target, he chose Portland, Oregon.

Portland

On May 28, 2020, three days after the killing of George Floyd, Portland protesters had gathered for the first of hundreds of protests that would last through the fall months.[23] Protests were part of the city's unique identity; it averaged approximately two hundred such demonstrations a year. It was no surprise to see the city's population, 80 percent white, take to the streets, as they did to express outrage over the murder of George Floyd and over police mistreatment of African Americans nationwide.

But it was not just solidarity over the blatant injustice of the Floyd killing that made Portland a hotbed of the Black Lives Matter protests. It was also the city's own history of police violence against Blacks.[24] In 2017, Portland police had shot and killed a seventeen-year-old Black teenager, Quanice Derrick Hayes.[25] In 2018 Portland police had shot and killed an unarmed Black man, Patrick Kimmons, and Portland State University police had killed another Black man, Jason Washington.[26] None of the officers in these cases were disciplined, charged, or otherwise held accountable.

Protesters in Portland began to gather at night outside the Justice Center in the downtown area of the city. For the most part, by all accounts, the demonstrations were peaceful. Some gave speeches, others chanted support for George Floyd. Many held up "Black Lives Matter" signs. On occasion, particularly late into the evenings, the demonstrations became rowdier as protesters graffitied buildings and vehicles near the Justice Center and clashed with local Portland police. In several instances, the encounters turned violent, with officers sending tear gas and rubber bullets into the crowd of protesters.

On June 5, the nonprofit accountability group Don't Shoot Portland filed a civil complaint in federal court against the local police, alleging the use of tear gas against protesters who "posed no threat of violence."[27] The complaint described the dangerous effects of the nerve gas, including "eye burning, excessive tearing, blurred vision and redness; runny nose, and nasal burning and swelling; mouth burning, irritation, difficulty swallowing and drooling; chest tightness, coughing, choking sensation, wheezing shortness of breath; burns and skin rash." The complaint cited studies showing that the gas was "linked to miscarriage and fetal harm" and was particularly dangerous during the COVID-19 pandemic as it attacked the respiratory system.

The federal judge, Marco Hernández, an Obama appointee, complied and issued a Temporary Restraining Order (TRO) on June 9 forbidding the use of tear gas except in exceptional circumstances "in which the lives or safety of the public or the police are at risk."[28] Meanwhile, the protests continued, with protesters tearing down statues of Thomas Jefferson and George Washington, and at times blocking traffic on the interstate highways, setting fires, and vandalizing property. The protesters called for cuts in the police budget and for police accountability. On June 16, tensions heightened as protesters occupied the Fremont Bridge spanning the Willamette River, hanging signs that said "Defund Police" and "No Justice, No Peace." That same day, in downtown Portland, a driver plowed into the protesters, injuring three people. The police responded to the protests using a variety of munitions. As a result, on June 26 as the violence intensified, the TRO was expanded to include additional crowd control munitions, including the launching devices for rubber balls, pepper spray, and Long Range Acoustic Devices.[29]

Over the Fourth of July weekend, despite the restraining order, the clashes took a turn for the worse. Unbeknownst to the public, on the day of the president's June 26 executive order on monuments and under its authorization, the federal government had deployed federal agents to the City of Portland in a secret DOJ operation titled Operation Diligent Valor.[30] Within weeks, it would be revealed that the more than one hundred federal agents sent to the city were from DHS—Rapid Deployment Teams, the Federal Protective Service, ICE, Customs and Border Protection—and from the Department of Justice, the U.S. Marshals Service.[31] While not the military itself, the agents who arrived in Portland wore military camouflage and gas masks and carried assault munitions—but displayed no visible insignia, masking their identities and the authority they carried. Reports surfaced of these mysterious agents attacking protesters who were blocks beyond the perimeter of the federal building, pulling them into vans, and taking them away.[32]

Local authorities were appalled by the appearance of the camouflaged and weaponized agents and by the escalation in violence. Before the Fourth of July weekend was over, the governor of Oregon, Kate Brown, and the mayor of Portland, Ted Wheeler, had each appealed to Washington to withdraw the federal agents, a request they would repeat numerous times. Their appeals fell on deaf ears. Trump was eager for his federal agents, as he had envisioned, to dominate the situation. Wheeler and Brown accused the agents of escalating the crisis.

The federal government not only refused to withdraw its agents but also to heed local law. In violation of the spirit of the court-ordered TRO, which applied to the local police, federal agents used tear gas, rubber bullets, batons, pepper spray, and other projectiles. On July 10, Judge Hernández's court order was extended to cover the federal agents as well as local police. Yet that evening, federal officers shot a woman in the head with a pink paintball, and shot a law student—clearly identified by her hat as a National Lawyers Guild observer—in the chest with a rubber bullet. Dressed in dark uniforms without insignia, it was nearly impossible to hold any person or any one agency accountable. In addition to the secrecy of anonymity, federal agents took advantage of bureaucratic porousness by joining with agents from other services. The Federal Protective Service, for example, roamed the streets well beyond the perimeters of the courthouse and other buildings, working with Customs and Border Protection to surveil and accost potential vandals. On the same day more federal troops arrived, with Trump announcing that local law enforcement could not keep control of the situation.

Over the following days, the standoff between the federal government and the city became as heated as that between the protesters and law enforcement. When DHS secretary Chad Wolf arrived in the city on July 16, he did not ask for a meeting with Mayor Wheeler; the county sheriff he had invited for a meeting declined. It was a sign of just how deep the division was between the federal government and both the city's officials and its citizens.[33] Wolf, capitalizing on the tensions, publicly excoriated the city officials and listed dozens of instances in which "violent anarchists" had caused destruction in the city.[34]

Tensions were further inflamed on July 19 when DHS issued a memo designed to further expand the authorities of the executive order on monuments. The new three-page memo authorized "expanded intelligence activities necessary to mitigate the significant threat to homeland security," and included not just protecting monuments but "Combating Recent Criminal Violence." In other words, it justified, as the legal experts Ben Wittes and Steve Vladeck summed it up, "intelligence gathering against ordinary Americans—most of whom had nothing to do with the underlying property damage, and many of whom were engaged in the most American of activities: peacefully protesting their government."[35]

In Portland, Trump had succeeded in sending in the very "occupying force" he had wished for. Far away from the hotbed and public scrutiny of DC, Portland offered a perfect staging ground for testing out the subtle tools crafted in the war on terror on the homeland.

Pleased with what was happening in Portland, Trump announced his intention to spread this aggressive, norms-breaking use of federal law enforcement to other cities in the country: New York, Chicago, Philadelphia, Detroit, Baltimore, and Oakland, California. Trump admitted outright that his agenda in deploying federal forces was political, as the mayors of these cities were, in his words, "liberal Democrats."

Events in Portland gave mayors elsewhere little hope of resistance to this expanded agenda. If the pleas of Mayor Wheeler and Governor Brown (and the protests of top national security officials) were not to be heeded, if restraints on law enforcement could be readily trespassed, and if secrecy could be embraced without repercussions, then what remained inviolable? What defense did local authorities have against the unique incursions of the Trump government in Portland, and potentially elsewhere in the country? The answer lay in the federal courts.

A Federal Court Steps In

On June 28, news reporters, photographers, and volunteer legal observers for the American Civil Liberties Union filed court papers claiming that they were being singled out and assaulted by police, even after they had identified themselves as press, and at times because they were press. Even before the first federal troops arrived, journalists documenting the protests had been directly targeted by the local police. Among others, the *Oregonian/Oregon Live* reporter Beth Nakamura was quoted in the lawsuit. Attaching a video of the confrontation, the complaint described her as being "slammed" with a "truncheon," all the while holding up her press pass, saying "press, press," in response to which the officer said, "I don't give a fuck."[36] As a result, news agencies and legal observers were suing the members of the local Portland Police Bureau "and other agencies working in concert" with it for fifteen violations, including of the First Amendment right to free speech and assembly and Fourth Amendment protection against unwarranted search and seizure, as their equipment had been confiscated on numerous occasions.

Three weeks later, Judge Michael Simon—an Obama appointee who, earlier in the Trump presidency, had issued a nationwide injunction halting the administration's requirement that immigrants prove they had health insurance or could pay for medical care in order to obtain visas—did what Judge Hernández had done with the use of tear gas and other weapons.[37] He issued a TRO. Simon added the DHS and the U.S. Marshals Service to the list of law enforcement agents prohibited from using force against journalists and legal observers.[38] The judge's order prohibited them from "arresting, threatening to arrest, or using physical force directed against any person whom they know or reasonably should know is a Journalist or Legal Observer, unless the federal agents have probable cause to believe that such individual has committed a crime." The order attempted to forestall any future claims by the federal officers to qualified immunity—a legal principle that aims to protect government employees from frivolous suits but that has historically been relied upon as a defense for the use of excessive force by law enforcement. Nor could they seize photographic audio or video-recording equipment, Judge Simon wrote. He referenced a decision by the Ninth Circuit—the court to which the case would be appealed if it went forward—which had concluded that "the Supreme Court has long recognized a qualified right of access for the press and public to observe government activities."[39]

Simon endeavored to defuse the conflict by insisting on clarity where there was imprecision. In his TRO forbidding assaults on journalists, Simon ordered the journalists and legal observers to wear visible identification, "a professional or authorized press badge or distinctive clothing that identifies the wearer as a member of the press." He also suggested green hats or blue vests for authorized legal observers.

The government lawyers called Simon's remedy "unworkable." "Under the chaotic circumstances of the protests," they argued, "it is difficult for officers, who are often wearing gas masks and laser protective goggles, to verify small indicia of press membership that may be present on certain members of crowds." Law enforcement could not be expected to restrain themselves in the midst of such confusion. It was an overt acknowledgment of the useful power of imprecision as a rationale for lawlessness. The order was in effect, but the government had already signaled its planned noncompliance.

As the government defiance continued, the importance of Portland as a template for the rest of the country grew. By summer's end, the government had deployed teams from sixteen different federal agencies to cities across the country, including Los Angeles, San Diego, San Francisco, Denver, Washington, DC, Miami, Detroit, St. Louis, Buffalo, New York City, Dallas, Houston, Seattle, and others. The outcome of the Portland battle would potentially cast its shadow across the country.

The "Draw Down"

Finally, on July 29, Governor Kate Brown, working through Vice President Mike Pence, brokered a deal with DHS acting secretary Chad Wolf. Having publicly accused federal agents of "pouring gasoline on a fire," Brown announced that officers with Customs and Border Protection and Immigration and Customs Enforcement would depart downtown Portland beginning on July 30.[40] It would be a "phased withdrawal," according to Brown, with some federal troops remaining on "standby."[41] The wording of the agreement thus allowed both sides to save face.

Video clips from clashes that lasted from July 29 into the morning of July 30 showed federal agents firing tear gas and less-lethal munitions at journalists standing on SW Main Street.[42] But in the days to come, the streets of Portland quieted down. July 31 was the city's first peaceful night since the protests had begun. Demonstrations continued, but the violence had subsided. The Oregon State Police had taken over the protection of the federal buildings as promised in the deal with the government, and for the most part stayed inside the courthouse, offering "little sign of presence."[43] Reportedly, Portland city police backed away from confrontations, and protesters restrained one another from acts of vandalism. The result, according to the press, was a night "without any major confrontations, violence or arrests."[44]

But even as a fragile peace ensued, the administration took up the tool of imprecision once again, sharpening it into disinformation.[45] Contradicting news headlines and Governor Brown's statement, Wolf announced that DHS was actually not withdrawing, saying the department would "continue to maintain our current, augmented federal law enforcement personnel in Portland" until they were certain that "federal properties will no longer be attacked and that the seat of justice in Portland will remain secure."[46] A DHS press release issued several days later credited the peace on Portland's streets to the presence of federal troops—not their withdrawal.[47] It portrayed Governor Brown as the obstructionist villain in the ongoing conflict who had "finally agreed to do what the Department of Homeland Security (DHS) has demanded for months: step up and work with federal authorities to stop the nightly criminal violence directed at the Hatfield Federal Courthouse in Portland."

The drawdown, so Wolf claimed, was not happening. It's a "myth" that "DHS forces are standing down and withdrawing."[48] From his perch at the White House, the president's senior advisor for policy, Stephen Miller, backed Wolf's account, telling Fox News's Tucker Carlson: "This is about the survival of this country, and we will not back down."[49]

Yet even as the Trump administration denied the withdrawal in public, it endeavored to use the deal to enhance its powers in Portland. On August 6, the Trump administration went back to federal court, arguing that due to the drawdown deal, the TRO restraining federal agents from targeting journalists and excusing journalists from dispersal orders should be removed. Judge Simon, referencing the remarks of federal officials who claimed the drawdown was a "myth," refused the government's appeal for the removal of the TRO. How could they claim they were not withdrawing and at the same time ask for a new ruling based on the fact of a withdrawal? Judge Michael Simon issued his ruling from the bench; the court order would stay in effect until

August 20.[50] By intentionally confusing the facts, the government had hurt its own cause.

Throughout August, violence escalated once again. Reports of legal observers being shot in the head with paintballs and rubber bullets, beaten with batons, pepper-sprayed, tear-gassed, and doused with water showed federal officers in defiance of the order and its intent. Judge Simon gave additional permanence to the restraining order, issuing a preliminary injunction, and emphasizing that unless there was actual evidence that a journalist or legal observer was engaged in a crime, the federal forces were "enjoined from arresting, threatening to arrest, or using physical force directed against any person whom they know or reasonably should know is a Journalist or Legal Observer." The judge pointed to a distinction between federal forces and local law enforcement, which had complied with the original restraining order and noted that "the City supports Plaintiffs' request for an injunction against the Federal Defendants." In so doing, he suggested that Portland was a unified front and that the conflict was between the federal government and Portland, not between local law enforcement and the protesters. His assertion downplayed local tensions in the service of the larger point— the federal government's attempt to occupy Portland.

The judge further addressed the problem of secrecy and confusion that had exacerbated the conflict. Simon reiterated his earlier order requiring journalists to wear insignia. But now he required the federal agents to do so as well. "The current identifying markings are not of sufficient visibility," Simon wrote. "The court does not find it credible that there is no possible location on the helmet or uniforms on which more visible markings can be placed." For the judge, identification would in and of itself help reduce "the very conduct against which plaintiffs have filed suit."[51]

After a summer of unmarked vans and black uniforms without insignia, the judge's ruling glimpsed the possibility that some return to peace on the streets might occur if clarity, transparency, and the law would be adhered to. But hopes in that direction were put on pause one week later, on August 27, when Judge Simon's injunction barring federal troops from assaulting journalists was overruled and lifted by a three-judge panel on the Ninth Circuit Court of Appeals while they considered in full the appeal in the case. (Notably, one of the judges on the circuit court had been replaced at the last minute, without explanation, by a Trump appointee.)[52]

Meanwhile, as the Ninth Circuit pondered the Portland journalists' case, the protests there continued. Michael Chertoff, former DHS secretary and co-chair of the group that had issued the letter of protest in the wake of the Lafayette Square conflict, decided to educate the nation about the wrongfulness of the government's strategy in the streets of Portland.

Chertoff versus Wolf

In a series of public appearances over the course of the summer, Chertoff lambasted the performance of DHS in Portland and other American cities. Chertoff's credentials for judging the actions of DHS agents were impeccable. He had not only led the Department of Homeland Security during George W. Bush's second term but he had coauthored the Patriot Act. He had been the U.S. attorney in New Jersey and a federal judge on the Third Circuit Court of Appeals, appointed by George W. Bush. His combined expertise and knowledge of the government and of the law, and his insights into powers claimed in the name of the war on terror, now abused in the name of the protests, were as legitimate an authority as one could ask for.

Chertoff's message: the agency that he had helped bring to life in the early years after 9/11 had taken a devastatingly wrong turn. "The execution of this," he said on the ABC News Powerhouse Podcast, referring to Portland, "has been a real problem." "They operate normally in a border environment . . . an almost quasi-military situation. That does not translate well into an urban environment with First Amendment protected demonstrators."[53] He accused the department of forgoing specificity and evidence, telling the *Washington Post*'s Greg Sargent that the government had turned its counterprotest mission into "a general roving opportunity to conduct police operations." The mission creep of the agency and the unrestrained enforcement behavior of DHS was, he said, "problematic legally as well as morally."[54]

Chertoff attacked the administration's use of secrecy specifically in an op-ed he wrote for the *New York Times*, condemning the practice of "agents operating in camouflage uniforms with no clear identifying insignia."[55] He castigated the president for "reveling in the use of brutal and aggressive force" and tied the activity in Portland to a wider misuse of DHS during the Trump administration, notably in invalidating Deferred Action for Childhood Arrivals (DACA) by ceasing to process applications. He called upon the "department's leadership" to "firmly and unequivocally reject efforts to hijack the agency for political purposes," and to display "the commitment to the rule of law and to restrained and measured operational behavior."

One by one, Chertoff had identified the subtle tools—imprecision, secrecy, bureaucratic porousness, and lawlessness—as together violating the very essence of the department's mission. The terrorism and counterterrorism expert Brian Jenkins recalled there were two things that DHS was expressly intended *not* to be: "a domestic intelligence agency nor a Napoleonic gendarmerie—neither a MI-5 agency like that in the U.K. nor a national police. And certainly not a Praetorian Guard or the President's police force."[56]

In Lafayette Square and in Portland, Trump had, however, done just that. As the first secretary of DHS Tom Ridge described it, the agency was acting in both venues as "the president's personal militia." Drawing a stark distinction between DHS at its inception and DHS under Trump, Ridge added, "It would be a cold day in hell before I would consent to a unilateral, uninvited intervention into one of my cities."[57]

Critics of DHS at the time of its creation had foreseen this potential for mission creep—now those who had run the agency were seeing it too. As many had argued in Congress during discussions over the Homeland Security Act in 2002, combining so many different departments—each with its own mission and each with its own authorities—into one agency was a prescription for the abuse of power. Richard Clarke was national coordinator for security, infrastructure protection, and counterterrorism for George W. Bush at the time the Department of Homeland Security was created; as he explained, DHS was riddled with problems of clarity of mission and distinctive powers from the onset. The absence of a cohesive organizing principle and "the sheer magnitude of the bureaucratic challenge overwhelmed the department's leaders."[58] Brian Jenkins concurred, saying that "the size and complexity of the department created an assemblage of authorities, which some asserted were all fungible—the authorities and rules of one of its operational components were considered interchangeable with the authorities and rules of another component, and the resources of one could be transferred to another."[59]

The cascade of criticism—coming now even from DHS's earliest leaders—nettled Chad Wolf. Appearing on August 6 before the Senate Homeland Security and Governmental Affairs Committee, Wolf said Ridge "did not know all of the facts." He had done a briefing with the two former secretaries, he assured the senators, and had "walked them through what was going on in Portland." The problem, Wolf continued to insist, was not DHS and its agents but Portland's leadership and the lack of cooperation that the federal agents had received from the local authorities.[60]

Wolf's briefing did not change Chertoff's mind; two weeks later, Chertoff appeared on PBS's *Amanpour and Company* and reiterated his concern, this time even more strongly, that DHS had been politicized on the streets of American cities.[61] Chertoff pointed to the wrongful embrace of bureaucratic porousness within the agency, and its accompanying disregard for professionalism and normative limits. "To send into the field, into the cities, people who are trained really to do operations at the border where you're dealing with violent drug gangs and who were not trained and equipped and didn't have rules of engagement that would be more appropriate when you're dealing with American citizens in the cities" was wrongheaded. Chertoff chastised the president for having "used rhetoric that was aimed essentially at labelling the entire exercise as a political exercise . . . deliberately messaging a view of how to use the organs of government that suggests they are to be subordinated to the personal political interests of the president which is the exact opposite of what the people who swear an oath to the Constitution have dedicated themselves to be."

As the summer turned to fall, Chertoff had laid down the gauntlet. The subtle tools of ever-expansive language leading to ever-expansive authorities, the confusing of bureaucratic distinctions, and the bypassing of norms had, to his mind, overtaken the law.

But Secretary Wolf was not backing down. Imprecision and bureaucratic porousness were the very tools he cherished as head of DHS. On September 9, in his tenth month as acting secretary, Wolf said as much when he delivered the annual State of the Homeland Address.[62] He began with reference to 9/11: "We cannot gather as family in September and fail to remember that day 19 years ago. The smoke has long since disappeared over New York, Shanksville, and the Pentagon. . . . But for us, the skies of September are never clear." His speech acknowledged the transformation that DHS had undergone. "Our challenges today are unimaginably different than those of our past. Threats shift. And so must we." But those critics who accused the department of "mission creep" and "politicization" were, Wolf said, but a "vocal and ill-informed minority" trying through their "baseless sensationalism" to deter the department from keeping the nation safe. "It's unsettling," he complained, that "these self-appointed experts rush to criticize the uniformed men and women of DHS working to save lives and defend federal property, even before they condemn the violent behavior of a rioting mob." DHS, Wolf boasted, "was established for years like this." He acknowledged the current transgression of norms and embraced them. "We're using authorities previously granted by Congress, but never before used as we face evolving and novel threats."

Wolf's blatant embrace of the newly weaponized subtle tools against protesters in Portland and elsewhere in the country was mirrored by DHS's constant ally, the Department of Justice. The same week that Wolf delivered his speech, Attorney General Barr was holding a conference call with the country's U.S. attorneys. He strongly encouraged the nation's federal prosecutors to file federal charges against the protesters, referencing Portland specifically as well as Seattle where local authorities had created a police-free zone around the protests in June.[63] In presenting the statutes that prosecutors could turn to, Barr added one that put the protests in a new category: sedition. Under the Seditious

Conspiracy statute, a person who has incited violence against the government with the goal of overthrowing it or destroying it can be punished by up to twenty years in prison.[64]

Clarifying the intent of his recommendation, Barr added his own spin to the fuzzy language that had accompanied references to the protesters. In place of the terrorists that Trump had referred to in the Rose Garden, in place of the violent anarchists that the DHS press release had identified, in place of the list of followers of Marxist ideology singled out in the executive order on monuments, Barr named "antifa." Short for antifascist, and often linked with antiracists, the term came into prominence in 2017 in a series of clashes between left-wing and right-wing extremists. But, in reality, antifa is "not an organization," as the historian and author Mark Bray—who wrote a book on antifa—explained, "rather it is a politics of revolutionary opposition to the far right." It is like feminism, Bray contends, "but neither antifa nor feminism is itself an organization."[65] Antifa was an imprecise enemy, and thus a useful enemy for a government bent on using imprecision to accomplish its end.

One week later, on September 17, the Department of Justice formalized Barr's encouragement to use sedition charges against protesters. The DOJ had already broken new legal ground in late August, charging protesters with "civil unrest," which DHS had initially been deployed to counter, a charge brand-new to Portland. Now, over the signature of Deputy Attorney General Jeffrey Rosen, who would succeed Barr in the last month of Trump's presidency, the DOJ issued a memo to U.S. attorneys about the sedition charge and its applicability to the protesters.[66] "The Attorney General and I recently discussed with you the need to consider the use of a variety of federal charges when they may be appropriate, including 'Seditious conspiracy.' . . . I want to re-emphasize that message." The applicability of the statute, the memo claimed, was broader than the prosecutors might have understood. "As was previously pointed out, Section 2384"—the section of the U.S. Criminal Code that makes seditious conspiracy a crime—"does not require proof of a plot to overthrow the U.S. Government, despite what the name might suggest." The memo made a pointed reference to Portland, with this example: "For instance, where a group has conspired to take a federal courthouse or other federal property by force." Willing to take the lead in launching sedition charges, Barr asked prosecutors at DOJ about the possibility of charging the mayor of Seattle with sedition.[67]

Before month's end, the federal occupation of Portland intensified, riding in on a new pretense. In the middle of September, the Black Lives Matter protests in Portland had quieted down a bit, in part due to wildfires whose smoke made protests untenable. But in late September, a new kind of protest appeared. The Proud Boys—a far-right white supremacist group that had gained momentum throughout 2020—had organized a rally in the Oregon city for Saturday, September 26. Earlier in the week President Trump had given the group a shout out during the first presidential debate, telling them, with the nation listening in, to "stand back and stand by." The protest fizzled as only a few hundred of the expected twenty thousand showed up. But in preparation for the rally, the U.S. Marshals deputized members of the Portland Police in anticipation of violence, and announced that the officers would remain deputized until the end of the year.

The deputizing took place in defiance of the rulings of the court, the sensibilities of former national security officials, and the preferences of local authorities. The DOJ and the U.S. Marshals deputized fifty-six local police officers and twenty-two country sheriff's deputies as federal agents, enabling them to arrest protesters on federal charges that carried heavier penalties than local convictions would.[68] When Mayor Wheeler asked the Portland U.S. Attorney's Office to reverse this, U.S. Attorney Billy Williams and U.S. Marshal Russ Burger refused, on the grounds that police needed better protection against protesters.[69] Within days, federal charges had been leveled against two dozen Black Lives Matter protesters.

The message was clear. As Trump, Barr, and Wolf had done at the border, so now they had done in an American city. And despite local opposition, court orders, and criticism from former national security officials, they were not backing down. Bureaucratic porousness between DHS and DOJ and ultimately between the federal government and local government, the bypassing of norms evident in creating new laws and regulations by decree, and ultimately, the reliance on linguistic imprecision to extend one category of authorities—i.e. those aimed at the border—to Black Lives Matter protesters, had combined to bring the worst of the war on terror onto the streets of American cities. The federal government's response to the protests in Portland was the ultimate example of the damage that the subtle tools, used in tandem, could wreak.

But, in an unexpected way, it was also an example of where some of the vulnerabilities of the subtle tools might lie.

The Subtle Tools, Blunted

On October 9, the Ninth Circuit, in a 2–1 decision, upheld Judge Simon's findings and amplified them. Having considered the Portland journalists' case and its arguments, the court reinstated the injunction against the federal guards' assaults on journalists and provided a comprehensive rebuke to the behavior of federal forces in Portland.[70] The court's revulsion at the proliferation of false statements, misinformation, and deceptions was matched by its conclusion that federal agents had not only overstepped their authority but also had violated the law in numerous ways. The decision thus ruled decisively against the subtle tools of imprecision and secrecy as much as against the overt expansion of the law and the widespread violation of norms.

The court chastised the federal government for the mission creep that had resulted from the aggressive use of the subtle tools. There is "a mountain of evidence," the judges wrote, "that the Federal Defendants routinely left federal property to engage in crowd control." The government forces had wrongfully taken it upon themselves "to disperse members of the public who are neither on federal property nor threatening it." The judges pointed out that the interpretation of the law by the federal defendants was in fact incorrect: "The Federal Defendants' suggestion that [the law] confers authority to take action to disperse members of the public who are neither on nor threatening federal property is dubious." Federal agents, the court opined, did not have the right to overstep the local authorities when it came to actions outside of federal property. That authority lay with local law enforcement.

In addition, the defendants from DHS and DOJ were held to account by the circuit court for violating the previous TRO from Judge Simon, as documented testimony and video clips had shown. "The record fully supports the district court's conclusion that the Federal Defendants' interest does not require dispersing plaintiffs. They have not threatened federal property, and the journalists, in particular, provide a vitally important service to the public."

The use of government agents as an "occupying force," violating rules and norms through secretive behavior and the spread of disinformation, was a nonstarter for the federal judges. It was therefore a rejection of those habits and policies that had sprouted and blossomed during the war on terror, and had now embedded themselves at home, under the aegis not of the military but of the Department of Homeland Security and the Department of Justice. Echoing the district court, the circuit court called for the restoration of clarity, precision, and honesty, and for honoring the bureaucratic distinctiveness between federal and local authorities. The circuit court drew on Simon's attempt to distinguish local law enforcement from the activities of federal agents. "In fact, the City supported entry of the instant preliminary injunction against the Federal Defendants, arguing '[t]he actions of [F]ederal [D]efendants are escalating violence, inflaming tensions in [Portland], and harming Portlanders who seek to engage in nonviolent protests in support of racial justice.'" It neglected a pronounced anger that the Black Lives Matter protesters espoused against Mayor Wheeler and the local police, but it nonetheless articulated the boundaries of the ordeal at hand.

The decision constituted the most resounding rejection of the subtle tools to date. Legally, and in terms of the national conversation, Portland was a consequential setback for Trump, Barr, and Wolf—and for the subtle tools. Mark Milley and the military establishment had set the tone with a firm refusal to play the role of occupying force that Trump had announced for them. Michael Chertoff and Tom Ridge had deplored the use of the Department of Homeland Security for its errant violations of norms and the law. The federal court judges had insisted on transparency and clarity. Together they had aligned with the civil libertarians who had taken the administration to court.

As the election approached, tensions between law enforcement and protesters in Portland escalated—but much as Barr had put the pieces in place for ramped up federal action, the use of law enforcement was local. On election day, Governor Brown asked the National Guard to be on standby in anticipation of unrest at Black Lives Matter protests. On the day after the election, the local sheriff declared a riot, and Brown did call in the Guard. Meanwhile, taking their protests to the polls, on Election Day Oregon voters approved a ballot measure to create a civilian-run police oversight board.[71] The problems had turned decidedly local.

The city of protests, Portland, would enter yet another new period of protests in 2021 with both antigovernment and Black Lives Matter activists continuing to demonstrate, sometimes with violence, uprooting the city and challenging local authorities with a new intensity. But the federal use of the subtle tools had moved on to a bigger target, namely, the election of 2020 and its aftermath.

9

The 2020 Elections

The election is absolutely being rigged by the dishonest and
distorted media pushing Crooked Hillary—but also at many
polling places—SAD.

DONALD TRUMP TWEET, OCTOBER 15, 2016

THE 2020 ELECTION and its aftermath carved deep fissures in the fab-
ric of American democracy, many owing to Donald Trump's weaponization of the subtle tools. Confounding reality through the abuse and degradation of language, interfering with bureaucratic procedures, and
violating norms and the law with unbridled dedication in the last year of
his presidency, the culture of governance that had been under attack since
9/11 began to collapse in unprecedented ways under the weight of 2020's
many crises and ultimately, under the impact of the election itself.

The Rise of COVID-19

The disruptive contours that would come to define the election season
began early in 2020 with the COVID-19 crisis. On January 18, Alex Azar,
secretary of health and human services, first briefed President Trump
on the newly discovered coronavirus, SARS-CoV-2. The news came two
weeks after the Soleimani strike and four days before opening arguments in Trump's impeachment trial. Sandwiched between the foreign

policy event that could have put the country on a war footing and the congressional investigation into a quid-pro-quo scheme with Ukraine, the news of the novel coronavirus appeared to arouse little interest from the president. On January 20, when the first case was found inside the United States, Trump was abroad, attending the World Economic Conference in Davos, Switzerland. He remained unconcerned, remarking two days later, "It's one person coming from China. It's going to be just fine."[1] Within weeks, the COVID-19 pandemic would knock the country off of its axis, destabilizing the economy, swamping public health systems, and infecting and killing first hundreds and then thousands, and by election day 2020, hundreds of thousands of Americans.

As the virus spread, President Trump continued to deny the potency and the threat of the virus, aided in part by Azar's reassurance that "the crisis was under control."[2] Meanwhile the virus was most heavily felt in the very same communities that had been subjected to the harsh policies of the Trump administration—racial and ethnic minorities. As a Centers for Disease Control and Prevention (CDC) fact sheet pointed out, "systemic health and social inequities have put many people from racial and ethnic monitories groups at increased risk of getting sick and dying from COVID-19." Crowded living and work conditions, multigenerational households, the high percentage of minorities in essential services, and preexisting medical conditions had created a heightened vulnerability to a disease whose prevention required social distancing and quarantine.[3]

The administration responded to the compounding crisis with imprecise, misleading, and confusing messaging. In February, the president said the virus would "disappear" and that the cases would "be down close to zero." Repeatedly in March and April, as cases rose into the hundreds of thousands and as deaths approached 66,000, Trump continued to insist that the virus was "going to go away."[4]

By summer, a brief period of control over the virus's spread had been established in some states. By late June, Connecticut and New York reported a decline in the number of cases.[5] In Michigan, where more than 6,000 deaths from COVID had occurred by the middle of June, officials reported a flattening in the rates of both new cases and deaths.[6] Yet the virus remained vigorous, "rounding upward again" in the early fall.[7]

COVID's impact on the election would be no less overwhelming than it had been on the nation's schools, where social distancing led to "hybrid" teaching nationwide and where small businesses and major retailers were closing their doors at an alarming rate. Retailers, bars, and restaurants were hit the hardest and by early fall, shutdowns had led to closures, layoffs, and bankruptcies from coast to coast.[8]

The recent fruits of the subtle tools—the militarization of the police, the marginalization of communities of color, the heightened racial tension, the confusion of facts versus lies, and an increasingly fragile relationship between the federal government and the states—had weakened the country, leaving it vulnerable to COVID and to the myriad challenges posed by the upcoming election.

One of the most obvious complications was that in-person, election-day voting would be much more hazardous during the time of COVID. But the rituals of the election season itself were also disrupted. The Republican and Democratic conventions, originally scheduled for June and July, respectively, were moved to August. Both were held virtually—although not without a fight from Trump and the Republican National Committee. Set on their plans for a fully attended in-person convention in Charlotte, North Carolina, they sought to move the event to Jacksonville, Florida, when the North Carolina state government insisted on public health measures at the convention, such as social distancing and mask wearing. Ultimately the Jacksonville plan fizzled as well.[9]

The normal setting for the debates was also derailed. The first debate between Donald Trump and the Democratic nominee Joe Biden, held on September 29, was in person, with social-distancing rules observed by a limited audience. Three days later, on October 2, Trump himself was hospitalized for COVID. Released from the hospital on October 5, he demanded that the second debate, scheduled for October 15, be held in person. When debate organizers would not comply, he refused to participate. A third in-person debate was held with social distancing in effect on October 22 at the Curb Event Center at Belmont University in Nashville, Tennessee.[10]

But the primary electoral impact of COVID was in the changes mandated in voting itself. By late spring, state election officials had begun to rethink the time-honored rules for voting in person, as health officials emphasized its dangers in the face of the pandemic. If voters were afraid to vote, low turnout could compromise the strength of the election. Instead of in-person voting, citizens would need to be able to vote by mail.

State election officials scrambled to reconfigure their voting procedures and regulations, setting up brand-new procedures and scheduling extended time frames for counting mail-in ballots. Bypassing procedure and norms now became a necessity, not a choice. State courts were approached with requests to allow extended voting policies in order to allow voters to avoid the long lines—and thus, potential exposure to COVID—of in-person voting. Some states—including Wisconsin, Michigan, Pennsylvania, North Carolina, and Georgia—sought to extend the deadlines for receiving mail-in ballots that had been postmarked by election day. Others prepared to set up early voting systems.

It was the perfect scenario in which to use the subtle tools, in accelerated Trump style, for an attack on the elections themselves, beginning with the embrace of imprecision and the express intention of breeding confusion and misinformation.

Seeds of Distrust

Even before new COVID-sensitive procedures were put into place for the elections, Trump endeavored to disrupt them. As early as May, he began to cast doubt on the integrity of the upcoming elections, warning that the COVID-responsive policies presaged a futile election. The sheer volume of mail-in ballots anticipated by local officials, he announced, meant that the election would likely be invalid. Voter fraud, he alleged, was sure to result. "There is NO WAY (ZERO!) that Mail-In Ballots will be anything less than substantially fraudulent. Mailboxes will be robbed, ballots will be forged & even illegally printed out & fraudulently signed."[11] By July, he was hinting that the election should be postponed, tweeting: "With universal Mail-in Voting (not Absentee Voting, which is good), 2020 will be the most INACCURATE AND FRAUDULENT Election in history. It will be a great embarrassment to the USA. Delay the Election until people can properly, securely and safely vote???"[12] But much as Trump's cries about voter fraud seem tied to the events of 2020, in fact they had been on his mind well before that.

Trump had begun to seed the ground for distrust in the country's elections four years earlier. In 2016, when he won the electoral vote in the presidential election, Trump had lost the popular vote. For him, this was an unacceptable reality; winning on both fronts was essential. While Trump accepted the election results and the presidency, in which 304 electoral votes legitimized his win, he refused to accept the validity of the popular vote, which he had lost by 2.9 million votes. He disputed the tally and claimed that the election was rigged, tweeting on November 16, 2016, his allegation of "Serious voter fraud in Virginia, New Hampshire and California."[13] Before the month was out, he had cast doubt on the popular vote count everywhere. "In addition to winning the Electoral College in a landslide," he tweeted, "I won the popular vote if you deduct the millions of people who voted illegally."[14] (It was an ironic twist, given that throughout his presidency, the legitimacy of the 2016 election would be at issue as proof of Russian interference aimed at aiding and abetting Trump's win continued to be revealed.)[15]

Even after he took office, Trump did not let up on his conviction that there had been voter fraud. He considered it imperative to look at systemic problems with the country's elections. In May 2017, five months after his inauguration, Trump appointed a Presidential Advisory Commission on Election Integrity. It was charged with looking into voter fraud. He appointed Vice President Pence and Kansas secretary of state Kris Kobach to head it. The commission ran into immediate obstacles as states refused to comply and a series of lawsuits alleged that the group was not adhering to required public disclosure rules.[16] Despite prodigious effort, the commission produced no evidence of fraud. Trump reluctantly dismantled the commission in January 2018, promising to send its work to the Department of Homeland Security (DHS).[17] In Kobach's words, "A decision was made in the middle of the day to pass the ball. The Department of Homeland Security is going to be able to move faster and more efficiently than a presidential advisory commission." The project ended without much explanation, and the White House director of information technology said in a sworn statement that the commission "did not create any preliminary findings."[18]

Trump nonetheless refused to give up on his claims of widespread, systematic fraud, and began to think about possible remedies. He discredited the 2018 midterm elections before they took place, warning voters on the eve of the election to "cheat at your own peril."[19] In Florida, when a Senate contest between Democratic incumbent Bill Nelson and Republican governor Rick Scott was so close that a recount was required, Trump urged intervention: "Don't worry Florida. I am sending much better lawyers to expose the FRAUD!"[20] Scott approached the chief judge of the Seventeenth Judicial Circuit Court, Jack Tuter. Claiming voter fraud, Scott asked Judge Tuter to authorize the impounding of the voting machines during the recount. The judge refused to consider the case, foreshadowing judicial responses to the 2020 elections. "I don't think I have any evidence to enter a mandatory injunction right now," he said, adding, "If someone in this lawsuit, or someone in this county has evidence of voter fraud or irregularities at the supervisors office, they should report it to their local law enforcement officer."[21]

The recount took place without machines being impounded, and the Republican candidate, Governor Scott, was declared the winner. The debate over the Florida seat ended there, but the process portended the strategy Trump would embrace in 2020.

Narrative of a Rigged Election

For Trump, chief cheerleader for the idea that the voting systems in the United States were both inept and untrustworthy, COVID was a boon for propelling that agenda forward. He began tweeting in earnest in May and June of 2020 about the danger of any new voting procedures. He further confused things by making a distinction that in reality did not exist, tweeting, "Absentee Ballots are fine. A person has to go through a process to get and use them. Mail-In Voting, on the other hand, will lead to the most corrupt Election is [sic] USA history. Bad things happen with Mail-Ins." Trump, who voted in Florida via absentee ballot, was apparently trying to criticize the practice whereby some states sent all voters mail-in ballots—rather than just sending to those who requested them. His criticism of mail-in ballots focused on several city council-member elections in Paterson, New Jersey, where in a special election in May 2020, the mayor had ordered all votes to be cast by mail. "Just look at Special Election in Patterson [sic], N.J. 19% of Ballots a FRAUD!" he tweeted. Ultimately, the New Jersey election ended up in court, where the New Jersey attorney general charged a winning councilmen with fraud.[22] In another special election, ordered to be held by the judge, the result was the same. Councilman Alex Mendez again won—by 9 votes, as opposed to his win of 245 votes in the May election. The attempts to subvert the election, although it had spread seeds of doubt in the electoral process and delayed the outcome of the election, had turned out to be a lot of trouble for naught.

As in Trump's other attempts at destabilizing existing law and policy, Attorney General William Barr was at the ready to support him. On June 1, on the same day that Barr accompanied Trump on his photo-op walk through Lafayette Square, the New York Times Magazine published an article in which Barr warned: "There are a number of foreign countries that could easily make counterfeit ballots, put names on them, send them in. And it'd be very hard to sort out what's happening."[23] Barr reiterated the claim later that month, telling NPR's Steve Inskeep that mail-in ballots would be especially vulnerable to both fraud and foreign influence. When Barr raised his concern about "counterfeiting," Inskeep followed up. "Did you have evidence to raise that specific concern?" "No, it's obvious," the attorney general answered. He offered no facts to bolster his public declarations about the threat to the election.[24]

Trump amplified the attorney general's comments, tweeting in all caps, "RIGGED 2020 ELECTION: MILLIONS OF MAIL-IN BALLOTS WILL BE PRINTED BY FOREIGN COUNTRIES, AND OTHERS. IT WILL BE THE SCANDAL OF OUR TIMES!"[25] Barr and Trump were once again weaponizing the subtle tool of imprecise language, sharpening it into a total disregard for clarity and facts. They recognized that imprecision in language could lead to confusion, and confusion could influence the voters and ultimately, undermine acceptance of the vote count.

In state after state, election officials tried to counter the president and the attorney general's predilection for statements that the election would be illegitimate.[26] In Colorado, where nearly all ballots would be cast by mail, election officials said there was "zero chance" voter fraud would happen, given the security precautions put in place. In Arizona, Texas, Maryland, and elsewhere, officials tried to tamp down the allegations of fraud and a compromised election.[27]

But the suspicions that Barr and Trump had embraced were soon to deepen, finding support elsewhere in the government and the country. Successfully casting confusion onto facts on the ground, the two-man team had wielded imprecision with vigor—and in the days to come, the subtle tool of bureaucratic porousness would bolster their efforts, turning doubts about the elections into outright distrust.

The Post Office

Given the expectation of a large volume of mail-in ballots, the post office would be playing an unprecedented role in the upcoming elections. The Postal Reorganization Act of 1970 had created a Board of Governors to help ensure that politics would not come to bear on the post office. Amended in 2006, the law laid out clear procedures pertaining to the staffing, oversight, and policy decisions of the agency. As the election approached, Trump pushed law and custom aside, seeing the postal service as a mechanism for creating his own advantages.

Soon after taking office, Trump had begun to replace the members of the post office board, and to fill vacancies left by Obama with Republican loyalists. In October 2017 Trump nominated Robert Duncan, former head of the Republican National Committee who led the political action committee tied to Mitch McConnell, as the chairman of the board. Then, on May 6, 2020, the Postal Service's Board of Governors appointed a new postmaster general, Louis DeJoy, who had raised an unprecedented $428 million for the Republican Party, and was also a generous Trump donor.[28] The two remaining board members with deeper ties to the agency and its institutional memory left, one resigning in protest over DeJoy's new policy directives, another being forced out.[29] By early summer 2020, the Board of Governors consisted of four Republicans and two Democrats—all Trump appointees and all Senate confirmed as required. The two Democratic appointments were mandated by law, which required that no more than five, of a possible ten positions, could be held by members of one party.

DeJoy's policy changes drastically and immediately cut back mail services across the country—despite a pandemic that left Americans more reliant than ever on at-home deliveries. DeJoy scheduled the dismantling and removal of 671 high-speed mail-sorting machines; prohibited customary late trips or extended hours for workers intending to make sure trucks were loaded and mail was not left behind; and forbade mail carriers from sorting mail before going on their delivery routes. DeJoy made the changes unilaterally, ignoring the legally mandated course for policy reform, which included running any such changes by the Postal Regulatory Commission. He claimed financial considerations as a main driver of the changes.

By the end of July, DeJoy was casting doubt on the mail-in voting policies devised by states. He circulated a memo to the secretaries of state across the country warning them that due to their election laws, "certain deadlines for requesting and casting mail-in ballots are incongruous with the Postal Service's delivery standards." In other words, the changes made to accommodate COVID meant that the post office could not in his estimation guarantee a fair election. "There was a risk," DeJoy wrote, "that ballots requested near the deadline under state law will not be returned by mail in time to be counted."[30] To address the problem, the Postal Service would be upping its rates and charging first-class postage for mail-in ballots. Whereas before, mass mailing rates had applied, now citizens would have to pay more to ensure that their votes would count.

In late summer 2020, with the election nearing, DeJoy made further changes. He issued a reorganization plan for personnel, including reassigning top executives and issuing requests for voluntary early retirements. By mid-August, yet more policy changes seemed to be afoot as reports of mailboxes being removed across the country raised further suspicion that the Postal Service was intentionally trying to subvert the election.

At a time when voting was made much harder by the threat of exposure to COVID, the government was making it even more difficult.

Both Congress and the individual states responded to the increasing sense of alarm over DeJoy's policies. On August 24, 2020, DeJoy, explaining his changes in the context of financial and management concerns, testified in a contentious hearing before the House Committee on Oversight and Reform. New York congresswoman Carolyn Maloney accused DeJoy of "extremely reckless" behavior given the restrictions imposed by COVID, and of trying to "hobble mail in voting." California congressman Ro Khanna addressed the psychological impact of DeJoy's disruptions. "What is the harm in just putting those machines back until election day, just for the peace of mind, for the confidence of the American people?"[31]

DeJoy stood up to his critics, assuring them that "We're very ready to handle the election mail." He even defended the removal of the mail-sorting machines, claiming, "We don't need the machines to process an election." Deflecting the blame, DeJoy said, "We will do everything within our power and structure to deliver ballots on time. But again, we remind them to request their ballot early and vote early."

The next day, the attorneys general for the states of New York, Hawaii, and New Jersey, as well as counsels for the city of New York, and the city and county of San Francisco filed suit in DC Federal Court against President Trump and Postmaster DeJoy, seeking a preliminary injunction to halt the new policies.[32] The suit challenged DeJoy's overhaul of the agency and argued that the changes constituted an attempt to disrupt state efforts to allow mail-in voting in the face of COVID. The delays Dejoy's changes had caused, the state and municipal lawyers argued, were "forcing voters to risk either disenfranchisement by voting by mail or their health by voting in person."

It was, they argued, an aggressive use of bureaucratic degradation in the service of voter suppression. The suit claimed that the Postal Service had become in essence "a political football set to undermine a federal election." The AGs suit claimed violations of the Elections Clause of the Constitution and of the law governing the process the postmaster general was required to follow before implementing such changes. As the

AGs suit reminded the court, "the U.S. Postal Service was required to seek an advisory opinion from the Postal Regulatory Commission prior to undertaking new nationwide policies," a process they had bypassed.

It was not the only case to mount a challenge to DeJoy's election-related policies. On August 18, the states of Washington, Colorado, Connecticut, Illinois, Maryland, Michigan, Minnesota, Nevada, New Mexico, Oregon, Rhode Island, Vermont, Virginia, and Wisconsin had filed suit claiming that the new postal policies consisted of constitutional and statutory violations, and seeking an injunction to halt the policies. On August 21, 2020, a similar suit was brought against DeJoy and Duncan by the states of Pennsylvania, California, Delaware, Maine, Massachusetts, North Carolina, and the District of Columbia, also seeking injunctive relief.[33]

All told, twenty-four states plus the District of Columbia filed suits and asked for preliminary injunctions. In each case, federal judges ordered an immediate halt to DeJoy's policies. On September 17, the judge in the *Washington v. Trump* case granted a nationwide preliminary injunction, writing that "if there ever were a mandate for the need of a nationwide injunction, it is this case."[34] According to Judge Stanley Bastian, the evident attempt to interfere with the election was crystal clear. "It is easy to conclude," he wrote, that the changes constituted "an intentional effort on the part of the current Administration to disrupt and challenge the legitimacy of upcoming local, state, and federal elections, especially given that 72% of the decommissioned high speed mail sorting machines that were decommissioned were located in counties where Hillary Clinton receive[d] the most votes in 2016." Judge Bastian underscored the policy's deviation from the intent of the law. "DeJoy's actions fly in the face of Congress's intent to insulate the management of the Postal Service from partisan politics and political influence and acknowledgment that free and fair elections depend on a reliable mail service."

On September 27, Judge Emmet Sullivan in DC likewise granted an injunction, writing, "It is clearly in the public interest to mitigate the spread of COVID-19, to ensure safe alternatives to in-person voting, and to require that the USPS comply with the law." Further, Judge Sullivan emphasized the wrongfulness of the bureaucratic messiness by which the policies had come into being. "The equities balance in favor of Plaintiffs" because the preliminary injunction stopped policies "with respect to which an advisory opinion from the PRC [Postal Regulatory Commission] should have been obtained prior to implementation."[35] On September 28, a federal judge in the *Pennsylvania v. DeJoy* case granted an injunction as well.[36] And on September 25, a similar injunction granted by New York judge Victor Marrero ordered the Postal Service to treat all election mail as First Class or Priority mail.[37]

There was uniform agreement among federal judges handling these cases that the policies would have a negative impact on the election. Bureaucratic degradation and the violation of procedures required by law had led to distrust in the country's central governing norm—the electoral process.

Bypassing legally mandated process had taken on a life of its own in Trump's fourth year in office. Freed from the 9/11 context, the subtle tools were weaponized against the elections themselves. While injunctions had halted the policies nationwide, the controversy over the validity of the elections continued apace in the weeks leading up to the election. Attention would soon turn to an issue that went hand in hand with mail-in ballots—the implementation of new timelines for ballot counting to account for the volume of ballots expected.

COVID and Voting

As local officials made changes not just to how votes could be cast but how they would be counted, courts nationwide became embroiled in lawsuits. Republicans, fearing losses at the polls, asked courts to put limits on voting. Democrats, relying heavily on the votes of minorities and the elderly, asked to extend existing rules so that more votes could be counted. By late October, over three hundred lawsuits had been filed in forty-four states.[38]

Cases from Pennsylvania, North Carolina, Wisconsin, and Alabama reached the Supreme Court in October. Overall, the high court leaned toward expanding the rules on voting in order to accommodate the challenges posed by COVID. In North Carolina and Pennsylvania, the court ruled to allow ballots to be received up to nine days and three days, respectively, after the date of the election, reserving the right to revisit the case after the election. Writing six days before the election, Justice Samuel Alito explained, "There is simply not enough time at this late date to decide the question before the election."[39] Meanwhile, in a case in Rhode Island, the court had refused to intervene, leaving in place the state's decision to remove the requirement for two witnesses (or a notary public) for absentee ballots. But in two cases, the court ruled for more restrictive measures. In an Alabama case, the court blocked an order allowing voters to cast their ballots curbside. In a Wisconsin case, the court rejected a request for a six-day extension for the receipt of mail-in ballots.

Adding to fears of ballots not being counted were fears that they would not be cast due to voter intimidation. Many worried about disruption from the Proud Boys, whom Trump had told to "stand back and stand by" at his second debate, and other arms-bearing white supremacists. As a paper for Brookings concluded in late October, "the risk of violence appears to be growing." The paper's authors, terrorism experts Daniel Byman and Colin Clarke, listed the threats that could coalesce for trouble on election day as including "increasingly heated presidential rhetoric, political polarization, COVID-19-related anxiety, mobilization and counter-mobilization related to Black Lives Matter protests."[40]

As the incessant refrain from the president about fraudulent ballots and an invalid election escalated in the days leading up to the election, many expressed worry that Trump would invoke the Insurrection Act. Chairman of the Joint Chiefs Mark Milley reiterated his June pledge to keep the military out of civilian affairs, focusing now on the election in particular. "I foresee no role for the U.S. Armed Forces in this process," he wrote in late August in answer to questions posed by the House Committee on Armed Services.[41] In October, he told NPR's Steve Inskeep, "There's no role for the U.S. military in determining the outcome of a U.S. election."[42]

Fearing violence at the polls, Oregon governor Kate Brown, fresh on the heels of the heated protests in Portland, ramped up state protection, declared a state of emergency, and asked the National Guard to be on standby. Massachusetts and Texas also asked the National Guard to be on standby, while New Jersey and Wisconsin called up hundreds of citizen soldiers and airmen to work the election in an administrative capacity.[43]

The courts and the military had done their best to help deter the potential disruptions and confusion that Trump and his allies had sown. But there was one option that Trump held dear—his expectation that the Supreme Court, with three justices appointed by him, could eventually decide the election in his favor.

Amy Coney Barrett

While local authorities rallied in their efforts to ensure voting during the time of the COVID pandemic, Trump was handed yet another opportunity to bypass accepted norms as a means of ensuring a victory in the election. On September 18, Supreme Court justice Ruth Bader Ginsburg lost her many-year battle with cancer. On September 26, even before Ginsburg was buried, Trump nominated the Indiana law professor and federal appeals court judge Amy Coney Barrett to replace Ginsburg. Barrett's Supreme Court nomination was rushed to the floor of the Senate in anticipation of an election challenge. As Trump put it, "I think this will end up in the Supreme Court, and I think it's very important that we have nine justices."[44]

The timeline of Barrett's confirmation constituted a radical departure from tradition. Most recent confirmation hearings for the court had taken two to three months. Besides, the norm of not rushing a vote during the end of a presidential term had been established in 2016. In March of that year, President Obama, whose term would expire in November, had nominated Merrick Garland to the Supreme Court to replace Antonin Scalia who had died in February. Senate Majority Leader Mitch McConnell, however, successfully prevented the nomination from coming to a vote in the Senate, despite much opposition by Democrats and legal scholars at the time. Now, in the rush to have Barrett confirmed before the election, McConnell pushed the nomination through the Senate with record speed. Her confirmation took twenty-seven days.

By the time election day 2020 arrived, the disruptive politics of the Postal Service had largely been reversed, though the damage done by the removal of mailboxes and sorting machines remained. But the fear of violence and the threat of the Supreme Court putting its thumb on the scale were as vibrant as ever. By election day, the country was collectively holding its breath. There was a general sense that basic traditions and democratic processes, eroding since 9/11 and even more so since Trump had come to power, might not hold.

The Election and Its Aftermath

As election day approached, election officials nationwide prepared to counter potential outbreaks of violence. Police in Philadelphia, for example, were instructed to refrain from any assault or attacks on voters. In Michigan, where threats had been made against Governor Gretchen Whitmer—including the revelation of a violent right-wing extremist militia's plot to kidnap her in October—special measures were taken to train poll workers to handle disrupters. Elsewhere, police stood at the ready, but stayed physically away from the polls. Tensions in several voting venues arose over Republican poll watchers' complaints that they had insufficient access to the floor.[45]

Despite all the threats about violence, the day proceeded with relative calm. And the turnout was the largest in terms of total votes cast in U.S. history: 66.7 percent of eligible voters cast their ballots, a total of 159,633,396, including mail-in ballots, early voting, drop-off ballots, and election-day voting. Of total ballots, 64.1 percent voted by mail or cast their votes early. The proportion of votes cast surpassed that of the 2016 election between Hillary Clinton and Trump by 6.5 percent, the 2012 election between President Obama and Mitt Romney by 8.1 percent, and the 2008 election between Obama and McCain by 4.5 percent.[46]

With all the votes counted, Biden had won over 81 million votes, or 51.2 percent, with Trump trailing at 46.8 percent of votes. But it would take more than a week for the results to be fully counted in states as the counting of mail-in ballots continued.

Nonetheless, at 2:30 a.m. on the night of the election, with final tallies not expected for days, President Trump appeared in the East Room of the White House and addressed a room full of supporters and media. He declared victory—but also immediately began to cast doubts on the election. "Frankly, we did win this election," he told the group. In stark contrast to his months of imprecise language, he offered specific numbers. In Georgia, he cited a lead of 117,000 votes. In North Carolina, he boasted that he was up by 77,000, in Pennsylvania by 690,000, and in Michigan by "almost 300,000." "They're never gonna catch us," he insisted.[47]

Although they were specific, the numbers Trump cited were incorrect. Earlier in the evening, as most of the country was headed for bed, Trump was indeed up in the polls in Georgia, Pennsylvania, and Michigan, though by fractions of the numbers that he claimed. In North Carolina, Biden reportedly held the lead. But, more importantly, it was largely Democratic-leaning counties that still remained to be counted. As it turned out, Biden would win all but North Carolina.

With his false accounting of the election results that night and through the remaining two months of his presidency, Trump underscored the belief in the power of falsehoods that had carried him from his inauguration in 2017 to Election Day 2020. He had begun his presidency disputing media reports about the crowd size at his inauguration, his spokeswoman Kellyanne Conway insisting that the president held the right to define reality with his own "alternative facts."[48] With the 2020 election, the president's ability to provide his own facts seemed to have reached an end.

In the weeks following the election, two states, Georgia and Pennsylvania, conducted a recount of the presidential votes. The president continued to take to the bully pulpit, claiming the tallies were fraudulent and that he was expecting to continue in office. As the cases found their way into the courts, Trump egged them on: "I concede NOTHING! We have a long way to go. This was a RIGGED ELECTION!"

Rummaging through his box of subtle tools, Attorney General Barr once again stepped in to assist the president—as he had in the Mueller investigation, as he had at the border, and as he had in cities during the

Black Lives Matter protests. Now, Barr attempted to use the Department of Justice (DOJ) to support Trump's endeavor to discount the election results.

On November 9, the Monday following the election, Barr issued a memorandum authorizing assistant U.S. attorneys along with several divisions of the Department of Justice, including the FBI, to prioritize investigations of potential "vote tabulation irregularities."[49] It was a bold move. First, as he acknowledged in the memo, "the States have the primary responsibility to conduct and supervise elections under our Constitution and the laws enacted by Congress." Barr said he was, however, overriding the constitutional issues on the grounds that "the United States Department of Justice has an obligation to ensure that federal elections are conducted in such a way that the American people can have full confidence in their electoral process and their government." Second, he was departing from DOJ rules stating that no investigation take place "until the election in question has been concluded, its results certified, and all recounts and election contests concluded," which would not happen until December 14. And third, no investigation was supposed to take place without first consulting the Public Integrity Section's Elections Crime Branch.

Barr refused to abide by any of these rules, which—as he explained in the memo—were themselves inappropriate. Such a "passive and delayed enforcement approach" could result in "situations in which election misconduct cannot realistically be rectified." He had thereby taken it upon himself to authorize U.S. attorneys and other DOJ officials to bypass the law as well as the rules on procedure and timing. "I authorize you to pursue substantial allegations of voting and vote tabulation irregularities prior to the certifications."

The bypassing of norms had now reached a new operational level. The nation's top law enforcement official was blatantly casting aside established procedures and the law to achieve an expressly political end in the most sacred of America's democratic institutions—the election of the president.

The backlash against Barr's decision was immediate, and public. On November 10, the day after Barr issued his memo, the head of the DOJ's

Elections Crime Branch, Richard Pilger, resigned in protest. In 2017, Pilger had edited the most recent version of the guidelines pertaining to the election. "Having familiarized myself with the new policy and its ramifications," as stated in Barr's memo from the day before, Pilger wrote, "I must regretfully resign as Director."[50]

Meanwhile, some of the state attorneys general refused to comply with Barr's memo. On November 13, Minnesota's attorney general, Keith Ellison, joined by twenty-two other Democratic state attorneys general, disputed Barr's interruption of standing process, and specifically its view of federal versus state power.[51] "We are alarmed by your reversal of long-standing DOJ policy that has served to facilitate that function without allowing it to interfere with election results or create the appearance of political involvement in elections." The letter closed with a request that Barr withdraw his directive. "The people of the United States have spoken. The U.S. Department of Justice should not interfere with their choice, nor should it undermine confidence in the electoral process."

The dissension came not just from inside the Department of Justice, not just from state attorneys general, but from inside DHS as well. On November 12, the DHS official tasked with protecting the security of elections registered his opposition to Trump and Barr's campaign to prove fraud in the elections. Chris Krebs, the head of DHS's Cybersecurity and Infrastructure Security Agency (CISA), along with members of the Election Infrastructure Government Coordinating Council (GCC), issued a statement contradicting Trump's claims of fraud. "The November 3rd election was the most secure in American history," it read. "There is no evidence that any voting system deleted or lost votes, changed votes, or was in any way compromised." The statement promised that "election officials are reviewing and double checking the entire election process prior to finalizing the result." Krebs created a webpage called Rumor Control to help put the facts forward. The site contrasted "Rumor" and "Reality," disputing the kinds of allegations that Trump was making and emphasizing that ballots were decidedly secure.[52]

It was an important moment in the evolution of the culture of governance in America after 9/11. In this instance, the seemingly inevitable roll toward norm-breaking in law and policy had been, for the moment at least, interrupted. DHS had been Trump's loyal ally through thick and thin—at the border as existing law was trampled, and in the protests inside American cities as agents became the enemies of citizens. But now, in a department that had so consistently done his bidding, the president's antics encountered opposition. On November 17, Trump fired Krebs, announcing in a tweet that he had "terminated" him and calling Krebs's confidence in the elections "highly inaccurate." Days earlier, CISA's assistant director Bryan Ware had resigned as well, reportedly pressured to do so by the White House.[53]

As the bureaucracy began to reassert its integrity at the hands of individuals, the courts took up where they had left off before the elections. A total of eighty-six suits were brought in nine states, all but one of which judges either dismissed or ruled on in favor of the legitimacy of the election.[54] Citing a wide range of allegations of fraud and misconduct, all aiming to overturn the results of the election, the cases revealed a sense of desperation and a neglect of fact. A series of cases, for example, challenged signatures on ballots, some claiming that machines had made mistakes in signature verification, some that poll workers had failed to verify signatures. Other cases challenged the counting of absentee ballots and alleged duplicate voting. Others claimed voter fraud in the form of voting by noncitizens. In some cases, the numbers in question were not enough to make a difference in the overall tally.

Judges were summarily unconvinced by the arguments alleging fraud. One after another, the cases were dismissed for lack of evidence, as occurred in Georgia where the Trump campaign filed suit to prevent ballots received after 7 p.m. on election day from being counted. According to the judge, "there is no evidence" that election officials had "failed to comply with the law." Similarly, in Nevada, as elsewhere, a court found "no credible or reliable evidence" of voter fraud.[55] Judges around the country echoed similar rebukes. There was no there there.

Finally, one suit began to gain traction in a way that threatened to subvert the overall election results.

The Texas Suit

On December 7, Texas attorney general Ken Paxton filed suit in the Supreme Court against Georgia, Pennsylvania, Michigan, and Wisconsin—all battleground states in the election—claiming that the policies state authorities had implemented due to the pandemic had violated federal law.[56] The Supreme Court provides the first venue for a case when the dispute is between states, but this suit was unusual in the harm it was alleging. Customarily, such interstate cases resulted from disputes over a shared resource, such as water or water rights. But as with so much else in the 2020 election cycle, this was a departure from custom.

The Texas complaint alleged that "using the COVID-19 pandemic as a justification, government officials" in the four states, had "usurped their legislatures' authority and unconstitutionally revised their state's election statutes." It further alleged that Texas could bring suit on the grounds that fraudulent voting practices in one state can harm the rights of other states. The Texas suit was asking the Supreme Court to block the four states from casting their votes in the electoral college. Without these states, Biden would not win the election, falling short of the 270 electoral college votes needed to obtain office.

As Trump had done in his late election-night remarks, the suit cited numbers to give the impression of precision—but the numbers, not based in fact, seemed designed to elicit emotion rather than a change of mind based on fact. Based on Hillary Clinton's loss in those states in 2016 and Trump's numbers in 2016 and 2020, the suit absurdly claimed that "the statistical improbability of Mr. Biden winning the popular vote in these four States collectively is 1 in 1,000,000,000,000,000"—one in a quadrillion. This set the tone for the case as one of disrespect for figures and precision, with the speculation of probability substituted for the certainty of the vote counts themselves.

Despite its outlandish claims, the case nevertheless gained powerful supporters. On December 9, 17 Republican state attorneys general signed an amicus curiae brief supporting the Texas brief, arguing among other things that the COVID-related changes "removed protections that responsible actors had recommended for decades to guard against fraud and abuse in voting by mail."[57] In addition, 106 Republican House members also filed an amicus brief in support of the Texas lawsuit.

The next day, December 10, the attorneys general in the four states—all Democrats—responded to the claims of their Republican peers.[58] Their rebuttal disparaged the subtle tools, one by one. The Texas suit, having "no basis in law or fact," was a clear attempt to depart from customary process. The Pennsylvania attorney general argued that the disruption of process constituted "a seditious abuse of the judicial process." The Michigan attorney general rejected the Texas brief's lack of specifics and its reliance on "nothing more than a generalized grievance that the Clause was violated." The Wisconsin brief talked about the disrespect for the boundaries between state bureaucracies, noting that "Texas proposes an extraordinary intrusion" into the other states' elections.

Forming their own legal bloc, twenty states and the District of Columbia filed a brief supporting the assurances of the Democratic attorneys general of integrity in the election. Eighteen additional states signaled their support for a Supreme Court decision in the matter.[59]

On December 11, the Supreme Court issued a terse, two-paragraph order, declining to consider the complaint, ruling that "the State of Texas's motion for leave to file a bill of complaint is denied for lack of standing under Article III of the Constitution." The court explained that Texas had "no cognizable interest in the manner in which another State conducts its elections."[60] Although the Supreme Court did not share any further reasoning, the upshot was that there was no legal issue for the court to adjudicate.

Although the president and other Republican Party members would continue to contest vote counting in Pennsylvania and other states, the avenue of the courts had essentially been foreclosed. On December 14, as required by law, the electors met in their respective states and cast their votes, verifying Biden's victory.

That same day, Attorney General William Barr resigned, effective December 23. On December 1, Barr had publicly conceded that, despite his efforts to uncover evidence of voter fraud, investigations led to the conclusion that "we have not seen fraud on a scale that could have affected a different outcome in the election."[61] In his letter of resignation, submitted on the day he met with Trump to discuss the election results, Barr made scant reference to the election, referring only to "the Department's review of voter fraud allegations in the 2020 election and how these allegations will continue to be pursued." The remainder of the letter was a strong defense of the accomplishments of President Trump over the four years of his presidency, noting that "your record is all the more historic because you accomplished it in the face of relentless, implacable resistance."[62]

Uniformly rejected by the courts, deprived of his intrepid ally William Barr, and with a bureaucracy whose officials were defying his challenge of the elections, Trump—armed with his weaponized subtle tools—seemed to have lost his quest to overturn the election. His embrace of imprecision, alternative facts, and confusion had stumbled on the shoals of accuracy. The bypassing of law, regulations, and custom by DeJoy had faltered in the courts. The abrogation of procedural regularity in the appointment of Amy Coney Barrett had failed to overstep the separation of powers and succumb to bureaucratic porousness. Nor did the reliance on the U.S. attorney general to use the Department of Justice to interfere on behalf of the White House prove sufficient. All told, the attempt to wield the subtle tools in combination with one another in an effort to attack the elections had failed to overturn Biden's electoral victory.

But even as the courts showed that they would not be cowed by Trump and his attempts to upend process and defy norms, Trump looked for other ways to bypass the legal and procedural norms attached to the transfer of power. His attention turned to the transition process.

Transition

As Trump refused to accept the results of the election, so he refused to engage in one more set of procedural and legal norms—those that together constituted the transition process. The Presidential Transition Act of 1963 had mandated "the orderly transfer of the executive power" on inauguration day, which included funds, office space, communications services, and equipment for the transition of power. "Any disruption occasioned by the transfer of the executive power," the act warned, "could produce results detrimental to the safety and well-being of the United States and its people."[63]

As with so many elements of governance, the attacks of 9/11 colored thoughts about the transfer of power. It was not just facilities and funds that were of importance in the transfer, but intelligence as well. The 9/11 Commission Report had determined that one of the country's vulnerabilities to a future attack was a poorly handled transition period. The 2000 presidential election between George W. Bush and Al Gore, warranting a recount in Florida, had delayed the presidential transition for several weeks. Not until the Supreme Court intervened, halting the recount, did George Bush become president. The funding for transition activities was not released until December 14.

The 9/11 report pointed out scoldingly that "the dispute over the elections and the 36-day delay cut in half the normal transition period," and claimed that this delay "hampered the new administration in identifying, recruiting, clearing, and obtaining Senate confirmation of key appointees," hindering the National Security Council in its efforts to prevent terrorists from attacking the United States. On the grounds that "a catastrophic attack could occur with little or no notice," the report called for "the outgoing administration" to "provide the president-elect, as soon as possible after election day, with a classified, compartmented list that catalogues specific, operational threats to national security; major military or covert operations; and pending decisions on the possible use of force."[64]

When Obama came into office, experts worried that enemies would use the potential chaos and uncertainty of this first transition of power after 9/11 as an excuse for an attack. Experts agreed, as a Congressional Research Service report at the time pointed out, that "America's adversaries may perceive that the United States could be particularly vulnerable during a presidential transition."[65]

Although the Obama transition went relatively smoothly, lawmakers nevertheless continued to focus on the transition process and to create new mechanisms for protecting it against disruption. The Pre-Election

Presidential Transition Act of 2010 put into motion a plan to start the transition process much earlier. Previously, the time between the election and inauguration was the designated transition period. Going forward, plans for the transition would have to be drafted a year before the election, White House efforts to oversee the transfer of power were to begin no later than six months before the election, and candidates for president were to begin being briefed once they were nominated—not after election day.[66]

The Trump administration did take several of the functional steps toward the transition, as required by law, creating the proper White House teams to direct the transition, identifying workspace for Biden's transition team, and submitting updates to Congress in the months preceding the election.[67] But when it came to the allocation of funds for the transition to take place, Emily Murphy, the administrator of the General Services Administration responsible for approving the funds, withheld her approval. Citing the disputed results, she remained unwilling to formally "ascertain" the results of the election as required before releasing the funds. Finally, on November 23, nearly three weeks into the transition period, she assented.

But Trump and his administration found other ways to interfere with law and procedure. Funding aside, Trump continued to block Biden and his advisors from the very national security briefings that the 9/11 report had identified as essential to preserving national security. Biden's team met with intelligence officials at the Office of the Director of National Intelligence and the CIA. But when it came to military intelligence, there was a delay; meetings with officials at the National Security Agency, the Defense Intelligence Agency, and military intelligence departments had still not taken place by December 4, as the Department of Defense had reportedly "rejected or did not approve requests from the Biden team" for meetings.[68]

In addition to blocking the transfer of intelligence, Trump endeavored to plant seeds for disruption beyond his presidency. On October 21, he issued an executive order that created a brand-new category of government employee, called the "Excepted Service," or "Schedule F" employees. Civil servants could be reassigned to this newly created category, whereby they would lose their employment protections and could be fired at will. Moreover, political appointees under the executive order could be moved into this new category and thus occupy positions usually reserved for career civil servants.[69] The intention, experts surmised, was to "burrow" into the new administration with individuals loyal to Trump and his allies.

Ultimately, by delaying the transition, by laying the groundwork for future interventions, and by obstructing briefings, Trump was attempting to ensure that the damage wrought by the subtle tools could continue, even in his absence. But the implicit recognition that subterfuge was his only option revealed that the tools had lost some of their power.

While the collective use of the subtle tools to bypass norms, hijack legal procedures, corrupt the integrity of the bureaucracy, and turn language into lies had worked together to prolong Trump's attempt to discredit and overturn the election, the momentum aimed at undermining the election results was ultimately halted. The countervailing forces of law and norms that had prevailed in earlier eras of turmoil seemed finally, after nearly twenty years of compromising and degrading attacks by the subtle tools, abetted and stoked by fear, to have worn down the subtle tools, blunting their power. The overwhelming decisions by courts had set a tone that enough was enough. But it would take some guidance by the other branches of government and by the incoming administration to be sure that the cycles of American history that Arthur Schlesinger, Jr., had worried might one day collapse, would instead revive, albeit in potentially novel form.

CONCLUSION

Biden's Ground Zero

I believe that they will restore a bunch of norms . . . that I think have
been breached over the last four years.

BARACK OBAMA, NOVEMBER 16, 2020

ON WEDNESDAY JANUARY 6, 2021, at approximately 1:00 p.m., a joint
session of Congress met to certify the results of the election. Representative Paul Gosar from Arizona and Senator Ted Cruz from Texas rose
to object to the vote count from Arizona.[1] Although the objection was
novel, there was a process to follow, and the legislators dutifully did so.
As required, the House and Senate members retired to their separate
chambers to debate the objection.

A mile and a half away, at the Ellipse park, a different kind of norm-
breaking moment was unfolding. The president was addressing a protest
that had labelled itself a "Save America Rally." President Trump, the first
presidential candidate in U.S. history to refuse to accept his loss in an election, spoke to a crowd carrying Trump flags and yelling out "Stop the Steal."[2]
"We're going to walk down to the Capitol, and we're going to cheer on our
brave senators and congressmen and women, and we're probably not going
to be cheering so much for some of them. Because you'll never take back
our country with weakness. You have to show strength and you have to be
strong. We have come to demand that Congress do the right thing and only
count the electors who have been lawfully slated, lawfully slated."[3]

Within thirty minutes, the crowd had done as the president had urged, marching down Pennsylvania Avenue and joining protesters in front of the Capitol. Still yelling "Stop the Steal," some rushed the Capitol and entered the "People's House," armed with sticks and metal pipes, banging on doors and breaking windows. For almost six hours, the mob occupied the building, strutting through the corridors, vandalizing offices, and chanting racist slogans. One marched steadily back and forth with a Confederate flag, others brandished Trump flags, another wore a sweatshirt emblazoned with the words "Camp Auschwitz."

It was a far cry from June 1, when law enforcement officers from 26 different agencies had converged on protesters at Lafayette Square and used crowd-clearing weapons to dislodge protesters. Here, 1,400 Capitol Police officers were, it seemed, comparatively restrained, as well as alone, unsupported by other agencies.

Inside, the leadership of the House was whisked away by Capitol Police and the Secret Service. Those remaining in the House Chamber heard smoke grenades going off, smelled tear gas, and listened to screams of "Steal is Real," "USA!" and "Hang Mike Pence." Some, looking for a means of defense, broke off the legs of chairs. Colorado representative Jason Crow reached for the pen in his shirt pocket as a possible weapon. Others watched as guards barricaded the windows and doors. The members donned gas masks. Some called their families with messages of love, fearing they might not get out alive.

The siege lasted for six hours, ending when hundreds of law enforcement officers from the FBI, the Bureau of Alcohol, Tobacco, Firearms and Explosives, the U.S. Marshals Service, the Federal Protective Service, and the Secret Service arrived to offer assistance.[4] At 8:06 p.m., the country's legislators reentered the building, to resume where they had left off, determined to complete the day's business and to restore a sense of normalcy, however cosmetic or strained.

Nothing could have been further from the norms accompanying the presidential transfer of power from one administration to another. Trump had tried his best to overturn the election results by using the courts, interfering with the authorities and laws governing the election, and distorting language into lies to call the election "rigged" and its results fraudulent. Having failed, he now turned to his base, armed with the swaggering hope that he could still control efforts across government, aided by the tool of bureaucratic porousness. But in fact the bureaucracy was not, in this moment, susceptible to his efforts. William Barr had resigned, removing a chief ally in using the Department of Justice to comport with Trump's wishes. The head of the Department of Homeland Security, Chad Wolf, had resigned, after being declared ineligible by the Government Accountability Office to hold the post he had occupied for well over a year. Slowly but surely, rules and regulations were catching up with Trump's determination to defy norms at will, without consequences.

It was a pivotal moment for the subtle tools, tools that the government had deployed in the days of fear following 9/11 and that had taken on frightening new power as the years progressed, uncoupled more and more from the war on terror context. In many ways, the reaction to January 6 and the policies enacted in the weeks and months that followed constituted a forceful repudiation of the subtle tools, and a recognition of their destructive power—especially in the hands of a president eager to sharpen and wield them. Yet, the question remained, would this be enough to disempower the tools entirely?

A New Era?

Inside and outside the Capitol, witnesses and observers struggled to settle upon terms to describe the events of January 6. At first, those in the invading group were referred to as protesters and their activity as a protest. But as the day turned violent, the use of the word "protest" began to be replaced. It seemed more like a siege, or a coup, or a riot. The term "protester" likewise seemed inadequate. By mid-afternoon, some media were starting to call them violent protesters, rioters, and a pro-Trump mob. By evening, insurrectionists.

By the time the legislators reconvened, one word had taken over—"terrorists." And to ensure that the term connoted a new chapter of terrorism, they were referred to as "domestic terrorists." The persistence of the word "terrorist," so often used to connote "Islamic terrorist," was now being used to describe Americans who embraced a far right-wing white supremacist ideology. It was a sign that, with the January 6 attack, the country might be moving from the terms of 9/11 to a new reference point—yet the category of "domestic terrorist" seemed only slightly more specific than its 9/11-related predecessor. As former senator Russell Feingold had warned after 9/11 of the dangers of imprecise terminology for unleashing vast and unconstitutional powers for law enforcement, so now he warned again: "We must not . . . confuse the need for a force-ful response with the need for new law-enforcement powers."[5]

Indeed, many legislators, recognizing the horror of the moment, ac-knowledged January 6, as the end of an era. As Pearl Harbor had been the referent for 9/11, now 9/11 became the referent for the Capitol at-tack. Of the congresspersons who were trapped inside on January 6, ninety-four had been in office on 9/11, and many immediately remem-bered that day. The similarities were hard to ignore. In 2001, as in 2021, they were rushed off by security guards to secure locations in the build-ing, terrified that their lives were in danger. Only this time the enemy who threatened, armed with sticks and metal pipes, was inside the Capi-tol, not in a weaponized plane threatening from the outside. As Steny Hoyer, a Democratic congressman from Maryland, would state when Congress reassembled in the early evening, "Little did I know that this Capitol would be attacked by the enemy within. I was here on 9/11 when we were attacked by the enemy without."[6] The Republican congress-woman Ann Wagner, who had been the co-chair of the Republican National Committee on 9/11, claimed, "this is 1,000 times worse than even that was in terms of my emotions and feelings."[7] Several congres-sional members who had served in Iraq and Afghanistan compared the Capitol takeover to their experiences in the war on terror. Smelling the tear gas, hearing the screaming of threats, and being caught in the chaos of the evacuation, Florida republican Michael Waltz and Colorado democratic congressman Jason Crow were reminded of their deploy-ments in the war on terror. Crow, a former Army Ranger, said, "I felt like I was back in Afghanistan."[8]

Emphasizing the new era that was dawning, Steny Hoyer said, "We grieved at Fort Sumter; we grieved on December 7, 1941; and we grieved on 9/11. And, yes, we grieved on January 6 of this year."[9] As a signifier of the country's most recent traumatic event, the initial reactions seemed to suggest that January 6 would replace 9/11. But whether or not it was a momentary break in the ethos that had evolved since 9/11, and whether or not the subtle tools would persist even in a newly defined context, remained to be seen.

Reaching for Normalcy and Norms

The insurrection had been the most extreme example of the bypassing of process, norms, and the law that evolved in the post 9/11 years. When legislators reconvened on the night of the insurrection, they were making a point—that they would not tolerate this level of norm-breaking. At 11:30 p.m., as the joint session to certify the election results reconvened, the legislators described the violations of the day as wrongful precisely for the norms they disrupted.

"We do not live in normal times," said Hawaii's senator Mazie Hirono.

How is it normal as we and the world watched in horror as an angry mob stormed the U.S. Capitol? . . . It is not normal when we have a President who lies every single day. . . . It is not normal when, in the middle of a pandemic that has claimed the lives of over 350,000 Americans, . . . we have a President who only seems to care about spreading conspiracies to undermine confidence in our elections and our democracy. It is not normal when duly elected Senators who took an oath to uphold the Constitution pull a stunt to try and nullify millions of votes in six States so that Donald Trump can remain President.

But as Hirono pointed out—the challenge was clear. "I call this effort a stunt because it is doomed to fail."[10] No matter how long it took, the Congress needed to certify the vote without further disruption.

The appeal to restoring norms resonated strongly after the watershed events of the day. Georgia senator Kelly Loeffler, fresh off her recount loss to Raphael Warnock, spoke for others: "When I arrived in Washington this morning, I fully intended to object to the certification of the electoral votes. However, the events that have transpired today have forced me to reconsider, and I cannot now, in good conscience, object to the certification of these electors. The violence, the lawlessness, and siege of the Halls of Congress are abhorrent and stand as a direct attack on the very institution my objection was intended to protect: the sanctity of the American democratic process."[11]

Over the long course of the war on terror, the escape from norms had escalated year after year, leading to this moment. As if mirroring the initial response to 9/11, the legislators stepped in with the conviction that the horrifically disruptive event should not deter the business of the day. As George Bush had told families to "go shopping" as a shorthand for resuming their lives, now the nation's lawmakers were intent on showing that they, too, could defy the destructive consequences of January 6.

It was an important moment. Not only did the proceedings resume but the attempts at further delay were countered. Six Republican senators— Ted Cruz, Josh Hawley, Cindy Hyde-Smith, John Kennedy, Roger Marshall, and Tommy Tuberville—and 121 of 210 House Republicans voted to contest the Arizona election results. But to no avail. At 3:24 a.m., on January 7, the certification was complete. Joe Biden was declared president. He would be inaugurated two weeks later, on January 20.

This sign of a potential return to normalcy was, however, overshadowed by the groundbreaking decision to impeach President Trump in his last days in office. On January 13, Trump was impeached for the second time, this time for fomenting the insurrection. The only time a president in American history had been impeached twice, it was a threshold moment. And yet, its ultimate significance remained to be seen. Would it signify the end of the practices of breaking norms and a firm embrace of the Constitution's emphasis on checks and balances, or would it merely provide a pause before such departures from norms and the law resumed yet again?

Two reminders of 9/11 that colored the post-January 6 days gave some indicators as to what the future would bring, and whether or not the subtle tools would outlive the era that had spawned them. First, in the second impeachment hearings, the voice of Liz Cheney, the Wyoming congresswoman and one of ten Republican House members to vote for impeachment, spoke for many who wanted impeachment. Cheney was the daughter of Bush's vice president Dick Cheney, who had orchestrated the extralegal "gloves off" policy of the post–9/11 era that led the torture policies of the time. Her objections to the behavior of Donald Trump put a fine point on the end of the war on terror period. While she remained an ardent defender of her father and his policies, she opposed the abuse of power that Trump signified. "There has never been a greater betrayal by a President of the United States of his office and his oath to the Constitution."[12] It was a remarkably ironic moment, suggesting that Trump was an anomaly rather than the product of an evolution in presidential powers that had been fueled by 9/11 and the subtle tools.

Notably, in a second reminder of the legacy of 9/11, a growing number of members of Congress called for an investigation into what had happened on January 6 along the lines of the independent, bipartisan commission which produced the 9/11 Commission Report in 2004. Terrorism and counterterrorism expert Brian Jenkins wrote that only such a commission could provide the deep dive into what had happened, what vulnerabilities were exposed, and who should be held accountable.[13] Within days of the inauguration, bipartisan support for a commission to study the causes and actors behind the insurrection had gained momentum in Congress.[14] On January 15, House Speaker Nancy Pelosi wrote a letter to Democrats in the House announcing her intentions "to get to the truth of how this happened." "Security, Security, Security," she titled her letter, repeating the word nine more times in her one page letter. The "next step," she wrote, "will be to establish an outside, independent 9/11- type Commission to 'investigate and report on the facts and causes relating to the January 6, 2021 domestic terrorist attack upon the United States Capitol Complex . . . and relating to the interference with the peaceful transfer of power.'"[15] Symbolically, it was a telling sign. The era of 9/11 as the country's most recent national security trauma seemed to have given way to the trauma of the Capitol riots. In Pelosi's words, the threat was now from within. But the emphasis on security remained paramount as did, in her plan for the commission, the template provided by the responses to 9/11.

President Biden and the Subtle Tools

Joe Biden's signature phrase, "let me be clear," was a hopeful sign. He tossed the phrase around in speeches, interviews, and tweets—with a casual air. Despite its informality, it was nonetheless a sign of respect for the clarity that had succumbed incrementally to imprecision, false-hoods, and misinformation over the course of two decades. And it was a potential baseline for reintroducing clarity into the business of government.

In his inaugural address on January 20, Biden reclaimed a word that had been used with utmost imprecision for nearly two decades—"terrorist." He was the first president since the attacks of 2001 to use the word "terror-ism" in an inaugural or State of the Union address without referencing Is-lamic terrorism directly or indirectly. But his use of it—in pledging to de-feat "political extremism, white supremacy, domestic terrorism"—was only slightly more specific than the more general term "terrorism," which had been used widely for nearly two decades now, amplifying voices opposed to immigrants and protesters at home as well as an increasing number of groups abroad. Biden's use of the term now left relatively wide open who and what concerns and causes would come to the attention of law enforce-ment in the Biden years in the name of security, while reinforcing the power of the word that had been sustained since 9/11.

Biden's inaugural address was in fact short on words, lasting only eleven minutes. In his own way, as inadvertently perhaps as with the phrase "let me be clear," Biden seemed to recognize the trouble that lan-guage, hobbled by its misuse and abuse in the war on terror and beyond, had wrought. "To overcome these challenges—to restore the soul and to secure the future of America—requires more than words."[16] To re-cover from the subtle tool's dependence on imprecision, clearer words, and importantly, transparent action, were needed.

Instinctively as well perhaps, Biden's first efforts were focused on pro-cess and detail. Even as the contested election persisted, he reverted to a belief in process, counseling audiences to be patient. "The process is working," he told an audience two days after the election. "The count is being completed. And we'll know very soon."[17]

His emphasis on process, however, came in the form of a mixed message. Biden issued an unprecedented number of executive orders (EOs) during his first month in office, more than twice the number issued by Clinton, Bush, or Obama. This ready reliance on executive orders as a necessary means for moving forward was a sign that a lengthier, legislative process for undoing the Trump policies was neither timely enough nor perhaps reliable enough for a restoration of congressional work as an initial pathway forward.

These first decrees covered areas in which Trump had proved most destructive to law and norms.[18] Biden ordered a halt to the Muslim ban and a repeal of the presidential executive orders on law enforcement activities against immigrants in the interior and at the border. He issued an EO strengthening DACA (Deferred Action for Childhood Arrivals) and another halting deportations at the border and another ordering a stop to border construction. Several themes were running through his executive orders, among them a respect for tolerance; a proactive attempt to address the many dimensions of the COVID crisis; and a determination to address climate change.

Yet, much as they leapfrogged over legislative process, Biden's executive orders displayed in their details a heightened regard for establishing and following procedural norms. Weaving itself throughout each and every one of these directives was a robust attention to process. Executive orders normally set out intentions, name the agencies and official positions to be involved, and perhaps the programs to be included. Biden's executive orders, longer on average than those of his predecessors, were much more detailed and specific. For example, when it came to COVID relief, Biden issued not one but eighteen executive orders, each one packed with specific instructions to officials at the Departments of the Treasury, Education, State, and Defense, as well as to the Joint Chiefs and the Office of the Director of National Intelligence, detailing the work to be done, the kind of reporting and thus transparency required, and the results intended.

As the executive orders indicated, Biden was beginning his presidency by acknowledging the bureaucratic damage that the subtle tools had wrought—but he was also signaling an unwillingness to dispense entirely with the subtle tools. As with the reliance on executive orders, so too the convenience of bypassing process in appointments proved irresistible. For his secretary of defense, he appointed General Lloyd Austin, who had been retired for only four years, and who therefore required a waiver from Congress. Biden thus repeated the departure from norms and the law that Trump had made in appointing his first secretary of defense, General James Mattis.

Likewise, when it came to matters of personnel and bureaucracy, Biden recognized the damage to the bureaucracy that Trump had accomplished with broad strokes—but seemed to determine that only similarly broad strokes could undo that damage. He summarily revoked the Schedule F reclassifications of government employees, immediately replacing Trump's codification of the "spoils system," and restoring the customary merit system. And, in a gesture attesting to the breadth of his initial reforms, in a virtual ceremony, Biden himself swore in one thousand federal appointees, who pledged to be "decent, honorable, and smart." Similarly wide in scope, once Secretary of Defense Austin was sworn in, he began to purge at least forty-two boards throughout the Department of Defense, firing every member on every board, both last-minute Trump appointees and earlier administrations' appointments.[19] With this broad swipe at the entire category of employees, the subtle tool of imprecision and its allowances for expansive, rather than individually applied policies proved desirable, deemed essential for taking initial healing steps forward.

Finally, Biden's early days were colored by his addressing of the subtle tool of secrecy. From his first days in office, he pledged to honor transparency. While not going as far as Obama had when he issued a presidential memorandum on transparency, Biden signaled a respect for the media and the public's right to know. His White House press secretary, Jen Psaki, promised a return to daily press briefings, a custom that had long been abrogated by Trump whose White House at one point went nearly a year without a formal briefing. In addition, Psaki vowed to adhere to facts, alluding to the "alternative facts" and disinformation that had characterized those press interactions that did occur during the Trump years.

Essentially, President Biden was laying claim to his own Ground Zero. His decision to clear the decks before moving on was an explicit recognition of the harms the subtle tools had wrought, coming to fruition on January 6. Biden's plan was to start again, to "Build Back Better." His early rhetorical nod to clarity, his process-oriented executive orders, and his promise of public accountability signaled a possible change of direction away from the use of the subtle tools. But, as the two decades since 9/11 had shown, those tools were persistent, compelling, and still available should Biden or others choose to pick them up once again, even for new policy directives.

Questions about restoring and rebuilding inevitably call to mind the image of the pendulum swing or the historical cycles that Arthur Schlesinger, Jr., had reflected upon, cycles careening back and forth or evolving incrementally between eras of liberalism and conservativism, of private interest and public purpose, of adherence to constitutional principles and abuses of power.

But the lessons of the post–9/11 years suggest a different historical framework through which to accurately view the course of American political history, one tied less to ideologies, political proclivities, and policies, one bound instead to cataloging the culture of governance. These last twenty years suggest that the true course of American politics and history is apparent in *how* events happened as much as in *what* happened. It wasn't just the fact that the AUMF, the Patriot Act, and the Homeland Security Act gave new authorities to law enforcement and military strategy, it was that the subtle tools, beginning with imprecise language and leading to the disruption of norms and law, colored the creation and implementation of those authorities, transforming the culture of governance in the country.

In the past, after periods of intense trauma—wars, egregious presidential misdeeds, and civil unrest—the country has sometimes recovered, sometimes stumbled, and sometimes failed. The Civil War was followed after a brief and incomplete period of Reconstruction by the lasting injustices and unlawfulness of Jim Crow. The Nixon presidency and the Watergate scandal introduced a path to reform in laws which privileged oversight and accountability. The unrest of the civil rights movement led to some gains, like the Voting Rights Act and Civil Rights Bill, and some inexcusable losses, like the war on drugs, mass incarceration, and the return of the death penalty.

The questions facing us now include: What will be the aftermath of the 9/11 era that culminated in the Trump presidency and its destructive attacks on democracy? Will Americans—policymakers and the public—disavow the subtle tools through policy and procedural reform, or will we continue to use them to carve a path away from the rule of law and the respect for constitutional norms? Will we take to heart the true lesson left by the aftermath of 9/11—that the culture of governance lies at the heart of democracy? Will we honor clarity, transparency, bureaucratic integrity, and the respect for law and norms, or succumb instead to the lure of imprecision, secrecy, bureaucratic porousness, and the violation of law and custom? Or, have the subtle tools become so ingrained and effective that they have been become indispensable?

One thing seems certain. Only if the subtle tools are laid to rest will the future of democracy in America have its best chance.

ACKNOWLEDGMENTS

THERE ARE SEVERAL PEOPLE without whose help and encouragement this book would not have come into being. At the top of the list is Joshua Dratel who for decades now has been my legal mentor, my co-author, my sounding board, and my friend. Our constant conversations are a story unto themselves. My brother Richard Greenberg has fielded question after question, provided wise advice, and shared his own brilliant insights into the complex stories retold here. My wonderful children Adam Sticklor and Katherine Roberts, lights of my life, and their spouses Jessica Stilling Sticklor and William Roberts, have encouraged me along despite the distances of COVID, engaging my digressions about one issue or another, all the while more certain than I was that the book would reach completion on schedule. Thanks to Addison and Jackie for their wondrous presence. Gary Greenberg and Susan Powers were supportive as always, while Gary's remarkable writings inspired me along. Thanks to Lola Goldberg for her sisterly support. Thanks to my dad Larry Greenberg and Jo Thune-Larsen for their constant encouragement.

I am deeply indebted to my editor Bridget Flannery-McCoy, who helped in incalculable ways to make this book the best it could be. Her talent for envisioning the deeper possibilities of the narrative was extraordinary. Her encouragement, her inspiration, her trust in me, and her delight in seeing the manuscript evolve made all the difference.

I want to thank Julia Tedesco, my invaluable research assistant on the book, for her amazing research skills, her indefatigable commitment to detail, and her insightful understanding of the things that matter most to me. I am grateful as well for her indispensable help in keeping the Center on National Security thriving during this time.

My Fordham Law students and the Center on National Security's summer interns from around the country were generous beyond compare. My thanks go to Fordham Law students Abigail Krusemark, Sophia Porotsky, Robert Griffith, Dylan McGowan, Graham Streich, Jake Weber, and Joseph Del Vicario; to Fordham College students Thomas Reuter and Olivia Quartell; and to Fordham alum Jonathan Alegria. Thanks as well to Sarah Viola for her research. Thanks also to the wonderful research assistants from our national student summer college fellows program: Andrew Tobin, Ariadna Chua, Avery Ostro, Daniel Oestericher, and Parker Lewin. And special thanks to Alexandra Laguardia and Sofia Cimballa for their unwavering help during the school year as well as over the summer. My gratitude as well to Dan Humphreys for his lasting support.

I am beyond grateful to the many friends and colleagues who so generously fielded questions despite their busy schedules. Thanks to Ali Soufan for his vast knowledge, brilliant insights, and belief in me; to Michel Paradis for his laser-like grasp of the details that matter and his patience with my questions; to Brian Jenkins for his deep understanding of the complex issues at play; to John Berger for his stellar advice and guidance throughout; and to Jonathan Stevenson for sharing his superb grasp of policy and politics. A special thanks to John Brennan for his kindness and generosity both over the book and in our work together at CNS. Thanks to Jameel Jaffer for his generous and thoughtful explanations. Thanks to Neal Katyal, Carol Rosenberg, Hooman Majd, Donald Glascoff, Stanley Arkin, Stephen Holmes, David McCraw, Colin Clarke, and Tom Durkin for taking the time to help me think through some of the more complex issues in the book. Thanks to Peter and Cora Weiss for their love and their reflections on the challenges of our times. And thanks to Francesca Laguardia, Jennifer Indig, and Jacqueline Barkett—on their own paths now—who continue to inspire me about the future. My thanks to Russell Feingold for sharing his insights into the early war-on-terror years. My very deep gratitude goes to Vinnie Viola for sharing his wisdom and his vision with me for so many years. I am grateful to Elliott Millenson for his wise counsel over many years. My thanks to Ed Stroz and to Sally

Spooner for their enthusiastic engagement with the Center and their continuing friendship. I am grateful for the support of Dean Matthew Diller and the Fordham School of Law. My very special thanks go to Tom Engelhardt for his mentorship and his trust in me.

I am forever blessed by the friendship of Karma Kreizenbeck, whose belief in me has nurtured me through endless numbers of projects for decades. My deep thanks to Pat Bernard for her constant friendship over the years.

Above all, my gratitude goes to my husband Danny Goldberg, who always knows how to tilt the earth so that the bright side faces up. His love, encouragement, and guidance have been a gift from the heavens.

NOTES

Introduction

This chapter's epigraph derives from George W. Bush, "Statement by the President in His Address to the Nation," The White House, September 11, 2001, https://georgewbush-whitehouse.archives.gov/news/releases/2001/09/20010911-16.html (last accessed July 10, 2020).

1. Richard D. White, "George Tenet and the Last Great Days of the CIA," *Public Administration Review* 68, no. 3 (2008): 420–27, https://doi.org/10.1111/j.1540-6210.2008.00879.x (last accessed July 10, 2020).

2. "How the World Has Changed," Pew Research Center's Global Attitudes Project, Pew Research Center, December 19, 2001, https://www.pewresearch.org/global/2001/12/19/how-the-world-has-changed/ (last accessed July 10, 2020).

3. Michael Kruse, "What Trump and Clinton Did on 9/11," *Politico*, September 10, 2016, https://www.politico.com/magazine/story/2016/09/trump-hillary-clinton-september-11-911-attacks-nyc-214236 (last accessed February 20, 2021).

4. "Joint Resolution to Authorize the Use of United States Armed Forces against Those Responsible for the Recent Attacks Launched against the United States (AUMF of 2001)," Public Law 107-40 (September 18, 2001): 224–25. "Uniting and Strengthening America by Providing Appropriate Tools Required to Intercept and Obstruct Terrorism Act (USA Patriot Act) of 2001," Public Law 107-56 (October 26, 2001), https://www.govinfo.gov/content/pkg/PLAW-107publ56/pdf/PLAW-107publ56.pdf (last accessed July 10, 2020).

5. "Human Cost of Post-9/11 Wars: Direct War Deaths in Major War Zones, Afghanistan and Pakistan," 20 Years of War: A Cost of War Research Series, Watson Institute, Brown University (November 13, 2019), https://watson.brown.edu/costsofwar/files/cow/imce/papers/2019/Direct%20War%20Deaths%20COW%20Estimate%20November%2013%202019%20FINAL.pdf (last accessed February 20, 2021).

6. Adam Nagourney, "Obama Wins Election," *The New York Times*, November 4, 2008.

7. Barack Obama, *A Promised Land* (Crown, 2020), 579–88.

8. Arthur M. Schlesinger Jr., *The Cycles of American History* (Boston: Houghton Mifflin Harcourt, 1999), vii.

9. Ibid., 9.

10. Ibid., 8.

11. Ibid., 9–10.

12. Ibid, 92.

13. George Orwell, "Politics and the English Language," https://www.orwell.ru/library/essays/politics/english/e_polit/ (last accessed February 20, 2021).

Chapter 1: Ground Zero

This chapter's epigraph derives from House Debate, "Authorizing Use of United States Armed Forces against Those Responsible for Recent Attacks against the United States," 107th Cong., 1st Sess., September 14, 2001, H5638–H5681, https://www.congress.gov/congressional-record/2001/9/14/house-section/article/H5638-4 (last accessed July 10, 2020).

1. Dan Barry, "A Day of Terror: Hospitals; Pictures of Medical Readiness, Waiting and Hoping for Survivors to Fill Their Wards," *New York Times*, September 12, 2001, https://www.nytimes.com/2001/09/12/us/day-terror-hospitals-pictures-medical-readiness-waiting-hoping-for-survivors.html (last accessed July 10, 2020). Dan Barry, "After the Attacks: The Search; A Few Moments of Hope in a Mountain of Rubble," *New York Times*, September 13, 2001, https://www.nytimes.com/2001/09/13/us/after-the-attacks-the-search-a-few-moments-of-hope-in-a-mountain-of-rubble.html (last accessed July 10, 2020).

2. Joel Achenbach, "The Man Who Feared, Rationally, That He'd Just Destroyed the World," *The Washington Post*, July 23, 2015.

3. Donald J. Trump, "Donald Trump after 9/11 on NBC," *NBC*, September 13, 2001, https://www.youtube.com/watch?v=+J9774d7QI5I (last accessed July 10, 2020).

4. Alexander Hamilton, James Madison, and John Jay, *The Federalist Papers* (Dublin, OH: Coventry House Publishing, 2015).

5. Ibid., No. 37, 173.

6. R. W. Emerson, *Nature* (James Monroe and Company, 1849), 15.

7. Arthur M. Schlesinger Jr., "Politics and the American Language," *American Scholar* 43, no. 4 (Autumn 1974): 553–62.

8. George Orwell, "Politics and the English Language," https://www.orwell.ru/library/essays/politics/english/e_polit/ (last accessed February 20, 2021).

9. Arthur M. Schlesinger Jr., *The Cycles of American History* (Boston: Houghton Mifflin Harcourt, 1999), 433.

10. George W. Bush, "Statement by the President in His Address to the Nation," The White House, September 11, 2001, https://georgewbush-whitehouse.archives.gov/news/releases/2001/09/20010911-16.html (last accessed July 10, 2020). Katherine Seelye and Elisabeth Bumiller, "After the Attacks: The President; Bush Labels Aerial Terrorist Attacks 'Acts of War,'" *New York Times*, September 13, 2001, https://www.nytimes.com/2001/09/13/us/after-the-attacks-the-president-bush-labels-aerial-terrorist-attacks-acts-of-war.html (last accessed July 10, 2020).

11. Senate Session, *C-SPAN*, September 12, 2001, https://www.c-span.org/video/?165972-3%2Fus-senators-condemn-911-terrorist-attacks-2001 (last accessed July 10, 2020).

12. David Banks, Photograph, Washington, DC, 2001, *NPR*, https://legacy.npr.org/news/specials/americatransformed/gallery/dc_vigil/010912.dcvigil.slide10.html (last accessed July 10, 2020).

13. *Senate Congressional Record*, "Terrorist Attacks against the United States," 107th Cong., 1st Sess., 2001, vol. 147, no. 118 (September 12, 2001), https://www.congress.gov/crec/2001/09/12/CREC-2001-09-12.pdf (last accessed July 10, 2020).

14. Ibid.

15. Joint Resolution to Authorize the Use of United States Armed Forces against Those Responsible for the Recent Attacks Launched against the United States (AUMF of 2001), Public Law 107-40 (September 18, 2001) (hereafter AUMF of 2001).

16. Debate, "Authorizing Use of United States Armed Forces against Those Responsible for Recent Attacks against the United States," *House Congressional Record*, 107th Cong., 1st Sess. (September 14, 2001), H5638–H5681, https://www.congress.gov/congressional-record/2001/9/14/house-section/article/H5638-4 (last accessed July 10, 2020).

17. Authorization for the Use of Military Force, (AUMF), September 18, 2001, https://www.congress.gov/107/plaws/publ40/PLAW-107publ40.pdf (last accessed February 20, 2021).

18. Ibid.

19. George W. Bush, "Address to a Joint Session of Congress and the American People," The White House, September 20, 2001, https://georgewbush-whitehouse.archives.gov/news/releases/2001/09/20010920-8.html (last accessed July 20, 2020).

20. Joint Resolution Declaring That a State of War Exists between the Imperial Government of Japan and the Government and the People of the United States and Making Provisions to Prosecute the Same, Public Law 77-328, *U.S. Statutes at Large* 55 (1941), 795, https://www.loc.gov/law/help/statutes-at-large/77th-congress/session-1/c77s1ch561.pdf (last accessed July 10, 2020).

21. "Transcript of Tonkin Gulf Resolution (1964)," *OurDocuments.gov*, https://www.ourdocuments.gov/doc.php?flash=false&doc=98&page=transcript (last accessed July 10, 2020).

22. *Senate Congressional Record*, "Use of Force Authorized by the President," October 1, 2001, S9948, https://www.congress.gov/crec/2001/10/01/CREC-2001-10-01-pt1-PgS9948-2.pdf (last accessed July 10, 2020). Shayana Kadidal, "The $1.6 Trillion Blank Check," *The Daily Outrage* (blog), Center for Constitutional Rights, September 27, 2016, https://ccrjustice.org/home/blog/2016/09/27/16-trillion-blank-check (last accessed July 10, 2020).

23. Russell Feingold, *While America Sleeps: A Wake-Up Call for the 9/11 Era* (New York: Crown, 2012), 22.

24. Ibid., 22.

25. Ibid., 23.

26. John C. Yoo, "The President's Constitutional Authority to Conduct Military Operations against Terrorists and Nations Supporting Them," Memorandum Opinion for the Deputy Counsel to the President, September 25, 2001, https://fas.org/irp/agency/doj/olc092501.html (last accessed July 10, 2020).

27. Ibid.

28. Charlie Savage, *Power Wars: The Relentless Rise of Presidential Authority and Secrecy* (New York: Little, Brown 2015), 69.

29. Bush, "Address to a Joint Session of Congress and the American People," September 20, 2001.

30. Barbara Lee, "Congresswoman Lee Applauds House Passage of Her Provision to Sunset the 2001 Military Authorization," June 19, 2019, https://lee.house.gov/news/press-releases/congresswoman-lee-applauds-house-passage-of-her-provision-to-sunset-the-2001-military-authorization (last accessed July 10, 2020).

31. Steve Coll, *Directorate S: The C.I.A. and America's Secret Wars in Afghanistan and Pakistan* (New York: Penguin, 2018), 134.

32. Stephen Holmes, "In Case of Emergency: Misunderstanding Tradeoffs in the War on Terror," *California Law Review* 97, no. 2 (April 2009): 301–55.

33. Karen J. Greenberg, *The Least Worst Place: Guantanamo's First 100 Days* (Oxford: Oxford University Press, 2009), 152.

34. Ibid., 40.

35. Janis Karpinski, *One Woman's Army: The Commanding General of Abu Ghraib Tells her Story* (New York: Miramax Books, 2005), 183–205.

36. Office of the Inspector General of the Department of Defense, Report No. 06-INTEL-10, "Evaluation Report," August 25, 2006, https://fas.org/irp/agency/dod/abuse.pdf (last accessed July 10, 2020).

37. Joint Resolution to Authorize the Use of United States Armed Forces against Iraq (AUMF of 2002), Public Law 107-243, *U.S. Statutes at Large* 116 (2002), https://www.congress.gov/107/plaws/publ243/PLAW-107publ243.pdf (last accessed July 10, 2020).

38. Trevor McCrisken, "Ten Years on: Obama's War on Terrorism in Rhetoric and Practice," *International Affairs* 87, no. 4 (2011): 781–801, https://www.jstor.org/stable/20869759?seq=1 (last accessed July 10, 2020). United States Department of Justice, "Department of Justice Withdraws Enemy Combatant Definition for Guantanamo Detainees," Press Release, March 13, 2009, https://www.justice.gov/opa/pr/department-justice-withdraws-enemy-combatant-definition-guantanamo-detainees (last accessed July 10, 2020). Oliver Burkeman, "Obama Administration Says Goodbye to 'War on Terror,'" *The Guardian*, March 25, 2009, https://www.theguardian.com/world/2009/mar/25/obama-war-terror-overseas-contingency-operations (last accessed July 10, 2020).

39. Scott Wilson and Al Kamen, "'Global War on Terror' Is Given a New Name," *Washington Post*, March 25, 2009, https://www.washingtonpost.com/wp-dyn/content/article/2009/03/24/AR2009032402818.html (last accessed July 10, 2020). Congressional Research Service, "Summary of S. 553 (112th): Detention of Unprivileged Enemy Belligerents Act," March 10, 2011, https://www.govtrack.us/congress/bills/112/s553/summary (last accessed July 10, 2020).

40. Barack Obama, "Remarks by the President in Address to the Nation on the Way Forward in Afghanistan and Pakistan," United States Military Academy at West Point, West Point, New York, The White House, December 1, 2009, https://obamawhitehouse.archives.gov/the-press-office/remarks-president-address-nation-way-forward-afghanistan-and-pakistan (last accessed July 10, 2020).

41. Danielle Kurtzleben, "CHART: How the U.S. Troop Levels in Afghanistan Have Changed under Obama," *NPR*, July 6, 2016, https://www.npr.org/2016/07/06/484979294/chart-how-the-u-s-troop-levels-in-afghanistan-have-changed-under-obama (last accessed July 10, 2020).

42. Press Release, United States Department of Justice, "Department of Justice Withdraws Enemy Combatant Definition," March 13, 2009. "Respondents' Memorandum Regarding the Government's Detention Authority Relative to Detainees Held at Guantanamo Bay," *In Re: Guantanamo Bay Detainee Litigation*, March 13, 2009, https://www.justice.gov/sites/default/files/opa/legacy/2009/03/13/memo-re-det-auth.pdf (last accessed March 25, 2021).

43. Ibid.

44. Human Rights First, "Guantanamo by the Numbers," October 10, 2018, https://www.humanrightsfirst.org/resource/guantanamo-numbers (last accessed February 14, 2021).

45. Karen J. Greenberg, "Drone Strikes and the Law: From Bush-Era Detention to Obama-Era Targeted Killing," in *Drones and the Future of Armed Conflict: Ethical, Legal, and Strategic*

Implications, ed. David Cortright, Rachel Fairhurst, and Kristen Wall, 126–46 (Chicago: University of Chicago Press, 2015). Jameel Jaffer, *The Drone Memos: Targeted Killing, Secrecy, and the Law* (New York: New Press, 2010).

46. Micah Zenko, "Obama's Final Drone Strike Data," *Council on Foreign Relations*, January 20, 2017, https://www.cfr.org/blog/obamas-final-drone-strike-data (last accessed July 10, 2020). Spencer Ackerman, "Trump Ramped Up Drone Strikes in America's Shadow Wars," *Daily Beast*, November 26, 2018, https://www.thedailybeast.com/trump-ramped-up-drone-strikes-in-americas-shadow-wars (last accessed July 10, 2020). Ken Dilanian and Courtney Kube, "Trump Administration Wants to Increase CIA Drone Strikes," *NBC News*, September 17, 2017, https://www.nbcnews.com/news/military/trump-admin-wants-increase-cia-drone-strikes-n802311 (last accessed July 10, 2020).

47. "Trump Revokes Obama Rule on Reporting Drone Strike Deaths," *BBC News*, March 7, 2019, https://www.bbc.com/news/world-us-canada-47480207 (last accessed April 2, 2021).

48. United States Department of Justice, Memorandum for the Attorney General, "Applicability of Federal Criminal Laws and the Constitution to Contemplated Lethal Operations against Shaykh Anwar al-Aulaqi," July 16, 2010, https://fas.org/irp/agency/doj/olc/aulaqi.pdf (last accessed July 10, 2020). Jaffer, *Drone Memos*, 23.

49. Barack Obama, "Remarks by the President at the National Defense University," National Defense University, Fort McNair, Washington, DC, The White House, May 23, 2013, https://obamawhitehouse.archives.gov/the-press-office/2013/05/23/remarks-president-national-defense-university (last accessed July 10, 2020).

50. "Fact Sheet: U.S. Policy Standards and Procedures for the Use of Force in Counterterrorism Operations Outside the United States and Areas of Active Hostiles," Press Release, The White House, May 23, 2013, https://obamawhitehouse.archives.gov/the-press-office/2013/05/23/fact-sheet-us-policy-standards-and-procedures-use-force-counterterrorism (last accessed July 10, 2020). Directorate of National Intelligence, "Summary of Information regarding U.S. Counterterrorism Strikes outside Areas of Active Hostilities," https://www.dni.gov/files/documents/Newsroom/Press%20Releases/DNI+Release+on+CT+Strikes+Outside+Areas+of+Active+Hostilities.PDF (last accessed July 10, 2020). Amnesty International, "'Will I Be Next?' Us Drone Strikes in Pakistan," Report, 2013, https://www.amnesty.org/download/Documents/12000/asa330132013en.pdf (last accessed July 10, 2020).

51. Jameel Jaffer, "A Less-Secret Drone Campaign," *ACLU*, June 29, 2016, www.aclu.org/blog/national-security/targeted-killing/less-secret-drone-campaign (last accessed July 10, 2020).

52. Caitlyn Oprysko, "White House Claims Victory in Freeing Syria from ISIS Control," *Politico*, March 22, 2019, https://www.politico.com/story/2019/03/22/donald-trump-isis-syria-1232488 (last accessed July 10, 2020).

53. United States Department of State, "Report on the Legal and Policy Frameworks Guiding the United States' Use of Military Force and Related Security Operation," October 2019, https://www.state.gov/wp-content/uploads/2019/10/Report-to-Congress-on-legal-and-policy-frameworks-guiding-use-of-military-force-.pdf (last accessed July 10, 2020).

54. David Welna, "Trump Has Vowed to Fill Guantanamo with 'Some Bad Dudes'—But Who?" *NPR*, November 14, 2016, https://www.npr.org/sections/parallels/2016/11/14/502007304/trump-has-vowed-to-fill-guantanamo-with-some-bad-dudes-but-who (last accessed July 10, 2020).

55. Donald J. Trump, "President Donald J. Trump's State of the Union Address Speech," Transcript, The White House, January 30, 2018, https://trumpwhitehouse.archives.gov/briefings-statements/president-donald-j-trumps-state-union-address/ (last accessed January 21, 2021). Executive Order No. 13823, "Protecting America through Lawful Detention of Terrorists," *Federal Register* (January 30, 2018), https://www.federalregister.gov/documents/2018/02/02/2018-02261/protecting-america-through-lawful-detention-of-terrorists (last accessed July 20, 2020).

56. Aaron Nelson, "Trump's Claim of 'Enemy Combatants' Pouring across Southern Border Worries Advocates," *San Antonio Express-News*, April 2, 2018, https://www.expressnews.com/news/local/article/Trump-s-claim-that-enemy-combatants-are-12800248.php (last accessed July 10, 2020).

57. "Bipartisan Lawmakers Introduce Bill to Limit Further Expansion of 2001 Authorization for Use of Military Force," *The Hill*, July 9, 2020, https://thehill.com/blogs/congress-blog/politics/506621-bipartisan-lawmakers-introduce-bill-to-limit-further-expansion (last accessed July 10, 2020).

58. Limit on the Expansion of the Authorization for Use of Military Force Act, H.R.7500, 116th Cong. (July 9, 2020), https://www.congress.gov/bill/116th-congress/house-bill/7500/text?r=73&s=1 (last accessed July 10, 2020).

Chapter 2: The Patriot Act

This chapter's epigraph derives from *House Congressional Record*, vol. 147, no. 37, October 12, 2001, https://www.congress.gov/107/crec/2001/10/12/CREC-2001-10-12-house.pdf (last accessed February 16, 2021).

1. Russ Feingold, "Statement on Anti-Terrorism Bill Clip," *C-SPAN*, filmed October 25, 2001, 1:56, https://www.c-span.org/video/?c4640421/user-clip-statement-anti-terrorism-bill-clip (last accessed July 10, 2020).

2. Uniting and Strengthening America by Providing Appropriate Tools Required to Intercept and Obstruct Terrorism (USA Patriot Act) Act of 2001, H.R. 3162, 107th Cong. (October 26, 2001), https://www.govinfo.gov/content/pkg/PLAW-107publ56/pdf/PLAW-107publ56.pdf (last accessed February 14, 2021).

3. *House Congressional Record*, "Patriot Act of 2001," https://fas.org/sgp/congress/2001/h101201.html (last accessed February 14, 2021).

4. Anti-Terrorism Act of 2001, H.R. ___, 107th Cong., 1st Sess., introduced in House September ___, 2001, https://www.epic.org/privacy/terrorism/ata2001_text.pdf (last accessed July 10, 2020).

5. Ibid.

6. Russell Feingold, *While America Sleeps: A Wake-Up Call for the 9/11 Era* (New York: Crown, 2012), 160, 163.

7. The ACLU provided a detailed overview of the long-standing wishes of law enforcement for the powers granted in the Patriot Act. "Surveillance under the USA/Patriot Act," https://www.aclu.org/other/surveillance-under-usapatriot-act (last accessed February 14, 2021). David Stout, "Bush Urges Congress to Keep Patriot Act Intact," *New York Times*, June 9, 2005, https://www.nytimes.com/2005/06/09/politics/bush-urges-congress-to-keep-patriot-act-intact.html (last accessed July 10, 2020). Louis Fortis, "Russ Feingold Looks Ahead to 2016," *Shepherd Express*, June 30, 2015, https://shepherdexpress.com/news/features/russ-feingold-looks-ahead-2016/ (last accessed July 10, 2020). Karen J. Greenberg, *Rogue Justice: The Making of the Security State* (New York: Crown, 2016), 30.

8. Russell Feingold, *While America Sleeps*, 164–65. Author interview with Russell Feingold, August 4, 2020.

9. Author interview with Russell Feingold, August 4, 2020.

10. *House Congressional Record*, vol. 147, no. 37, October 12, 2001, https://www.congress.gov /107/crec/2001/10/12/CREC-2001-10-12-house.pdf (last accessed February 16, 2021).

11. Ibid.

12. Ibid.

13. Ibid.

14. Alexander Hamilton, James Madison, and John Jay, *The Federalist Papers*, No. 62 (Dublin, OH: Coventry House Publishing, 2015), 306.

15. Cristina D. Lockwood, "Defining Indefiniteness: Suggested Revisions to the Void for Vagueness Doctrine," *Cardozo Public Law, Policy and Ethics Journal* (Spring 2010), https:// heinonline.org/HOL/LandingPage?handle=hein.journals/cardplp8&div=11&id=&page= (last accessed July 10, 2020).

16. *Papachristou v. City of Jacksonville*, 405 U.S. 156 (1972), https://supreme.justia.com/cases /federal/us/405/156/#tab-opinion-1949589 (last accessed March 5, 2021).

17. *House Congressional Record*, October 12, 2001.

18. Feingold, *While America Sleeps*, 157–58.

19. *House Congressional Record*, October 12, 2001.

20. Feingold, *While America Sleeps*, 155, 158.

21. *House Congressional Record*, October 12, 2001.

22. U.S. Department of Justice, Office of the Inspector General, *A Review of the Federal Bureau of Investigation's Use of National Security Letters, IG Report I*, March 2007, https://oig.justice .gov/reports/2014/s1410.pdf (last accessed July 10, 2020).

23. Ibid., 17.

24. Eric Lichtblau, "U.S. Uses Terror Law to Pursue Crimes from Drugs to Swindling," *New York Times*, September 28, 2003, https://www.nytimes.com/2003/09/28/us/us-uses-terror-law -to-pursue-crimes-from-drugs-to-swindling.html.

25. Ibid.

26. U.S. Department of Justice, "Report from the Field: The USA Patriot Act at Work," July 2004, https://www.justice.gov/archive/olp/pdf/patriot_report_from_the_field0704.pdf (last accessed July 10, 2020).

27. Ryan Singel, "FBI Misuses, Underreports Patriot Act Power: Audit," *Wired*, June 5, 2017, https://www.wired.com/2007/03/fbi-misuses-und/ (last accessed July 10, 2020).

28. Michael German and Michelle Richardson, "Reclaiming Patriotism: A Call to Reconsider the Patriot Act," ACLU, March 2009, https://www.aclu.org/sites/default/files/pdfs /safefree/patriot_report_20090310.pdf (last accessed February 15, 2021). Department of Justice, Office of the Inspector General, "A Review of the FBI's Use of National Security Letters: Assessment of Corrective Actions and Examination of NSL Usage in 2006," March 2008, https://oig.justice.gov/reports/2014/s1410a.pdf (last accessed February 15, 2021).

29. Department of Justice, Office of the Inspector General, "A Review," 129–30.

30. David Cole, "Testimony of Professor David Cole Before the United States Senate Committee on the Judiciary on the USA Patriot Act," March 10, 2005, https://www.judiciary.senate.gov /imo/media/doc/Cole%20Testimony%20051005.pdf (last accessed July 10, 2020).

31. "Oversight of the USA Patriot Act," *Senate Congressional Record*, 109th Cong., 1st Sess. J-109-10, April 5, 2005, https://www.govinfo.gov/content/pkg/CHRG-109shrg24293/pdf /CHRG-109shrg24293.pdf (last accessed July 10, 2020).

32. In 2004, aware of the growing reliance on the Patriot Act for abusive practices, the ACLU worked with other nongovernmental organizations to try to gain passage of a bill that would counter the expansive uses of the USA Patriot Act. Titled the "Civil Liberties Restoration Act," it never even got a hearing on the floor of the House. "Civil Liberties Restoration Act of 2004," *Senate Congressional Record*, S.2528, 108th Cong., June 16, 2004, https://www.congress.gov/bill /108th-congress/senate-bill/2528/all-actions?r=7&overview=closed&s=1#tabs (last accessed July 10, 2020). ACLU, "ACLU Applauds Introduction of Civil Liberties Restoration Act; Measure Restores Freedom, Protects Security," Press Release, June 16, 2004, https://www.aclu.org /press-releases/aclu-applauds-introduction-civil-liberties-restoration-act-measure-restores -freedom (last accessed July 10, 2020).

33. "Four More Years: PATRIOT Provisions Renewed," Center for Democracy and Technology, June 2, 2011, https://cdt.org/insights/four-more-years-patriot-provisions-renewed/ (last accessed February 22, 2021).

34. *ACLU v. Clapper*, 785 F.3d 787 (2d Cir. 2015), https://pdfserver.amlaw.com/nlj/NSA_ca2 _20150507.pdf (last accessed July 10, 2020).

35. Ibid.

36. Ibid.

37. Uniting and Strengthening America by Fulfilling Rights and Ensuring Effective Discipline over Monitoring (USA Freedom Act) of 2015, H.R. 2048, 114th Cong., June 2, 2015, https://www .congress.gov/bill/114th-congress/house-bill/2048/text (last accessed July 10, 2020).

38. Charlie Savage, "Trump Administration Asks Congress to Reauthorize N.S.A.'s Deactivated Call Records Program," *New York Times*, August 15, 2019, https://www.nytimes.com/2019 /08/15/us/politics/trump-nsa-call-records-program.html (last accessed July 10, 2020).

39. Ibid. Office of the Director of National Intelligence, "Statistical Transparency Report regarding Use of National Security Authorities for Calendar Year 2016," April 2017, https://www .documentcloud.org/documents/3688538-FISA-Transparency-Report-April-2017.html (last accessed July 10, 2020). Charlie Savage, "N.S.A. Triples Collection of Data from U.S. Phone Companies," *New York Times*, May 4, 2018, https://www.nytimes.com/2018/05/04/us/politics /nsa-surveillance-2017-annual-report.html (last accessed July 10, 2020). Office of the Director of National Intelligence, "Statistical Transparency Report regarding Use of National Security Authorities for Calendar Year 2017," April 2018, https://www.dni.gov/files/documents/icotr /2018-ASTR—-CY2017—-FINAL-for-Release-5.4.18.pdf (last accessed July 10, 2020). Timothy B. Lee, "Trump Tweet Throws House Surveillance Debate into Chaos," *Ars Technica*, May 27, 2020, https://arstechnica.com/tech-policy/2020/05/in-surprise-tweet-trump-urges -republicans-to-vote-against-spying-bill/ (last accessed July 10, 2020).

40. Cole, "Testimony Before the United States Senate Committee on the Judiciary on the USA Patriot Act" (2010).

41. Lavie Mutanganshuro, "Rwanda Grants Asylum to Stateless Man from US," *New Times*, Rwanda, July 25, 2020. https://www.newtimes.co.rw/news/rwanda-grants-asylum-stateless -man-us (last accessed July 10, 2020).

42. Author interview with Russell Feingold, August 4, 2020.

Chapter 3: Homeland

This chapter's epigraph derives from *House Congressional Record*, July 17, 2001, https://www.govinfo.gov/content/pkg/CHRG-107hhrg83173/pdf/CHRG-107hhrg83173.pdf.

1. George W. Bush, "Address to a Joint Session of Congress and the American People," The White House, September 20, 2001, https://georgewbush-whitehouse.archives.gov/news/releases/2001/09/20010920-8.html (last accessed July 10, 2020).

2. Executive Order No. 13228, "Establishing the Office of Homeland Security and the Homeland Security Council," October 8, 2001, http://www.gpo.gov/fdsys/pkg/CFR-2002-title3-vol1/pdf/CFR-2002-title3-vol1-eo13228.pdf (last accessed July 10, 2020).

3. Department of Defense, "Report of the Quadrennial Defense Review," May 1997, https://www.files.ethz.ch/isn/32542/qdr97.pdf (last accessed July 20, 2020).

4. James Traub, "The Dark History of Defending the 'Homeland,'" *New York Times*, April 5, 2016, https://www.nytimes.com/2016/04/10/magazine/the-dark-history-of-defending-the-homeland.html (last accessed July 10, 2020).

5. Peggy Noonan, "Rudy's Duty," *Wall Street Journal*, June 14, 2002, https://www.wsj.com/articles/SB1022418750653241949 (last accessed July 10, 2020).

6. Mickey Kaus, "The Trouble with 'Homeland,'" *Slate*, June 14, 2002, https://slate.com/news-and-politics/2002/06/homeland-is-a-creepy-morale-sapping-word-let-s-drop-it.html.

7. Author interview with Russell Feingold, August 4, 2020.

8. I. M. Destler and Ivo H. Daalder, "Promise and Problems: President Bush's Homeland Security Department," *Brookings*, June 1, 2002, https://www.brookings.edu/articles/promise-and-problems-president-bushs-homeland-security-department/ (last accessed July 10, 2020).

9. George W. Bush, "Remarks by the President in Address to the Nation," June 6, 2002, https://georgewbush-whitehouse.archives.gov/news/releases/2002/06/20020606-8.html (last accessed March 8, 2021).

10. David Von Drehle and Mike Allen, "Bush Plan's Underground Architects," *Washington Post*, June 9, 2002, https://www.washingtonpost.com/archive/politics/2002/06/09/bush-plans-underground-architects/c9aec880-ac51-4f18-bc49-1da583f52981/ (last accessed July 10, 2020).

11. "The Homeland Security Act of 2002, Days 1 and 2," H.R. 5005, *Archive*, July 15–16, 2002, https://archive.org/stream/gov.gpo.fdsys.CHRG-107hhrg83172/CHRG-107hhrg83172_djvu.txt (last accessed July 10, 2020).

12. George W. Bush, "The Department of Homeland Security," June 2002, https://www.dhs.gov/sites/default/files/publications/book_0.pdf (last accessed July 10, 2020).

13. *House Congressional Record*, "Hearing on the Homeland Security Act of 2002, Day 3," 107th Cong., 2nd Sess. (2002), 60–63, https://www.govinfo.gov/content/pkg/CHRG-107hhrg83173/pdf/CHRG-107hhrg83173.pdf (last accessed July 10, 2020).

14. "Homeland Security Act of 2002, Days 1 and 2," H.R. 5005.

15. Homeland Security Act of 2002, Public Law 107-296, U.S. Statutes at Large (2002), https://www.dhs.gov/sites/default/files/publications/hr_5005_enr.pdf (last accessed July 10, 2020). United States Department of Homeland Security, Office of the Inspector General, "DHS Is Slow to Hire Law Enforcement Personnel," October 31, 2016, https://www.oig.dhs.gov/sites/default/files/assets/2017/OIG-17-05-Oct16.pdf (last accessed July 10, 2020).

16. Russell Feingold, *While America Sleeps: A Wake-Up Call for the 9/11 Era* (New York: Crown, 2012), 157.

17. David Heyman and James Jay Carafano, "DHS 2: Rethinking the Department of Homeland Security," Center for Strategic and International Studies, December 13, 2004, https://csis -website-prod.s3.amazonaws.com/s3fs-public/legacy_files/files/media/csis/pubs/041213 _dhsv2.pdf (last accessed February 15, 2021).

18. Ibid., 7.

19. DHS Office of the Inspector General, "An Assessment of the Proposal to Merge Customs and Border Protections with Immigration and Customs Enforcement, November 2005, https:// www.oig.dhs.gov/assets/Mgmt/OIG_06-04_Nov05.pdf (last accessed March 6, 2021).

20. DHS Office of the Inspector General, "Semiannual Report to the Congress," April 1, 2005–September 30, 2005, https://www.oig.dhs.gov/sites/default/files/assets/SAR/OIG_SAR _Apr05_Sep05.pdf (last accessed January 7, 2021). Condoleezza Rice, *No Higher Honor: A Memoir of My Years in Washington* (New York: Simon and Schuster, 2011), ccclvi.

21. U.S. Government Accountability Office, *Coast Guard: Observations on the Preparation, Response, and Recovery Missions Related to Hurricane Katrina*, GAO-06-903, July 31, 2006, https://www.govinfo.gov/content/pkg/GAOREPORTS-GAO-06-903/html/GAOREPORTS -GAO-06-903.htm (last accessed July 10, 2020).

22. Tom Ridge and Larry Bloom, *The Test of Our Times: America under Siege . . . And How We Can Be Safe Again* (New York: St. Martin's Press, 2009), 223–24.

23. United States Department of Homeland Security, Office of the Inspector General, "A Performance Review of FEMA's Disaster Management Activities in Response to Hurricane Katrina," OIG-06-32, March 2006, https://www.oig.dhs.gov/assets/Mgmt/OIG_06-32_Mar06 .pdf (last accessed January 24, 2021). House of Representatives Select Bipartisan Committee to Investigate the Preparation for and Response to Hurricane Katrina, "A Failure of Initiative," 109th Cong., 2nd Sess., Report 109-377, February 2006, https://www.congress.gov/109/crpt /hrpt377/CRPT-109hrpt377.pdf (last accessed January 24, 2021).

24. DHS Office of the Inspector General, "Semiannual Report to the Congress," 2005. Michael Chertoff, *Homeland Security: Assessing the First Five Years* (Philadelphia: University of Pennsylvania Press, 2009).

25. DHS Office of the Inspector General, "A Performance Review of FEMA's Disaster Management Activities," 2006.

26. Chertoff, *Homeland Security*, 7.

Chapter 4: President Trump and the Subtle Tools

This chapter's epigraph derives from "Confirmation Hearing on the Nomination of Hon. William Pelham Barr to be Attorney General of the United States," Committee on the Judiciary, https://www.congress.gov/116/chrg/CHRG-116shrg36846/CHRG-116shrg36846.htm (last accessed February 17, 2021).

1. Donald J. Trump, "Inaugural Address," January 20, 2017, https://www.pbs.org/newshour /politics/transcript-read-president-trumps-full-inaugural-address (last accessed February 15, 2021).

2. Ibid.

3. John Gramlich, "John Kelly's Military Background Is Unusual for a White House Chief of Staff," Pew Research, August 10, 2017, https://www.pewresearch.org/fact-tank/2017/08/10/john-kellys-military-background-is-unusual-for-a-white-house-chief-of-staff/ (last accessed July 10, 2020).

4. Senate Judiciary Committee, "Nomination of Steven Engel to be AAG for the OLC," Submitted May 17, 2017, Questions for the Record, https://www.judiciary.senate.gov/imo/media/doc/Engel%20Responses%20to%20QFRs.pdf (last accessed July 10, 2020).

5. Nomination Hearing, Stephen Gill Bradbury and Elizabeth Erin Walsh, Senate Committee on Commerce, Science, and Transportation, June 28, 2017, https://www.commerce.senate.gov/2017/6/nomination-hearing (last accessed February 15, 2021).

6. Senate Committee on Commerce, Science and Transportation, Nomination Hearing, June 28, 2017, https://www.commerce.senate.gov/2017/6/nomination-hearing (last accessed July 10, 2020).

7. Carol Rosenberg and Julian E. Barnes, "Gina Haspel Observed Waterboarding at C.I.A. Black Site, Psychologist Testifies," *New York Times*, May 3, 2022, https://www.nytimes.com/2022/06/03/us/politics/cia-gina-haspel-black-site.html (last accessed, July 6, 2022).

8. National Security Act of 1947, Public Law 235, 61 § 496 (July 26, 1947), https://www.dni.gov/index.php/ic-legal-reference-book/national-security-act-of-1947 (last accessed March 5, 2021).

9. Kathleen J. McInnis, "Statutory Restrictions on the Position of Secretary of Defense: Issues for Congress," *CRS Report*, January 5, 2017, updated January 26, 2021 as "The Position of Secretary of Defense: Statutory Restrictions and Civilian-Military Relations," https://fas.org/sgp/crs/natsec/R44725.pdf (last accessed February 15, 2021).

10. Richard Blumenthal, "Remarks," Senate Armed Services Committee, January 12, 2017, https://www.armed-services.senate.gov/imo/media/doc/17-03_01-12-17.pdf (last accessed July 10, 2020).

11. "An Act to Provide for an Exception to a Limitation Against Appointment of Persons as Secretary of Defense within Seven Years of Relief from Active Duty as a Regular Commissioned Officer of the Armed Forces," S. 84, 115th Cong. 1st Sess. (January 18, 2017), https://www.govinfo.gov/content/pkg/BILLS-115s84enr/pdf/BILLS-115s84enr.pdf (last accessed July 10, 2020).

12. Public Law 89–554, §1, September 6, 1966, 80 Stat. 378m, 5 U.S.C. §3110. Employment of relatives; restrictions, https://uscode.house.gov/view.xhtml?req=(title:5%20section:3110%20edition:prelim)%20OR%20(granuleid:USC-prelim-title5-section3110)&f=treesort&edition=prelim&num=0&jumpTo=true (last accessed July 10, 2020).

13. Office of Legal Counsel, "Re: 'Application of 5 US. C. § 3110 to Two Proposed Appointments by the President to Advisory Committees,'" Memorandum, September 17, 2009, https://www.justice.gov/olc/page/file/1009476/download (last accessed July 10, 2020). Josh Gerstein, "DOJ Releases Overruled Memos Finding It Illegal for Presidents to Appoint Relatives," *Politico*, October 3, 2017, https://www.politico.com/story/2017/10/03/justice-department-legal-memos-presidents-appoint-relatives-243395 (last accessed July 10, 2020).

14. Annie L. Owens, "Thwarting the Separation of Powers Doctrine in Interbranch Information Disputes," *Yale Law Journal* 130, 2020–21, https://www.yalelawjournal.org/forum/thwarting -the-separation-of-powers; Auth. of Individual Members of Cong. to Conduct Oversight of the Exec. Branch, 41 Op. O.L.C., slip op. at 1, May 1, 2017, https://www.justice.gov/olc/file/1085571 /download (last accessed March 6, 2021).

15. Office of Legal Counsel, "Application of the Anti-Nepotism Statute to a Presidential Appointment in the White House Office," Memorandum, January 17, 2017, https://www.justice .gov/opinion/file/930116/download (last accessed July 10, 2020).

16. Owens, "Thwarting the Separation of Powers Doctrine."

17. Joel Rose, "How Trump Has Filled High-Level Jobs Without Senate Confirmation Votes," *NPR*, March 9, 2020, https://www.npr.org/2020/03/09/813577462/how-trump-has -filled-high-level-jobs-without-senate-confirmation (last accessed February 22, 2021).

18. Nancy Cook, "Trump's Staffing Struggle: After 3 years, Unfilled Jobs Across the Administration," *Politico*, January 20, 2020, https://www.politico.com/news/2020/01/20/trumps -staffing-struggle-unfilled-jobs-100991 (last accessed February 22, 2021).

19. Chiqui Esteban, "Who's in Charge? Many Months of Acting Cabinet Secretaries," *Washington Post*, July 24, 2019, https://www.washingtonpost.com/politics/2019/07/24/whos-charge -many-months-acting-cabinet-secretaries/?arc404=true (last accessed July 10, 2020). Kathryn Dunn Tenpas, "Tracking Turnover in the Trump Administration," *Brookings*, October 2020, https://www.brookings.edu/research/tracking-turnover-in-the-trump-administration/ (last accessed July 10, 2020). Kathryn Dunn Tenpas, "And Then There Were Ten: With 85% Turnover across President Trump's A Team, Who Remains?" *Brookings*, April 13, 2020, https://www .brookings.edu/blog/fixgov/2020/04/13/and-then-there-were-ten-with-85-turnover-across -president-trumps-a-team-who-remains/ (last accessed July 10, 2020). Kathryn Dunn Tenpas, "Why Is Trump's Staff Turnover Higher Than the 5 Most Recent Presidents?" *Brookings*, January 19, 2018, https://www.brookings.edu/research/why-is-trumps-staff-turnover-higher-than -the-5-most-recent-presidents/ (last accessed July 10, 2020).

20. *CBS Face the Nation*, February 3, 2019, https://www.facebook.com/FaceTheNation /posts/i-like-acting-because-i-can-move-so-quickly-it-gives-me-more-flexibility-preside /2299978093387347/ (last accessed July 10, 2020).

21. Daniel Schorn, "Ex-FBI Chief on Clinton's Scandals," *CBS News*, October 6, 2005, https://www.cbsnews.com/news/ex-fbi-chief-on-clintons-scandals/ (last accessed July 10, 2020).

22. Andrew Kent, "Congress and the Independence of Federal Law Enforcement," *University of California at Davis Law Review* 52, no. 1927 (2019), https://ir.lawnet.fordham.edu/cgi /viewcontent.cgi?article=2024&context=faculty_scholarship.

23. Jack Goldsmith, "Independence and Accountability at the Department of Justice," January 30, 2018, https://www.lawfareblog.com/independence-and-accountability-department -justice (last accessed February 15, 2021).

24. Brennan Center for Justice, "Proposals for Reform: National Task Force on Rule of Law and Democracy," October 2, 2018, https://www.brennancenter.org/sites/default/files/publications /TaskForceReport_2018_09_.pdf (last accessed July 10, 2020).

25. Goldsmith, "Independence and Accountability."

26. Barton Gellman, *Angler: The Cheney Vice Presidency* (New York: Penguin Press, 2008).

27. U.S. Department of Justice, Office of the Inspector General, "A Review of Various Actions by the Federal Bureau of Investigation and Department of Justice in Advance of the 2016 Election," June 2018.

28. James Comey Interview, Executive Session Committee on the Judiciary, Joint with the Committee on Oversight and Government Reform, U.S. House Of Representatives, December 17, 2018, https://d3i6fh83elv35t.cloudfront.net/static/2018/12/Comey-interview-12-17-18 -redacted.pdf (last accessed February 15, 2021).

29. James Comey, Statement for the Record, Senate Selection Committee on Intelligence, June 8, 2017, https://www.politico.com/story/2017/06/07/james-comey-trump-russia -testimony-2017-239253 (last accessed February 15, 2021).

30. Ibid.

31. Ibid.

32. Jessica Taylor, "Attorney General Sessions to Recuse Himself from Any Trump Campaign Investigation," NPR, March 2, 2017, https://www.npr.org/2017/03/02/518198749/attorney -general-sessions-to-recuse-himself-from-any-trump-campaign-investigation (last accessed February 15, 2021).

33. "Trump Interview with Lester Holt," NBC News, May 11, 2017, https://www.nbcnews.com /nightly-news/video/pres-trump-s-extended-exclusive-interview-with-lester-holt-at-the-white -house-941854787582 (last accessed July 10, 2020).

34. Memorandum, "Transparency and Open Government," The White House, January 21, 2009, https://obamawhitehouse.archives.gov/the-press-office/transparency-and-open -government (last accessed July 10, 2020).

35. Conor Friedersdorf, "The Obama Administration's Abject Failure on Transparency," The Atlantic, February 2, 2012, https://www.theatlantic.com/politics/archive/2012/02/the-obama -administrations-abject-failure-on-transparency/252387/ (last accessed July 10, 2020).

36. Barack Obama, A Promised Land (New York: Crown, 2020), 356.

37. National Archives FOIA Annual Reports, Archives.gov, https://www.archives.gov/foia /reports (last accessed January 21, 2020).

38. The White House, Executive Order 13526—Classified National Security Information, December 29, 2009, https://obamawhitehouse.archives.gov/the-press-office/executive-order -classified-national-security-information#:~:text=This%20order%20prescribes%20a%20 uniform,to%20defense%20against%20transnational%20terrorism (last accessed February 15, 2021).

39. "'This Week' Transcript: Barack Obama," This Week with George Stephanopoulos, ABC News, January 10, 2009, https://abcnews.go.com/ThisWeek/Economy/story?id=6618199&page =1 (last accessed February 15, 2021).

40. Spencer Ackerman, "Senate Torture Report to Be Kept from Public for 12 Years after Obama Decision," The Guardian, December 12, 2016, https://www.theguardian.com/us-news /2016/dec/12/obama-senate-cia-torture-report-september-11-classified (last accessed July 10, 2020). Spencer Ackerman, "No Looking Back: The CIA Torture Report's Aftermath," The Guardian, September 11, 2016, https://www.theguardian.com/us-news/2016/sep/11/cia-torture -report-aftermath-daniel-jones-senate-investigation (last accessed July 10, 2020).

41. Jameel Jaffer, "Government Secrecy in the Age of Information Overload," Harvard Kennedy School's Shorenstein Center, November 6, 2017, https://shorensteincenter.org/jameel -jaffer-salant-lecture-2017/ (last accessed July 10, 2020).

42. National Archives FOIA Annual Reports. Steven Aftergood, "Was Obama Administration the Most Transparent or the Least?" November 20, 2017, https://fas.org/blogs/secrecy/2017/11/obama-transparency/ (last accessed July 10, 2020).

43. Jaffer, "Government Secrecy."

44. Information Security Oversight Office, Annual Report to the President, https://www.archives.gov/isoo/reports (last accessed July 10, 2020).

45. History of FOIA, *Electronic Frontier Foundation*, https://www.eff.org/issues/transparency/history-of-foia (last accessed July 10, 2020).

46. National Archives FOIA Annual Reports. Aftergood, "Was Obama Administration the Most Transparent?"

47. Joe Gould, "Trump Benched Mattis before His House Hearing: What Happened?" *Defense News*, January 13, 2017, https://www.defensenews.com/congress/2017/01/13/trump-benched-mattis-before-his-house-hearing-what-happened/ (last accessed July 10, 2020); Ana Radelat, "Despite CT Lawmakers' Opposition, Congress Approves Mattis Waiver," *CT Mirror*, January 13, 2017, https://ctmirror.org/2017/01/13/despite-ct-lawmakers-opposition-congress-approves-mattis-waiver/ (last accessed July 10, 2020).

48. John Bolton, *The Room Where It Happened: A White House Memoir* (New York: Simon and Schuster, 2020), 154.

49. Matt Stieb, "Trump Really Doesn't Like It When His Staff Takes Notes," *New York Magazine*, April 22, 2019, https://nymag.com/intelligencer/2019/04/trump-really-doesnt-like-it-when-his-staff-takes-notes.html (last accessed July 10, 2020).

50. Adam Smith, "The Pentagon's Getting More Secretive—and It's Hurting National Security," *Defense One*, October 28, 2018, https://www.defenseone.com/ideas/2018/10/pentagons-getting-more-secretive-and-its-hurting-national-security/152345/ (last accessed July 10, 2020). Juliet Eilperin, Josh Dawsey, and Brady Dennis, "White House Blocked Intelligence Agency's Written Testimony Calling Climate Change 'Possibly Catastrophic,'" *Washington Post*, June 8, 2019, https://www.washingtonpost.com/climate-environment/2019/06/08/white-house-blocked-intelligence-aides-written-testimony-saying-human-caused-climate-change-could-be-possibly-catastrophic/ (last accessed July 10, 2020).

51. David Rohde, "William Barr, Trump's Sword and Shield," *New Yorker*, January 13, 2020, https://www.newyorker.com/magazine/2020/01/20/william-barr-trumps-sword-and-shield (last accessed July 10, 2020).

52. Smith, "Pentagon's Getting More Secretive." Gould, "Trump Benched Mattis."

53. Josh Lederman, "William Barr Once Warned of Need for 'Political Supervision' at Justice Department," *NBC News*, January 14, 2019, https://www.nbcnews.com/politics/justice-department/william-barr-once-warned-need-political-supervision-justice-department-n958576 (last accessed July 10, 2020).

54. UVA Miller Center, "Barr Exam," December 7, 2018, https://millercenter.org/barr-exam (last accessed July 10, 2020).

55. William Barr, "Mueller's 'Obstruction' Theory," Memorandum to Steven Engel and Rod Rosenstein, https://int.nyt.com/data/documenthelper/549-june-2018-barr-memo-to-doj-mue/b4c05e39318dd2d136b3/optimized/full.pdf (last accessed January 23, 2021).

56. Office of Legal Counsel, "Re: 'Military Interrogation of Alien Unlawful Combatants Held outside the United States,'" Memorandum, March 14, 2003, https://www.aclu.org

/sites/default/files/pdfs/safefree/yoo_army_torture_memo.pdf (last accessed July 10, 2020).

57. Barr, "Mueller's 'Obstruction' Theory."

58. Jennifer Rubin, "What to Make of William Barr's Memo?" *Washington Post*, December 21, 2018, https://www.washingtonpost.com/opinions/2018/12/21/what-make-william-barrs-memo/ (last accessed July 10, 2020). Andrew C. McCarthy, "Barr Memo Is a Commendable Piece of Lawyering," *National Review*, December 20, 2018, https://www.nationalreview.com/2018/12/the-barr-memo-is-a-commendable-piece-of-lawyering/ (last accessed July 10, 2020). Jonathan Hafetz & Brett Max Kaufman, "William Barr's Unsolicited Memo to Trump about Obstruction of Justice," *ACLU*, January 11, 2019, https://www.aclu.org/blog/civil-liberties/executive-branch/william-barrs-unsolicited-memo-trump-about-obstruction-justice (last accessed July 10, 2020). Daniel Hemel and Eric Posner, "Bill Barr Just Argued Himself Out of a Job," *New York Times*, December 21, 2018, https://www.nytimes.com/2018/12/21/opinion/william-barr-attorney-general-memo-trump.html (last accessed July 10, 2020).

59. Rohde, "William Barr, Trump's Sword and Shield."

60. Barr, "Mueller's 'Obstruction' Theory."

61. Robert S. Mueller, "Report on the Investigation into Russian Interference in the 2016 Presidential Election," United States Department of Justice, March 2019, https://www.justice.gov/storage/report.pdf (last accessed July 10, 2020), 8.

62. Randolph D. Moss, Office of Legal Counsel, Department of Justice, "A Sitting President's Amenability to Indictment and Criminal Prosecution," October 16, 2000, https://www.justice.gov/file/19351/download (last accessed February 15, 2021) For 1973 opinion, see Robert G. Dixon, Jr., "Office of Legal Counsel, Re: Amenability of the President, Vice President and other Civil Officers to Federal Criminal Prosecution while in Office," September 24, 1973, https://fas.org/irp/agency/doj/olc/092473.pdf (last accessed February 15, 2021).

63. William Barr to Lindsey Graham et al., March 24, 2019, https://www.lawfareblog.com/document-attorney-general-barr-letter-mueller-report (last accessed February 15, 2021).

64. Letter to House Judiciary Committee Chairman from Pat Cipollone, The White House, May 7, 2019, https://int.nyt.com/data/documenthelper/812-cipollone-letter-mcgahn/6500f55136eae0eebaf3/optimized/full.pdf (last accessed July 10, 2020).

65. Office of Legal Counsel, "Re: 'Testimonial Immunity before Congress of the Former Counsel to the President,'" Memorandum, May 20, 2019, https://d3i6fh83elv35t.cloudfront.net/static/2019/05/McGahn_Opinion_5_20_19_FINAL_002_..01.pdf (last accessed July 10, 2020). Letter to Charles J. Cooper, The White House, October 25, 2019, https://www.justsecurity.org/wp-content/uploads/2019/10/White-House-letter-to-Kupperman-10-25-19-1.pdf (last accessed July 10, 2020).

66. Letter to Speaker of the House et al., The White House, October 8, 2019, https://assets.documentcloud.org/documents/6459967/PAC-Letter-10-08-2019.pdf (last accessed July 10, 2020).

67. Letter to Chairman of Senate Select Committee on Intelligence and Chairman of House Permanent Committee on Intelligence, August 12, 2019, https://www.justsecurity.org/wp-content/uploads/2019/11/ukraine-clearinghouse-whistleblower-complaint-aug-12-2019.pdf (last accessed July 10, 2020).

68. Office of Legal Counsel "Re: 'Urgent Concern' Determination by the Inspector General of the Intelligence Community,'" Memorandum, September 3, 2019, https://www.justice.gov /olc/opinion/file/1205711/download (last accessed July 10, 2020).

69. Ibid.

70. Josh Gerstein and Kyle Cheney, "Appeals Court Pushes Arguments into 2021," *Politico*, October 15, 2020, https://www.politico.com/news/2020/10/15/appeals-court-mcgahn-house -subpoena-429638 (last accessed February 15, 2021).

71. Kayla Goggin, "McGahn Subpoena Case Returns to Full DC Circuit," *Courthouse News*, October 15, 2020, https://www.courthousenews.com/mcgahn-subpoena-case-returns-to-full -dc-circuit/ (last accessed January 21, 2021).

72. Eric Lichtblau, "Report Says Gonzales Mishandled Classified Items," *New York Times*, September 2, 2008, https://www.nytimes.com/2008/09/03/washington/03justice.html (last accessed July 10, 2020).

73. Melissa Quinn, "The Internal Watchdogs Trump Has Fired or Replaced," *CBS News*, May 19, 2020, https://www.cbsnews.com/news/trump-inspectors-general-internal-watchdogs -fired-list/ (last accessed July 10, 2020).

74. Charlie Savage, "Endorsing Trump's Firing of Inspector General, Barr Paints Distorted Picture," *New York Times*, April 10, 2020, https://www.nytimes.com/2020/04/10/us/politics /barr-inspector-general-firing.html (last accessed July 10, 2020).

75. Inspector General Vacancy Tracker, *Project on Government Oversight*, May 5, 2020, https:// www.pogo.org/database/inspector-general-vacancy-tracker/ (last accessed July 10, 2020).

76. Memorandum, "Transparency and Open Government."

77. Jaffer, "Government Secrecy."

Chapter 5: The Muslim Ban

This chapter's epigraph derives from Neal Katyal, "Oral Argument," *Trump v. Hawaii* (April 25, 2018), https://www.supremecourt.gov/oral_arguments/argument_transcripts/2017/17-965 _3314.pdf (last accessed July 10, 2020).

1. "Here's Donald Trump's Presidential Announcement Speech," *Time*, June 16, 2015, https:// time.com/3923128/donald-trump-announcement-speech/ (last accessed July 10, 2020). Jenna Johnson and Abigail Hauslohner, "'I Think Islam Hates Us': A Timeline of Trump's Comments about Islam and Muslims," *Washington Post*, May 20, 2017, https://www.washingtonpost.com /news/post-politics/wp/2017/05/20/i-think-islam-hates-us-a-timeline-of-trumps-comments -about-islam-and-muslims/ (last accessed July 10, 2020). Jessica Taylor, "Trump Calls for 'Total and Complete Shutdown of Muslims Entering' U.S.," *NPR*, December 7, 2015, https://www.npr .org/2015/12/07/458836388/trump-calls-for-total-and-complete-shutdown-of-muslims -entering-u-s (last accessed July 10, 2020). Brian Bennett and Noah Bierman, "White House Aides Who Wrote Trump's Travel Ban See It as Just the Start," *Los Angeles Times*, January 30, 2017, https://www.latimes.com/politics/la-na-pol-trump-immigration-20170130-story.html (last accessed July 10, 2020).

2. Executive Order No. 13769, "Protecting the Nation from Foreign Terrorist Entry into the United States," *Federal Register* (January 27, 2017), https://www.federalregister.gov/documents

/2017/02/01/2017-02281/protecting-the-nation-from-foreign-terrorist-entry-into-the-united
-states (last accessed January 21, 2021). United States Department of Homeland Security, "Fact
Sheet: Protecting the Nation from Foreign Terrorist Entry to the United States," January 29,
2017, https://www.dhs.gov/news/2017/01/29/protecting-nation-foreign-terrorist-entry-united
-states (last accessed July 10, 2020).

3. United States Department of Justice, "Attorney General Prepared Remarks on The National Security Entry-Exit Registration System," June 6, 2002, https://www.justice.gov/archive
/ag/speeches/2002/060502agpreparedremarks.htm (last accessed July 10, 2020).

4. United States Department of Homeland Security, "Removal of Regulations Relating to
Special Registration Process for Certain Nonimmigrants," *Federal Register*, vol. 81, no. 247 (December 23, 2016), https://www.govinfo.gov/content/pkg/FR-2016-12-23/pdf/2016-30885.pdf
(last accessed July 10, 2020).

5. "Visa Waiver Program Improvement and Terrorist Travel Prevention Act of 2015," H.R.
158, 114th Cong. 1st Sess., Introduced in Senate December 9, 2015, https://www.congress.gov
/bill/114th-congress/house-bill/158 (last accessed July 10, 2020).

6. J. David Goodman and Ron Nixon, "Obama to Dismantle Visitor Registry before Trump
Can Revive It," *New York Times*, December 22, 2016, https://www.nytimes.com/2016/12/22
/nyregion/obama-to-dismantle-visitor-registry-before-trump-can-revive-it.html (last accessed
July 10, 2020).

7. Peter Bergen, *Trump and His Generals: The Cost of Chaos* (New York: Penguin Press, 2019),
98. "Defense Secretary Mattis Working on Ban Exemption List for Iraqis," *USMC Life*, January 30, 2017, https://usmclife.com/defense-secretary-mattis-working-ban-exemption-list
-iraqis/ (last accessed July 10, 2020).

8. Ryan Devereaux, Murtaza Hussain, and Alice Speri, "Trump's Muslim Ban Triggers
Chaos, Heartbreak, and Resistance," *The Intercept*, January 29, 2017, https://theintercept.com
/2017/01/29/trumps-muslim-ban-triggers-chaos-heartbreak-and-resistance/ (last accessed
Jan. 10, 2021).

9. Amicus brief, *Trump v. Hawaii* (March 30, 2018), https://www.courthousenews.com/wp
-content/uploads/2018/03/Trump-Travel-SCOTUS-States-AMICUS.pdf (last accessed
July 10, 2020). Michael D. Shear, Nicholas Kulish, and Alan Feuer, "Judge Blocks Trump Order
on Refugees amid Chaos and Outcry Worldwide," *New York Times*, January 28, 2017, https://
www.nytimes.com/2017/01/28/us/refugees-detained-at-us-airports-prompting-legal
-challenges-to-trumps-immigration-order.html (last accessed July 10, 2020).

10. Sirine Shebaya, "The Permanent Muslim Ban," *Georgetown Immigration Law Journal*. 32, no. 2
(Winter 2018), https://go.gale.com/ps/anonymous?id=GALE%7CA545714289&sid
=googleScholar&v=2.1&it=r&linkaccess=abs&issn=08914370&p=AONE&sw=w (last accessed
July 10, 2020). Michael D. Shear, "New Order Indefinitely Bars Almost All Travel From Seven Countries," *New York Times*, September 24, 2017, https://www.nytimes.com/2017/09/24/us/politics
/new-order-bars-almost-all-travel-from-seven-countries.html (last accessed March 25, 2021).

11. Proclamation No. 9645, "Enhancing Vetting Capabilities and Processes for Detecting
Attempted Entry into the United States by Terrorists or Other Public-Safety Threats," *Federal
Register* (September 24, 2017), https://www.govinfo.gov/content/pkg/DCPD-201700685/pdf
/DCPD-201700685.pdf (last accessed January 21, 2021).

12. Stephen Vladeck, "The Solicitor General and the Shadow Docket," *Harvard Law Review*, November 8, 2019, 135–38, https://harvardlawreview.org/wp-content/uploads/2019/11/123-163 _Online.pdf (last accessed July 10, 2020). ACLU Washington, "Timeline of the Muslim Ban," https://www.aclu-wa.org/pages/timeline-muslim-ban (last accessed July 10, 2020).

13. *Hamdan v. Rumsfeld*, 548 U.S. 557 (2006), https://supreme.justia.com/cases/federal/us /548/557/#tab-opinion-1962145 (last accessed February 22, 2021).

14. *Holder v. Humanitarian Law Project*, 2009 U.S. S. Ct Briefs, No. 08-1498 (August 24, 2009), https://www.supremecourt.gov/opinions/09pdf/08-1498.pdf (last accessed February 20, 2021).

15. "Brief for the Respondents," *Holder v. Humanitarian Law Project*, https://www.justice.gov /osg/brief/holder-v-humanitarian-law-projhumanitarian-law-proj-v-holder-brief-merits (last accessed February 19, 2021).

16. *Holder v. Humanitarian Law Project*, 561 U.S. (2010), https://www.supremecourt.gov /opinions/09pdf/08-1498.pdf (last accessed February 20, 2021).

17. Ibid.

18. "Oral Argument," *Trump v. Hawaii*, https://www.oyez.org/cases/2017/17-965 (last accessed February 19, 2021).

19. Ibid.

20. 8 U.S. Code § 1152 - Numerical limitations on individual foreign states, https://www.law .cornell.edu/uscode/text/8/1152. 8 U.S. Code §1182 - Inadmissable Aliens, https://www.law .cornell.edu/uscode/text/8/1182.

21. Amicus brief, *Trump v. Hawaii* (March 30, 2018), https://www.clearinghouse.net/chDocs /public/IM-HI-0004-0344.pdf (last accessed February 20, 2021).

22. *Trump v. Hawaii*, 138 S. Ct. 2392, 2420 (2018), https://www.supremecourt.gov/opinions /17pdf/17-965_h315.pdf (last accessed February 20, 2021).

23. Ibid.

Chapter 6: Crisis at the Border

This chapter's epigraph derives from William Barr, "Oral History," Miller Center, April 5, 2001, https://millercenter.org/the-presidency/presidential-oral-histories/william-p-barr-oral -history (last accessed February 26, 2021).

1. Donald J. Trump, "Remarks at the Department of Homeland Security," United States Department of Homeland Security, January 25, 2017, https://www.govinfo.gov/content/pkg /DCPD-201700513/html/DCPD-201700513.htm (last accessed February 26, 2021).

2. Jeh C. Johnson, "Record of Progress and Vision for the Future," United States Department of Homeland Security, Exit Memo, January 5, 2017, https://obamawhitehouse.archives.gov /administration/cabinet/exit-memos/department-homeland-security (last accessed February 26, 2021).

3. Franklin Foer, "How Trump Radicalized ICE," *The Atlantic*, September 2018, https://www .theatlantic.com/magazine/archive/2018/09/trump-ice/565772/ (last accessed February 26, 2021). Paul Bedard, "ICE Chief: 80% Jump in Illegal Targets, Readies National 'Sanctuary' Crackdown," *Washington Examiner*, July 18, 2017, https://www.washingtonexaminer.com/ice-chief-80 -jump-in-illegal-targets-readies-national-sanctuary-crackdown (last accessed February 26, 2021).

4. U.S. Senate Committee on Homeland Security and Governmental Affairs, "Pre-hearing Questionnaire," December 29, 2016, https://www.hsgac.senate.gov/imo/media/doc/Kelly%20 PreHearing%20Questions-2016-12-28-SIGNED.pdf (last accessed February 26, 2021).

5. "Donald Trump Announces a Presidential Bid," *Washington Post*, June 16, 2015, https:// www.washingtonpost.com/news/post-politics/wp/2015/06/16/full-text-donald-trump -announces-a-presidential-bid/ (last accessed February 26, 2021).

6. "President Trump at the Department of Homeland Security for Swearing-In and Executive Orders," *C-SPAN*, January 25, 2017, https://www.c-span.org/video/?c4652540/user-clip -trump-signs-border-wall-order (last accessed February 26, 2021). Kyle Balluck and Rebecca Savransky, "Trump Taps Kelly for DHS Chief," *The Hill*, December 12, 2016, https://thehill.com /homenews/campaign/309905-trump-nominates-kelly-as-dhs-chief (last accessed February 26, 2021).

7. Pamela Brown, Kevin Liptak, Jamie Gangel, Tal Kopan, and Lauren Fox, "John Kelly: Immigration 'Hardass,'" *CNN*, January 18, 2018, https://www.cnn.com/2018/01/17/politics /john-kelly-immigration/index.html (last accessed February 26, 2021).

8. Jacob Soboroff, *Separated: Inside American Tragedy* (New York: HarperCollins, 2020), 43. Wolf Blitzer interview with John Kelly, "The Situation Room with Wolf Blitzer," *CNN*, March 6, 2017, https://www.cnn.com/videos/politics/2017/03/06/john-kelly-dhs-trump-travel-ban -wiretap-tsr-intv-full.cnn (last accessed March 23, 2021).

9. Julie Hirschfeld Davis and Michael D. Shear, *Border Wars: Inside Trump's Assault on Immigration* (New York: Simon and Schuster, 2019), 57.

10. Adam Goodman, *The Deportation Machine: America's Long History of Expelling Immigrants* (Princeton, NJ: Princeton University Press, 2020), 176–77. Julia Preston, "Deportation Nation," *New York Review of Books*, October 2020, https://www.nybooks.com/articles/2020/10 /08/deportation-nation/ (last accessed February 26, 2021). Alex Nowrasteh, "Deportation Rates in Historical Perspective," *CATO*, September 16, 2019, https://www.cato.org/blog /deportation-rates-historical-perspective (last accessed February 26, 2021).

11. Patrisia Macías-Rojas, "Immigration and the War on Crime: Law and Order Politics and the Illegal Immigration Reform and Immigrant Responsibility Act," *Journal on Migration and Human Security* 6, no. 1 (2018): 1–25.

12. Adam Goodman, *The Deportation Machine: America's Long History of Expelling Immigrants*, 179; Douglas Massey, Jorge Durand, and Karen Pren, "Why Border Enforcement Backfired," *American Journal of Sociology* 121, no. 5 (March 2016): 1557–600 (last accessed February 26, 2021).

13. Muzaffar Chishti, Sarah Pierce, and Jessica Bolter, "The Obama Record on Deportations: Deporter in Chief or Not?" Migration Policy Institute, January 26, 2017, https://www .migrationpolicy.org/article/obama-record-deportations-deporter-chief-or-not (last accessed February 26, 2021).

14. Kerk Semple, "Advocates in New York Scramble as Child Deportation Cases Are Accelerated," *New York Times*, August 4, 2014, https://www.nytimes.com/2014/08/05/nyregion /advocates-scramble-as-new-york-accelerates-child-deportation-cases.html?_r=1 (last accessed February 26, 2021).

15. Ibid. Chishti, Pierce, and Bolter, "Obama Record on Deportations."

16. Safia Samee Ali, "Obama's 'Rocket Docket' Immigration Hearings Violate Due Process, Experts Say," *NBC*, October 27, 2016, https://www.nbcnews.com/news/us-news/obama-s -rocket-docket-immigration-hearings-violate-due-process-experts-n672636 (last accessed February 26, 2021).

17. Preston, "Deportation Nation."

18. Chishti, Pierce, and Bolter, "Obama Record on Deportations."

19. Jeh Johnson, "Security Communities," United States Department of Homeland Security, Memo, November 20, 2014, https://www.dhs.gov/sites/default/files/publications/14_1120 _memo_secure_communities.pdf (last accessed February 26, 2021). American Immigration Council, Fact Sheet, "Immigration Detainers under the Priority Enforcement Program," January 25, 2017, americanimmigrationcouncil.org/research/immigration-detainers-under-priority -enforcement-program (last accessed February 26, 2021). Jeh Johnson, "Policies for the Apprehension, Detention and Removal of Undocumented Immigrants," United States Department of Homeland Security, Memo, November 20, 2014 (last accessed February 26, 2021), https:// www.dhs.gov/sites/default/files/publications/14_1120_memo_prosecutorial_discretion.pdf.

20. Josh Gerstein, "Obama Administration Rebukes Sanctuary Cities," February 24, 2016, *Politico*, https://www.politico.com/story/2016/02/obama-immigration-sanctuary-cities-219754 (last accessed February 26, 2021).

21. Jonathan Blitzer, "A Trump Official behind the End of DACA Explains Himself," *New Yorker*, November 10, 2017, https://www.newyorker.com/news/news-desk/trump-official -behind-the-end-of-daca-explains-himself.

22. *United States v. Texas*, 136 S. Ct. 2271 (2016) https://www.supremecourt.gov/opinions /15pdf/15-674_jhlo.pdf (last accessed February 26, 2021). Adam Liptak & Michael D. Shear, "Supreme Court Tie Blocks Obama Immigration Plan," *New York Times*, June 23, 2016, https:// www.nytimes.com/2016/06/24/us/supreme-court-immigration-obama-dapa.html (last accessed February 26, 2021).

23. Jonathan Blitzer, "A Trump Official behind the End of DACA Explains Himself.".

24. David Rogers, "Under 16 and Ordered Deported—with No Lawyer," *Politico*, November 18, 2015, https://www.politico.com/story/2015/11/under-16-and-ordered-deported-with-no -lawyer-215944 (last accessed February 26, 2021).

25. Executive Order No. 13767, "Border Security and Immigration Enforcement Improvements," *Federal Register* (January 25, 2017), https://www.federalregister.gov/documents/2017 /01/30/2017-02095/border-security-and-immigration-enforcement-improvements (last accessed February 26, 2021).

26. Julia Ainsley, "Only Six Immigrants in Terrorism Database Stopped by CBP at Southern Border from October to March, *NBC News*, January 7, 2019, https://www.nbcnews.com/politics /immigration/only-six-immigrants-terrorism-database-stopped-cbp-southern-border-first -n955861 (last accessed February 26, 2021).

27. Executive Order No. 13767, "Border Security and Immigration Enforcement Improvements."

28. Department of Homeland Security, Office of the Inspector General, DHS OIG Highlights, DHS Training Needs for Hiring 15,000 Border Patrol Agents and Immigration Officers, November 26, 2018, https://www.oig.dhs.gov/sites/default/files/assets/2018-11/OIG-19-07 -Nov18.pdf (last accessed February 26, 2021).

29. Executive Order No. 13768, "Enhancing Public Safety in the Interior of the United States," *Federal Register* (January 25, 2017), https://www.federalregister.gov/documents/2017/01/30/2017-02102/enhancing-public-safety-in-the-interior-of-the-united-states (last accessed February 26, 2021).

30. Stephen Piggott, "Jeff Sessions: Champion of Anti-Muslim and Anti-Immigrant Extremists," Southern Poverty Law Center, November 19, 2016, https://www.splcenter.org/hatewatch/2016/11/18/jeff-sessions-champion-anti-muslim-and-anti-immigrant-extremists (last accessed February 26, 2021).

31. Emily Bazelon, "Department of Justification," *New York Times*, February 28, 2017, https://www.nytimes.com/2017/02/28/magazine/jeff-sessions-stephen-bannon-justice-department.html (last accessed February 26, 2021).

32. Davis and Shear, *Border Wars*, 107.

33. Ibid., 198.

34. United States Department of Homeland Security, Memorandum from John F. Kelly to Kevin McAleenan et. al, "Rescission of November 20, 2014 Memorandum Providing for Deferred Action for Parents of Americans and Lawful Permanent Residents ('DAPA')," June 15, 2017, https://www.dhs.gov/news/2017/06/15/rescission-memorandum-providing-deferred-action-parents-americans-and-lawful (last accessed February 26, 2021).

35. Davis and Shear, *Border Wars*, 168–69. United States Department of Justice, Office of Public Affairs, "Statement by Attorney General Sessions on the RAISE Act," Press Release, August 2, 2017, https://www.justice.gov/opa/pr/statement-attorney-general-sessions-raise-act (last accessed February 26, 2021).

36. Lisa Riordan Seville and Hannah Rappleye, "Trump Admin Ran 'Pilot Program' for Separating Migrant Families in 2017," *NBC*, January 29, 2018, https://www.nbcnews.com/storyline/immigration%20-border-crisis/trump-admin-ran-pilot-program-separating-migrant-families-2017-n887616 (last accessed February 26, 2021). United States Department of Justice, Office of Public Affairs, "Attorney General Announces Zero-Tolerance Policy for Criminal Illegal Entry," Press Release, April 6, 2018, https://justice.gov/opa/pr/attorney-general-announces-zero-tolerance-policy-criminal-illegal-entry (last accessed February 26, 2021).

37. United States Department of Justice, Remarks, "Attorney General Sessions Delivers Remarks Discussing the Immigration Enforcement Actions of the Trump Administration," May 7, 2018, https://www.justice.gov/opa/speech/attorney-general-sessions-delivers-remarks-discussing-immigration-enforcement-actions (last accessed February 26, 2021).

38. Daniel Kanstroom, "Criminalizing the Undocumented: Ironic Boundaries of the Post-September 11th 'Pale of Law,'" Boston College Law School Faculty Papers, January 1, 2004, https://lawdigitalcommons.bc.edu/cgi/viewcontent.cgi?article=1153&context=lsfp (last accessed February 26, 2021).

39. American Immigration Council, "Prosecuting People for Coming to the United States," January 10, 2020, https://www.americanimmigrationcouncil.org/research/immigration-prosecutions (last accessed February 26, 2021).

40. Catherine E. Shoichet, "'Zero Tolerance' a Year Later: How the US Family Separations Crisis Erupted," *CNN*, April 5, 2019, https://www.cnn.com/interactive/2019/04/us/immigrant-family-separations-timeline/ (last accessed February 26, 2021).

41. Foer, "How Trump Radicalized ICE."

42. Julia Preston, "The Immigration Crisis Jeff Sessions Leaves Behind," The Marshall Project, November 7, 2018, https://www.themarshallproject.org/2018/11/07/the-immigration-crisis-jeff-sessions-leaves-behind (last accessed February 26, 2021). Colleen Long, "Immigration Judges Say New Quotas Undermine Independence," September 21, 2018, Associated Press, https://apnews.com/article/d8008f7a66a54562b612bd74156f2bed (last accessed February 26, 2021).

43. Stephen Vladeck, "The Solicitor General and the Shadow Docket," Harvard Law Review, November 8, 2019, https://harvardlawreview.org/2019/11/the-solicitor-general-and-the-shadow-docket/ (last accessed February 26, 2021).

44. Nicole Einbinder, "How the Trump Administration Is Rewriting the Rules for Unaccompanied Minors," PBS, February 13, 2018, https://www.pbs.org/wgbh/frontline/article/how-the-trump-administration-is-rewriting-the-rules-for-unaccompanied-minors/ (last accessed February 26, 2021).

45. Lisa Riordan Seville and Adiel Kaplan, "AG Barr Using Unique Power to Block Migrants from U.S., Reshape Immigration Law," NBC, July 31, 2019, https://www.nbcnews.com/politics/immigration/ag-barr-using-unique-power-block-migrants-u-s-reshape-n1036276 (last accessed February 26, 2021). Adiel Kaplan, "AG Barr Issues 2 Decisions Limiting Ways Immigrants Can Fight Deportation," NBC, October 29, 2019, https://www.nbcnews.com/politics/immigration/ag-barr-issues-2-decisions-limiting-ways-immigrants-can-fight-n1073026 (last accessed February 26, 2021). Kim Bellware, "On Immigration, Attorney General Barr Is His Own Supreme Court: Judges and Lawyers Say That's a Problem," Washington Post, March 5, 2020, https://www.washingtonpost.com/immigration/2020/03/05/william-barr-certification-power/ (last accessed February 26, 2021). Andrew R. Arthur, "AG Certification Explained," Center for Immigration Studies, November 5, 2019, https://cis.org/Arthur/AG-Certification-Explained (last accessed February 26, 2021).

46. Matter of A-B-, 27 I&N Dec. 316 (A.G. 2018), https://www.justice.gov/eoir/page/file/1070866/download (last accessed February 28, 2021).

47. Seville and Kaplan "AG Barr Using Unique Power." Elizabeth Montano, "The Rise and Fall of Administrative Closure in Immigration Courts," Yale Law Journal 129 (2019–2020), https://www.yalelawjournal.org/forum/the-rise-and-fall-of-administrative-closure-in-immigration-courts (last accessed February 26, 2021).

48. Kristen Bialik, "ICE Arrests Went Up in 2017, with Biggest Increases in Florida, Northern Texas, Oklahoma," Pew Research, February 8, 2018, https://www.pewresearch.org/fact-tank/2018/02/08/ice-arrests-went-up-in-2017-with-biggest-increases-in-florida-northern-texas-oklahoma/ (last accessed February 26, 2021).

49. U.S. Immigrations and Customs Enforcement Agency, "Fiscal Year 2018 ICE Enforcement and Removal Operations Report," https://www.ice.gov/doclib/about/offices/ero/pdf/eroFY2018Report.pdf (last accessed February 26, 2021).

50. Einbinder, "How the Trump Administration Is Rewriting the Rules."

51. "President Trump at the Department of Homeland Security," C-SPAN, January 25, 2017, https://www.c-span.org/video/?422704-1/president-trump-visits-homeland-security-department (last accessed February 26, 2021).

52. Trump, "Remarks at the Department of Homeland Security."

53. Soboroff, *Separated*, 35.

54. United States Department of Justice, "Memorandum for All Federal Prosecutors, Attorney General of the United States," April 11, 2018, https://www.justice.gov/opa/press-release/file/956841/download (last accessed February 26, 2021).

55. Office of the Inspector General, Department of Justice, "Review of the Department of Justice's Planning and Implementation of Its Zero Tolerance Policy and Its Coordination with the Departments of Homeland Security and Health and Human Services," January 2021, https://oig.justice.gov/sites/default/files/reports/21-028_0.pdf (last accessed February 28, 2021).

56. Michael D. Shear, Katie Benner, and Michael S. Schmidt, "'We Need to Take Away Children,' No Matter How Young, Justice Dept. Officials Said," *New York Times*, October 6, 2020, https://www.nytimes.com/2020/10/06/us/politics/family-separation-border-immigration-jeff-sessions-rod-rosenstein.html (last accessed February 26, 2021). Office of the Inspector General, "Review of the Department of Justice's Planning and Implementation of Its Coordination with the Departments of Homeland Security and Health and Human Services," January 2021, https://oig.justice.gov/sites/default/files/reports/21-028_0.pdf (last accessed February 26, 2021).

57. Karen J. Greenberg, "No Fairy Tale: The Trump Administration's Declaration of Inhuman Rights," *TomDispatch*, July 25, 2019, https://tomdispatch.com/karen-greenberg-what-the-child-detentions-at-the-border-really-tell-us/ (last accessed February 26, 2021).

58. Stipulated Settlement Agreement, *Flores v. Reno*, No.CV 85-4544-RJK (Px) (C.D. Cal. Jan. 17, 1997), https://www.aclu.org/sites/default/files/assets/flores_settlement_final_plus_extension_of_settlement011797.pdf (last accessed February 28, 2021).

59. Human Rights First, "The Flores Settlement and Family Incarceration: A Brief History and Next Steps," October 30, 2018, https://www.humanrightsfirst.org/resource/flores-settlement-and-family-incarceration-brief-history-and-next-steps (last accessed March 30, 2021).

60. Davis and Shear, *Border Wars*, 243.

61. Gus Bova, "Journalists Blocked from Attending Secretive Immigration Tent Courts," *Texas Observer*, September 11, 2019, https://www.texasobserver.org/immigration-court-tent-laredo-trump-migrant-protection-protocols-mexico/ (last accessed February 26, 2021). PBS, "Media Fight Access Restrictions on Child Detention Centers," *PBS*, June 26, 2018, https://www.pbs.org/newshour/nation/media-fight-access-restrictions-on-child-detention-centers (last accessed February 26, 2021). ACLU, "Lawsuit: ICE Detention Centers Deny Detainees Contact with Attorneys," ACLU, December 17, 2018, https://www.aclusocal.org/en/press-releases/lawsuit-ice-detention-centers-deny-detainees-contact-attorneys (last accessed February 26, 2021).

62. Sheri Fink, "Migrants in Custody at Hospitals Are Treated Like Felons, Doctors Say," *New York Times*, June 10, 2019, https://www.nytimes.com/2019/06/10/us/border-migrants-medical-health-doctors.html (last accessed February 26, 2021); Wendy Fry, "U.S. Officials Deny Access to Doctors Seeking to Give Flu Shots to Migrant Children," *Los Angeles Times*, December 10, 2019, https://www.latimes.com/california/story/2019-12-10/cbp-denies-access-doctors-vaccinations-migrant-children (last accessed February 26, 2021); Veronica Rocha, Elise

Hammond, and Mike Hayes, "Doctors Describe How They Were Prevented from Establishing 'Continuity of Care' to Migrants," *CNN*, July 2, 2019, https://www.cnn.com/politics/live-news /immigration-crisis-us-border-july-2019/h_251521f29dbb877369ea8b100f8bb4dd (last accessed February 26, 2021).

63. "Sen. Merkley Denied Tour of Detention Center for Unaccompanied Immigrant Children," *Washington Post*, June 4, 2018, https://www.washingtonpost.com/video/politics /sen-merkley-denied-tour-of-detention-center-for-unaccompanied-immigrant-children/2018 /06/04/17fe9b60-680a-11e8-a335-c4503d041eaf_video.html (last accessed February 26, 2021). Philip Bump, "Legislators Were Turned Away from ICE Detention Centers: The Administration Has the Right to Do That," *Washington Post*, June 21, 2018. https://www.washingtonpost.com /news/politics/wp/2018/06/21/legislators-were-turned-away-from-ice-detention-centers-the -administration-has-the-right-to-do-that/ (last accessed February 26, 2021).

64. Keep Families Together Act, S.3036, introduced June 7, 2018, https://www.congress.gov /bill/115th-congress/senate-bill/3036 (last accessed February 26, 2021). Stephanie Murray, "11 Senators Demand an Update on Separated Kids," *Politico*, July 2, 2018, https://www.politico.com /story/2018/07/02/separated-families-democrats-letter-690699 (last accessed February 26, 2021).

65. Kate Bennett, "Melania Trump 'Hates to See' Children Separated from Their Families at Borders," *CNN*, June 18, 2018, https://www.cnn.com/2018/06/17/politics/melania-trump -children-separated-immigration/index.html, (last accessed February 26, 2021).

66. Julia Ainsley and Jacob Soboroff, "Trump Cabinet Officials Voted in 2018 White House Meeting to Separate Migrant Children, Say Officials," *NBC*, August 20, 2020, https://www .nbcnews.com/politics/immigration/trump-cabinet-officials-voted-2018-white-house-meeting -separate-migrant-n1237416, (last accessed February 26, 2021).

67. Adolfo Flores, "Border Patrol Said There Wasn't Room for More Immigrant Kids. The Shelter Agency Says Otherwise," *Buzzfeed News*, July 10, 2019, https://www.buzzfeednews.com /article/adolfoflores/border-patrol-immigrant-kids-beds-hhs-orr-facilities (last accessed February 26, 2021).

68. Department of Justice, Office of the Inspector General, "Review of the Department of Justice's Planning and Implementation of Its Zero Tolerance Policy and Its Coordination with the Departments of Homeland Security and Health and Human Services," January 2021, https://oig.justice.gov/sites/default/files/reports/21-028_0.pdf (last accessed February 26, 2021). Julia Ainsley, Jacob Soboroff, and Phil Heisel, "Justice Officials Drove Family Separation Policy, Draft Watchdog Report Says," *NBC News*, October 7, 2020, https://www.nbcnews.com /news/us-news/justice-department-officials-drove-family-separation-policy-watchdog-report -says-n1242375 (last accessed February 26, 2021). Julia Ainsley and Jacob Soboroff, "Justice Officials Respond to Report on Family Separation by Blaming Trump, Expressing Regret," *NBC News*, January 14, 2021, https://www.nbcnews.com/politics/immigration/justice-officials -respond-new-report-family-separation-blaming-trump-expressing-n1254278 (last accessed February 26, 2021).

69. American Immigration Council, "Prosecuting People for Coming to the United States," January 10, 2020, https://www.americanimmigrationcouncil.org/research/immigration -prosecutions (last accessed February 26, 2021).

70. John Gramlich, "How Border Apprehensions, ICE Arrests and Deportations Have Changed under Trump," Pew Research, March 2, 2020, https://www.pewresearch.org/fact-tank/2020/03/02/how-border-apprehensions-ice-arrests-and-deportations-have-changed-under-trump/ (last accessed February 26, 2021).

71. Einbinder, "How the Trump Administration Is Rewriting the Rules."

72. Bea Bischoff, "A Startling New Legal Opinion from William Barr Could Doom Thousands of Asylum-Seekers," *Slate*, April 17, 2019, https://slate.com/news-and-politics/2019/04/william-barr-asylum-bond-policy-trump-cruelty.html (last accessed February 26, 2021).

73. Board of Immigration Appeals, Interim Decision #3893, "*Matter of L-E-A*, Respondent," 27 I&N Dec. 40 (BIA 2017), May 24, 2017, https://www.justice.gov/eoir/page/file/969456/download (last accessed February 26, 2021).

74. "*Matter of L-E-A-*: Attorney General Overrules Finding of Family as a Social Group," *Harvard Law Review*, February 10, 2020, https://harvardlawreview.org/2020/02/matter-of-l-e-a/ (last accessed February 26, 2021).

75. Seville and Kaplan, "AG Barr Using Unique Power," Board of Immigration Appeals, Interim Decision #3959, "*Matter of L-E-A*, Respondent," 27 I&N Dec. 581 (A.G. 2019), July 29, 2019, https://www.justice.gov/file/1187856/download (last accessed February 26, 2021).

76. Kaplan, "AG Barr Issues 2 Decisions"; Seville and Kaplan, "AG Barr Using Unique Power."

77. Barr, "Oral History."

Chapter 7: The Deadly Strike

This chapter's epigraph derives from The White House, "Report on the Legal and Policy Frameworks Guiding the US Use of Military Force and Related National Security Operations," December 2016, https://www.justsecurity.org/wp-content/uploads/2016/12/framework.Report_Final.pdf.

1. Phil Helsel, Ken Dilanian, and Josh Lederman, "U.S. Airstrike Kills Top Iran General, Qassem Soleimani, at Baghdad Airport," *NBC*, January 3, 2020, https://www.nbcnews.com/news/world/airstrike-kills-top-iran-general-qassim-suleimani-baghdad-airport-iraqi-n1109821.

2. "Factbox: Reactions to the Killing of Iranian General in a U.S. Air Strike," Reuters, January 2, 2020, https://www.reuters.com/article/us-iraq-security-blast-reaction-factbox/factbox-reactions-to-the-killing-of-iranian-general-in-a-u-s-air-strike-idUSKBN1Z2070 (last accessed February 25, 2021). Colin Dwyer, "How the World Is Reacting to the U.S. Assassination of Iran's Qassem Soleimani," *NPR*, January 3, 2020, https://www.npr.org/2020/01/03/793289176/how-is-the-world-reacting-to-the-u-s-assassination-of-irans-qassem-soleimani (last accessed February 25, 2021).

3. Michael R. Gordon and David E. Sanger, "Deal Reached on Iran Nuclear Program; Limits on Fuel Would Lessen with Time," *New York Times*, July 14, 2015, https://www.nytimes.com/2015/07/15/world/middleeast/iran-nuclear-deal-is-reached-after-long-negotiations.html (last accessed February 25, 2021).

4. "Scientists' Letter to Obama on Iran Nuclear Deal," *New York Times*, August 8, 2015, https://www.nytimes.com/interactive/2015/08/08/world/document-iranletteraug2015.html (last accessed February 25, 2021).

5. "Kerry Defends Nuclear Deal before Skeptical Senate," *New York Times*, July 24, 2015, https://www.nytimes.com/2015/07/24/world/middleeast/john-kerry-defends-iran-nuclear-deal-before-skeptical-senate.html (last accessed February 25, 2021).

6. Robert Einhorn, "Debating the Iran Nuclear Deal: A Former American Negotiator Outlines the Battleground Issues," *Brookings*, August 12, 2015, https://www.brookings.edu/research/debating-the-iran-nuclear-deal-a-former-american-negotiator-outlines-the-battleground-issues/ (last accessed February 25, 2021).

7. "Live Updates: Netanyahu Addresses Congress," *Washington Post*, March 3, 2015, https://www.washingtonpost.com/blogs/liveblog-live/liveblog/live-updates-netanyahu-addresses-congress/?itid=lk_inline_manual_2 (last accessed February 25, 2021).

8. "Iran Nuclear Deal: Key Details," *BBC*, June 11, 2019, https://www.bbc.com/news/world-middle-east-33521655. "UN Security Council Resolutions on Iran," *Arms Control*, https://www.armscontrol.org/factsheets/Security-Council-Resolutions-on-Iran (last accessed August 24, 2020). Matthew Weybrecht, "State Department Affirms That Iran Deal is Only a Political Commitment," November 28, 2015, https://www.lawfareblog.com/state-department-affirms-iran-deal-only-political-commitment (last accessed April 4, 2021).

9. Katherine Krueger, "Trump on Iran Threat: They were 'Dying' before US Made Them a 'World Power,'" *Talking Point Memo*, September 6, 2016, https://talkingpointsmemo.com/livewire/donald-trump-downplays-iran-threat-nuclear-deal (last accessed February 25, 2021).

10. Sarah Begley, "Read Donald Trump Speech to AIPAC," *TIME*, March 21, 2016, https://time.com/4267058/donald-trump-aipac-speech-transcript/ (last accessed February 25, 2021).

11. "Representative Mike Pompeo on Iran Nuclear Agreement," *C-SPAN*, July 14, 2015, https://www.c-span.org/video/?326986-4/washington-journal-representative-mike-pompeo-r-ks (last accessed February 25, 2021).

12. "CIA Chief Pompeo Says He Warned Iran's Soleimani over Iraq Aggression," Reuters, December 2, 2017, https://www.reuters.com/article/us-iran-pompeo/cia-chief-pompeo-says-he-warned-irans-soleimani-over-iraq-aggression-idUSKBN1DX02P (last accessed February 25, 2021).

13. David Sanger, "U.S. Imposes New Sanctions on Iran Over Missile Test," *New York Times*, February 3, 2017, https://www.nytimes.com/2017/02/03/us/politics/iran-sanctions-trump.html (last accessed February 25, 2021).

14. Ibid.; Donald J. Trump, "Remarks by President Trump on the Joint Comprehensive Plan of Action," The White House, May 8, 2018, https://www.whitehouse.gov/briefings-statements/remarks-president-trump-joint-comprehensive-plan-action/(last accessed February 25, 2021). United States Institute of Peace, "Iran's Defense Spending," June 17, 2020, https://iranprimer.usip.org/blog/2020/jun/17/iran%E2%80%99s-defense-spending.

15. Mike Pompeo, "After the Deal: A New Iran Strategy," Heritage Foundation, May 21, 2018, https://www.heritage.org/defense/event/after-the-deal-new-iran-strategy(last accessed February 25, 2021).

16. Ibid.

17. Michael Hirsh, "U.S. Intelligence Undercuts Trump's Case on Iran-al Qaeda Links," *Foreign Policy*, June 24, 2019, https://foreignpolicy.com/2019/06/24/u-s-intelligence-undercuts-trump-case-on-iran-al-qaeda-links (last accessed February 25, 2021).

18. Asfandyar Mir and Colin P. Clarke, "Making Sense of Iran and al-Qaeda's Relationship," *Lawfare*, March 21, 2021, https://www.lawfareblog.com/making-sense-iran-and-al-qaedas-relationship (last accessed March 22, 2021).

19. Stanley McChrystal, "Iran's Deadly Puppet Master," *Foreign Policy*, January 1, 2019, https://foreignpolicy.com/gt-essay/irans-deadly-puppet-master-qassem-suleimani/ (last accessed February 25, 2021).

20. Michael R. Gordon and Bernard E. Trainor, *The Endgame: The Inside Story of the Struggle for Iraq, from George W. Bush to Barack Obama* (New York: Vintage Books, 2012), 518. "Transcript: General David Petraeus," on "Face the Nation," *CBS*, January 5, 2020, https://www.cbsnews.com/news/transcript-general-david-petraeus-on-face-the-nation-january-5-2020/ (last accessed February 27, 2021).

21. Ali Soufan, "Qassem Soleimani and Iran's Unique Regional Strategy," *CTC Sentinel* 18, no. 10 (November 2018), https://ctc.usma.edu/qassem-soleimani-irans-unique-regional-strategy/ (last accessed February 25, 2021).

22. Dexter Filkins, "The Shadow Commander," *New Yorker*, September 23, 2013, https://www.newyorker.com/magazine/2013/09/30/the-shadow-commander (last accessed February 25, 2021). Adam Entous and Evan Osnos, "Qassem Suleimani and How Nations Decide to Kill," *New Yorker*, February 10, 2020, https://www.newyorker.com/magazine/2020/02/10/qassem-suleimani-and-how-nations-decide-to-kill (last accessed February 25, 2021)..

23. Soufan, "Qassem Soleimani and Iran's Unique Regional Strategy." Filkins, "Shadow Commander."

24. Filkins, "Shadow Commander."

25. Ben Rhodes, *The World As It Is: A Memoir of the Obama White House* (New York: Random House, 2018), 251.

26. Grace Panetta, "Why neither George W. Bush nor Barack Obama Tried to Kill Iranian Commander Qasem Soleimani," *Business Insider*, January 3, 2020, https://taskandpurpose.com/analysis/qassim-suleimani-bush-obama-trump (last accessed February 25, 2021).

27. Chris Whipple, *The Spy Masters: How the CIA Directors Shape History and the Future* (New York: Scribner, 2020), 318.

28. McChrystal, "Iran's Deadly Puppet Master."

29. Tom Kertscher, "Fact-Checking Trump's Claim That Obama Designated Iran's Soleimani a Terrorist but Did Nothing," *PolitiFact*, January 16, 2020, https://www.politifact.com/factchecks/2020/jan/16/donald-trump/fact-checking-trumps-claim-obama-designated-irans-/ (last accessed February 25, 2021).

30. United States Treasury, "Anti-Terrorism Designations; Iran Revolutionary Guard Corps Related Designations," October 11, 2011, https://www.treasury.gov/resource-center/sanctions/OFAC-Enforcement/Pages/20111011.aspx (last accessed July 10, 2020).

31. Christopher Dickey, Noga Tarnopolsky, Erin Banco, and Betsy Swan, "Why Obama, Bush, and Bibi All Passed on Killing Soleimani," *Daily Beast*, January 3, 2020, https://www.thedailybeast.com/why-obama-bush-and-bibi-all-passed-on-killing-qassem-soleimani (last accessed February 25, 2021). Reis Thebault, "Iranian Agents Once Plotted to Kill the Saudi Ambassador in D.C.: The Case Reads Like a Spy Thriller," *Washington Post*, January 4, 2020, https://www.washingtonpost.com/history/2020/01/04/iran-agents

-once-plotted-kill-saudi-ambassador-dc-case-reads-like-spy-thriller/ (last accessed February 25, 2021).

32. Dickey et al., "Why Obama, Bush, and Bibi All Passed."

33. Donald J. Trump, "Statement from the President on the Designation of the Islamic Revolutionary Guard Corps as a Foreign Terrorist Organization," Address, The White House, April 8, 2019, https://ir.usembassy.gov/statement-from-the-president-on-the-designation-of-the -islamic-revolutionary-guard-corps-as-a-foreign-terrorist-organization/ (last accessed February 25, 2021).

34. Daniel Byman, "Killing Iran's Qassem Suleimani Changes the Game in the Middle East," *Brookings*, January 3, 2020, https://www.brookings.edu/blog/order-from-chaos/2020/01/03 /killing-irans-qassem-suleimani-changes-the-game-in-the-middle-east/ (last accessed February 25, 2021).

35. "Gulf of Oman Tanker Attacks: What We Know," *BBC*, June 18, 2019, https://www.bbc .com/news/world-middle-east-48627014 (last accessed February 25, 2021).

36. Michael D. Shear, Eric Schmitt, Michael Crowley, and Maggie Haberman, "Strikes on Iran Approved by Trump, Then Abruptly Pulled Back," *New York Times*, June 20, 2019. Carol E. Lee and Kourtney Kube, "Trump Authorized Soleimani's Killing 7 Months Ago, with Conditions," *NBC News*, January 13, 2020, https://www.nbcnews.com/politics/national-security/trump -authorized-soleimani-s-killing-7-months-ago-conditions-n1113271 (last accessed February 25, 2021). Toluse Olorunnipa, Josh Dawsey, Karoun Demirjian, and Dan Lamothe, "'I Stopped It': Inside Trump's Last-Minute Reversal on Striking Iran," *Washington Post*, June 21, 2019, https:// www.washingtonpost.com/politics/i-stopped-it-inside-trumps-last-minute-reversal-on-striking -iran/2019/06/21/e016effe-9431-11e9-b570-6416efdc0803_story.html (last accessed February 25, 2021). Edward Wong, "Trump Imposes New Sanctions on Iran, Adding to Tensions," *New York Times*, June 24, 2019, https://www.nytimes.com/2019/06/24/us/politics/iran-sanctions.html (last accessed February 25, 2021). Shear et al., "Strikes on Iran Approved by Trump."

37. Corey Dickstein and Caitlin M. Kenney, "Pentagon to Send More Troops to Middle East amid 'Significant Escalation' from Iran," *Stars and Stripes*, September 20, 2018, https://www .stripes.com/news/us/pentagon-to-send-more-troops-to-middle-east-amid-significant -escalation-from-iran-1.599887 (last accessed February 25, 2021).

38. Elisha Fieldstadt, "U.S. Contractor Whose Killing in Iraq Was Cited by Trump Was Linguist with 2 Young Sons," *NBC News*, January 8, 2020, https://www.nbcnews.com/news/us-news/u-s -contractor-whose-killing-iraq-was-cited-trump-was-n1112266 (last accessed February 25, 2021).

39. Falih Hassan, Ben Hubbard, and Alissa J. Rubin, "Protesters Attack U.S. Embassy in Iraq, Chanting 'Death to America,'" *New York Times*, December 31, 2019, https://www.nytimes.com /2019/12/31/world/middleeast/baghdad-protesters-us-embassy.html (last accessed February 25, 2021).

40. Alex Ward, "Senate Confirms Army Gen. Mark Milley as New Joint Chiefs Chair," *Vox*, July 25, 2019, https://www.vox.com/2019/7/25/8930156/mark-milley-joint-chiefs-chair-dunford -trump (last accessed February 25, 2021).

41. Shane Harris, Josh Dawsey, Ashley Parker, and John Wagner, "Ratcliffe Withdraws from Consideration for Intelligence Chief Less Than a Week after Trump Picked Him," *Washington Post*, August 2, 2019, https://www.washingtonpost.com/politics/ratcliffe-withdraws-from

-consideration-for-intelligence-chief-trump-says/2019/08/02/9f3c42cc-b551-11e9-951e
-de024209545d_story.html (last accessed February 25, 2021).

42. Peter Baker, "Trump Ousts John Bolton as National Security Adviser," *New York Times*,
September 10, 2019, https://www.nytimes.com/2019/09/10/us/politics/john-bolton-national
-security-adviser-trump.html (last accessed February 25, 2021).

43. Robert C. O'Brien. *While America Slept: Restoring American Leadership to a World in
Crisis* (New York: Encounter Books, 2016).

44. The White House, "Report on the Legal and Policy Frameworks Guiding the United
States' Use of Military Force and Related National Security Operations," December 2016,
https://www.justsecurity.org/wp-content/uploads/2016/12/framework.Report_Final.pdf (last
accessed February 27, 2021).

45. Joshua Geltzer, "Important Report by White House on National Security Due Soon,"
Just Security, February 28, 2018, https://www.justsecurity.org/53156/important-report-white
-house-national-security-due/ (last accessed February 28, 2021).

46. White House, "Report on the Legal and Policy Frameworks Guiding the United States'
Use of Military Force and Related National Security Operations," March 2018, https://assets
.documentcloud.org/documents/4411804/3-18-War-Powers-Transparency-Report.pdf (last
accessed February 27, 2021).

47. Prabhjote Gill, "The Deadly Drone That Killed Qassem Soleimani Weighs as Much as
an African Elephant," *Business Insider*, January 6, 2020, https://www.businessinsider.in/defense
/news/the-deadly-drone-that-killed-qasem-soleimani-weighs-as-much-as-an-african-elephant
/articleshow/73124252.cms (last accessed February 25, 2021).

48. Jonathan Stevenson, "American Foreign Policy Is Broken: Suleimani's Killing Proves It,"
New York Times, January 4, 2020, https://www.nytimes.com/2020/01/04/opinion/trump
-soleimani-strike.html (last accessed February 25, 2021). Entous and Osnos, "Qassem Suleimani
and How Nations Decide to Kill."

49. Author interview with John Brennan, June 12, 2020, updated, March 1, 2021.

50. The World Staff, "Killing Soleimani Was a 'Hasty' Decision, Says Former Defense Under-
secretary," *The World*, January 7, 2020, https://www.pri.org/stories/2020-01-07/killing-soleimani
-was-hasty-decision-says-former-defense-undersecretary (last accessed March 1, 2021).

51. Ellen Cranley, "How Trump's Decision to Strike a Top Iranian Commander Unfolded at
Mar-a-Lago," *Business Insider*, January 4, 2020, https://www.businessinsider.com/trump
-planned-strike-iranian-soleimani-mar-a-lago-2020-1#as-news-of-the-successful-strike-broke
-thursday-night-trump-appeared-at-ease-3 (last accessed February 27, 2021). Veronica Stracqualursi, "Lindsey Graham Says He Was Briefed Ahead of Strike, while Democratic Leaders Were
Not," *CNN*, January 3, 2020, https://www.cnn.com/2020/01/03/politics/lindsey-graham
-suleimani-drone-strike/index.html (last accessed February 27, 2021).

52. Alice Friend, Mara Karlin, and Loren DeJonge Schulman, "Why Did the Pentagon Ever
Give Trump the Option of Killing Soleimani?" *Washington Post*, January 10, 2020 (last accessed
March 1, 2021).

53. Stevenson, "American Foreign Policy Is Broken."

54. "House Foreign Affairs Committee Hearing on U.S.-Iran Tensions," *C-SPAN*, January 14,
2020, https://www.c-span.org/video/?467944-1/house-foreign-affairs-committee-hearing-us

-iran-tensions (last accessed February 25, 2021). "US Attorney General Barr: Soleimani Killing Was 'Legitimate,'" *Al Jazeera*, January 13, 2020, https://www.aljazeera.com/news/2020/1/13/us -attorney-general-barr-soleimani-killing-was-legitimate (last accessed February 25, 2021).

55. "Dan Coats: US Intelligence Chief Leaves Trump Administration," *BBC*, July 29, 2019, https://www.bbc.com/news/world-us-canada-49147365 (last accessed February 25, 2021). "Watch Intel Chief Dan Coats Find Out about Putin's White House Invite," *NBC News*, July 19, 2018, https://www.nbcnews.com/video/watch-intel-chief-dan-coats-find-out-about-putin-s -white-house-invite-1281354307879 (last accessed February 25, 2021).

56. Joint Resolution to Authorize the Use of United States Armed Forces against Those Responsible for the Recent Attacks Launched against the United States, Public Law 107-40 (September 18, 2001) (hereafter, AUMF of 2001).

57. Melissa Quin, "David Petraeus: "Impossible to Overstate" Significance of Soleimani Strike," *CBS News*, January 5, 2020, https://www.cbsnews.com/news/general-david-petraeus -impossible-to-overstate-the-significance-of-soleimani-strike-face-the-nation/ (last accessed February 25, 2021). McChrystal, "Iran's Deadly Puppet Master."

58. "President Trump Statement on Death of Iranian Commander," *C-SPAN*, January 3, 2020, https://www.c-span.org/video/?467859-1/president-trump-speaks-air-strike-killed-iranian -commander (last accessed February 25, 2021).

59. Alex Pappas, "Trump Tells Fox News' Laura Ingraham 'Four Embassies' Were Targeted in Imminent Threat from Iran," *Fox News*, January 10, 2020, https://www.foxnews.com/politics /trump-tells-laura-ingraham-four-embassies-were-targeted-in-imminent-threat-from-iran (last accessed February 25, 2021).

60. Morgan Chalfant, "Trump Says Soleimani Was Plotting Attacks on Four U.S. Embassies," *The Hill*, January 10, 2020, https://thehill.com/homenews/administration/477740-trump-says -four-embassies-targeted-before-soleimani-strike (last accessed February 25, 2021).

61. Veronica Stracqualursi and Jennifer Hansler, "Pompeo: Strike on Soleimani Disrupted an 'Imminent Attack' and 'Saved American Lives,'" *CNN*, January 3, 2020, https://www.cnn.com /2020/01/03/politics/mike-pompeo-iran-soleimani-strike-cnntv/index.html (last accessed February 25, 2021).

62. Steve Inskeep and Robert O'Brien, "Transcript: NPR's Full Interview with NSC Adviser Robert O'Brien," *NPR*, January 9, 2020, https://www.npr.org/2020/01/09/794914963/transcript -nprs-full-interview-with-nsc-adviser-robert-o-brien (last accessed February 25, 2021).

63. Shannon Pettypiece, "Trump's Evolving Account of Soleimai's 'Imminent Threat,'" *NBC News*, January 10, 2020, https://www.nbcnews.com/politics/white-house/trump-s-evolving -account-soleimani-s-imminent-threat-n1113846 (last accessed February 25, 2021).

64. Bobby Allyn and Ari Shapiro, "Esper: U.S. Could Strike Iran or Proxies 'Where Legally Available and Appropriate,'" *NPR*, January 13, 2020, https://www.npr.org/2020/01/13/796102188 /esper-u-s-could-strike-iran-or-proxies-where-legally-available-and-appropriate (last accessed February 25, 2021).

65. Phil Stewart (writer) and Sandra Maler (editor), "Top U.S. General: Soleimani Was Planning 'Campaign' of Violence against U.S.," Reuters, January 2, 2020, https://www.reuters .com/article/us-iraq-security-usa-milley/top-u-s-general-soleimani-was-planning-campaign -of-violence-against-u-s-idUSKBN1Z222T (last accessed February 25, 2021).

66. Michael Pompeo, "The Restoration of Deterrence: The Iranian Example," Remarks, United States Department of State, January 13, 2020, https://hk.usconsulate.gov/n-2020011301 / (last accessed February 25, 2021).

67. William Barr, "News Conference on Pensacola Naval Base Shooting Investigation," C-SPAN, January 13, 2020, https://www.c-span.Sorg/video/?468125-1/attorney-general-pensacola -naval-base-shooting-act-terrorism (last accessed February 25, 2021).

68. Masood Farivan and Ken Bredemeier, "US Attorney General Calls Imminence of Iranian Threat 'a Red Herring,'" January 13, 2020, VOA, https://www.voanews.com/middle-east/voa -news-iran/us-attorney-general-calls-imminence-iranian-threat-red-herring (last accessed February 25, 2021).

69. Chris Strohm, "Soleimani Killing Was Justified as a Military Target, Barr Says," Bloomberg Quint, January 14, 2020, https://www.bloombergquint.com/politics/soleimani-killing-was -justified-as-a-military-target-barr-says (last accessed February 25, 2021).

70. Ibid.

71. Ari Shapiro and Mark Esper, "Transcript: NPR's Full Interview with Defense Secretary Mark Esper on Iran," NPR, January 14, 2020, https://www.npr.org/2020/01/14/796246147 /transcript-nprs-full-interview-with-defense-secretary-mark-esper-on-iran (last accessed February 25, 2021).

72. Ibid.

73. Matt Sczesny, "Former CIA Analyst Expects Iran to Retaliate, Won't Start Conventional War," WPTV, January 3, 2020, https://www.wptv.com/news/region-c-palm-beach-county /former-cia-analyst-expects-iran-to-retaliate-wont-start-conventional-war (last accessed February 25, 2021).

74. Javad Zarif (@JZarif), Twitter, January 7, 2020, 9:32 p.m., https://twitter.com/jzarif /status/1214736614217469953?lang=en (last accessed February 25, 2021). Bill Chappell, "109 U.S. Troops Suffered Brain Injuries in Iran Strike, Pentagon Says," NPR, February 11, 2020, https:// www.npr.org/2020/02/11/804785515/109-u-s-troops-suffered-brain-injuries-in-iran-strike -pentagon-says (last accessed February 25, 2021).

75. Nikki Carvajal, "Trump Vetoes Iran War Powers Resolution," May 6, 2020, https://www .cnn.com/2020/05/06/politics/trump-veto-iran-war-powers/index.html (last accessed February 27, 2021).

Chapter 8: The Black Lives Matter Protests

This chapter's first epigraph derives from Donald J. Trump (@RealDonaldTrump), Twitter, May 29, 2020, 12:53 a.m., https://twitter.com/realDonaldTrump/status/1266231100780744704 available at Michael S. Rosenwald, "'When the looting starts, the shooting starts': Trump quotes Miami police chief's notorious 1967 warning," Washington Post, May 29, 2020, https://www .washingtonpost.com/history/2020/05/29/when-the-looting-starts-the-shooting-starts-trump -walter-headley/ (last accessed February 23, 2021).

This chapter's second epigraph derives from Department of Homeland Security, "2020 State of the Homeland as Delivered by Acting Secretary Chad Wolf," September 9, 2020, https://www .dhs.gov/news/2020/09/09/2020-state-homeland (last accessed February 23, 2021).

1. Tou Thao, "Ex-Officer Charged in the Death of George Floyd, Released from Jail," *CBS Minnesota*, July 4, 2020, https://minnesota.cbslocal.com/2020/07/04/tou-thao-ex-officer-charged-in-the-death-of-george-floyd-released-from-jail (last accessed February 23, 2021). Derrick Bryson Taylor, "George Floyd Protests: A Timeline," *New York Times*, July 10, 2020, https://www.nytimes.com/article/george-floyd-protests-timeline.html (last accessed February 23, 2021).

2. Demonstrations and Political Violence in America: New Data for Summer 2020, ACLED, September 2020, https://acleddata.com/2020/09/03/demonstrations-political-violence-in-america-new-data-for-summer-2020/, (last accessed February 23, 2021). Tim Craig, "'The United States Is in Crisis': Report Tracks Thousands of Summer Protests, Most Nonviolent," *Washington Post*, September 3, 2020, https://www.washingtonpost.com/national/the-united-states-is-in-crisis-report-tracks-thousands-of-summer-protests-most-nonviolent/2020/09/03/b43c359a-edec-11ea-99a1-71343d03bc29_story.html (last accessed February 23, 2021).

3. Jill Colvin and Colleen Long, "Trump Tries a New Response after George Floyd's Death," Associated Press, May 28, 2020, https://apnews.com/article/89d86d28110b5f9a6d5a6dfib9f3be30 (last accessed February 23, 2021).

4. Mark Decambre, "President Trump Says George Floyd's Death Was 'Terrible' but Says 'More White People,' Die at Hands of Police Than Blacks in U.S.," *Market Watch*, July 15, 2020, https://www.marketwatch.com/story/president-trump-says-george-floyds-death-was-terrible-but-says-more-white-people-die-at-hands-of-police-than-blacks-in-us-2020-07-14 (last accessed February 23, 2021). Joanna Walters, "Trump Twists Stats on Police Brutality: 'More White People' Are Killed," *The Guardian*, July 14, 2020, https://www.theguardian.com/us-news/2020/jul/14/donald-trump-george-floyd-police-killings (last accessed February 23, 2021).

5. Taylor, "George Floyd Protests."

6. "Donald Trump Phone Call Transcript with Governors after Protests: 'You Have to Dominate' & 'Most of You Are Weak,'" *Rev*, June 1, 2020, https://www.rev.com/blog/transcripts/donald-trump-phone-call-transcript-with-governors-george-floyd-protests (last accessed February 23, 2021).

7. Daniel Dale, "Fact Check: Minnesota Governor, Not Trump, Called Out the National Guard," *CNN*, July 1, 2020, https://www.cnn.com/2020/07/01/politics/fact-check-trump-walz-minnesota-national-guard/index.html (last accessed February 23, 2021).

8. Jennifer Elsea, "The Posse Comitatus Act and Related Matters: A Sketch," Federation of American Scientists, updated November 6, 2018, https://fas.org/sgp/crs/natsec/R42669.pdf (last accessed February 23, 2021).

9. Nathan Baca, "New Video Shows Federal Police Holding Tear Gas Launchers, Rolling Stinger Grenade at Protesters," *WUSA9*, June 9, 2020, https://www.wusa9.com/article/news/local/protests/tear-gas-protesters-lafayette-square-park-police-new-video-evidence/65-c39fb767-b114-41d6-bcbb-530b3823d8e7/ (last accessed February 23, 2021). Philip Bump, "Timeline: The Clearing of Lafayette Square," *Washington Post*, June 5, 2020, https://www.washingtonpost.com/politics/2020/06/02/timeline-clearing-lafayette-square/ (last accessed February 23, 2021) (last accessed February 23, 2021).

10. Niels Lesniewski and Todd Ruger, "Trump Floats Invoking 1807 Insurrection Act to 'Dominate' Protests," *Roll Call*, June 1, 2020, https://www.rollcall.com/2020/06/01/trump-floats-invoking-1807-insurrection-act-to-dominate-protests/ (last accessed February 23, 2021).

11. Thomas Gibbons-Neff, Eric Schmitt, and Helene Cooper, "Aggressive Tactics by National Guard, Ordered to Appease Trump, Wounded the Military, Too," *New York Times*, June 10, 2020, https://www.nytimes.com/2020/06/10/us/politics/national-guard-protests.html (last accessed February 23, 2021).

12. Carol D. Leonnig, Matt Zapotosky, Josh Dawsey, and Rebecca Tan, "Barr Personally Ordered Removal of Protesters Near White House, Leading to Use of Force against Largely Peaceful Crowd," *Washington Post*, June 2, 2020, https://www.washingtonpost.com/politics/barr-personally-ordered-removal-of-protesters-near-white-house-leading-to-use-of-force-against-largely-peaceful-crowd/2020/06/02/0ca2417c-a4d5-11ea-b473-04905b1af82b_story.html (last accessed February 23, 2021).

13. "A Video Timeline of the Crackdown on Protesters before Trump's Photo Op," *Washington Post*, June 8, 2020, https://www.youtube.com/watch?v=JxYmILDyaoA (last accessed February 23, 2021). "Officer Contradicts Official Account of Clearing of Protesters from D.C.'s Lafayette Square," *Los Angeles Times* via Associated Press, July 27, 2020, https://www.latimes.com/world-nation/story/2020-07-28/officer-challenges-account-of-violent-clearing-of-protesters (last accessed February 23, 2021). Clare Hymes, "Barr Involved in Decision to Expand Perimeter around White House and Remove Protesters," *CBS*, June 2, 2020, https://www.cbsnews.com/news/attorney-general-william-barr-order-expand-white-house-perimeter-protesters/ (last accessed February 23, 2021). Lateshia Beachum, Meagan Flynn, and Meryl Kornfield, "As Protests Nationwide Continue Past Curfew, Tension Eases in Some Cities," June 2, 2020, https://www.washingtonpost.com/nation/2020/06/02/george-floyd-protests-live-updates/ (last accessed February 23, 2021).

14. JM Rieger, "How the Trump Administration Has Tried to Explain Clearing Protesters from Lafayette Square," *Washington Post*, September 17, 2020, https://www.washingtonpost.com/politics/2020/06/09/how-trump-administration-has-tried-explain-clearing-protesters-lafayette-square/ (last accessed February 23, 2021).

15. "Video Timeline of the Crackdown on Protesters," *Washington Post*.

16. Keith L. Alexander and Meryl Kornfield, "Among the More Than 411 Arrested during Protests in the District, Most Cases Involve Curfew Violations and Burglary," *Washington Post*, June 16, 2020, https://www.washingtonpost.com/local/public-safety/among-more-than-400-arrested-during-protests-in-the-district-most-cases-involve-curfew-violations-and-burglary/2020/06/14/ef7e2e82-ac93-11ea-94d2-d7bc43b26bf9_story.html (last accessed February 23, 2021).

17. "Statement of Gregory T. Monahan, Acting Chief United States Park Police, U.S. Department of the Interior Before the House Natural Resources Committee on Actions Taken to Protect Life and Property July 28, 2020," https://naturalresources.house.gov/imo/media/doc/Acting%20Chief%20Monahan%20-%20Written%20Testimony.pdf (last accessed February 27, 2021).

18. Rebecca Kheel, "Esper Seeks to Explain Participation in White House Photo-op," *The Hill*, June 3, 2020, https://thehill.com/policy/defense/500915-esper-seeks-to-explain-participation-in-white-house-photo-op (last accessed February 23, 2021).

19. Fred Kaplan, "The Generals Are Turning on Trump," *Slate*, June 11, 2020, https://slate.com/news-and-politics/2020/06/milley-trump-esper-civil-military.html (last accessed February 23, 2021).

20. "Statement of Homeland and National Security Leaders," *Just Security*, June 15, 2020, https://www.justsecurity.org/70783/statement-of-homeland-and-national-security-leaders/ (last accessed February 23, 2021). Zolan Kanno-Youngs, "G.O.P. Architects of the Post-9/11 Security Order Object to Trump's Heavy Hand," *New York Times*, June 17, 2020, https://www.nytimes.com/2020/06/17/us/politics/trump-protesters.html (last accessed February 23, 2021).

21. Executive Order 13933, "Protecting American Monuments, Memorials, and Statues and Combating Recent Criminal Violence," June 26, 2020, https://www.federalregister.gov/documents/2020/07/02/2020-14509/protecting-american-monuments-memorials-and-statues-and-combating-recent-criminal-violence (last accessed February 27, 2021).

22. Ken Klippenstein, "The Border Patrol Was Responsible for an Arrest in Portland," *The Nation*, July 17, 2020, https://www.thenation.com/article/society/border-patrol-portland-arrest/ (last accessed February 27, 2021). U.S. Customs and Border Protection, "Public Affairs Guidance: CBP Support to Protect Federal Facilities and Property," reprinted in Klipperstein, above.

23. "Protests in Portland: A Timeline: May 29–Nov 15, 2020," https://www.portlandoregon.gov/police/article/765145 (last accessed February 23, 2021).

24. Timelines DB, BLM Timeline, Timelines DB.com, http://www.timelinesdb.com/listevents.php?subjid=1811&dayinhist=0&date1=-99999999999&date2=99999999999&words=&title=BLM&fromrec=60 (last accessed January 4, 2021).

25. Maxine Bernstein, "Portland City Attorneys: Quanice Hayes, a 17-Year-Old Fatally Shot by Police, and His Mother Were Partly to Blame for His Death," *Oregon Live*, December 10, 2019, https://www.oregonlive.com/news/2019/12/portland-city-attorneys-say-quanice-hayes-a-17-year-old-fatally-shot-by-police-and-his-mother-were-partly-to-blame-for-his-death.html (last accessed February 23, 2021).

26. Lizzy Acker and Everton Bailey, "Jason Washington Took Friend's Gun Away to Prevent 'Poor Decision' before Portland State Cops Shot Him, Reports Say," *Oregon Live*, January 29, 2019, https://www.oregonlive.com/portland/2018/09/jason_washington_took_friends.html (last accessed February 23, 2021).

27. *Don't Shoot Portland v. City of Portland*, class action 3:20-cv-00917-HZ, filed June 5, 2020, https://www.classaction.org/news/class-action-looks-to-stop-portland-police-from-using-tear-gas-against-peaceful-protestors#embedded-document (last accessed February 23, 2021).

28. *Don't Shoot Portland v. City of Portland*, 465 F. Supp. 3d 1150 (D. Or. 2020), https://www.courtlistener.com/docket/17228658/29/dont-shoot-portland-v-city-of-portland/ (last accessed February 23, 2021).

29. Jonathan Levinson, Conrad Wilson, and Ryan Hass, "50 Days of Protest in Portland: A Violent Police Response: This Is How We Got Here," *Oregon Public Broadcasting*, July 19, 2020, https://www.opb.org/news/article/police-violence-portland-protest-federal-officers/. Jenny Young and Hannah Ray Lambert, "Protesters Rushed to Hospital after Being Hit by Car, Driver Arrested," *KOIN6News*, June 16, 2020, https://www.koin.com/news/protests/protests-portland-demonstration-black-lives-matter-blm-police-violence-march-rose-city-justice/ (last accessed February 28, 2021). *Don't Shoot Portland v. City of Portland*, class action 3:20-cv-00917-HZ, TRO Modification, filed June 26, 2020, https://www.documentcloud.org/documents/6958701-Stipulatedchangetemprestrainingorder.html (last accessed February 23, 2021).

30. Marissa Lang, Josh Dawsey, Devlin Barrett, and Nick Miroff, "Operation Diligent Valor: Trump Showcased Federal Power in Portland, Making a Culture War Campaign Pitch," *Washington Post*, July 24, 2020, https://www.washingtonpost.com/national/portland-protests -operation-diligent-valor/2020/07/24/95f21ede-cce9-11ea-89ce-ac7d5e4a5a38_story.html (last accessed February 23, 2021).

31. Gabriella Borter, "Court Documents Reveal Secretive Federal Unit Deployed for 'Operation Diligent Valor' in Oregon," Reuters, July 22, 2020, https://www.reuters.com/article /us-global-race-portland-valor/court-documents-reveal-secretive-federal-unit-deployed -for-operation-diligent-valor-in-oregon-idUSKCN24N2SH (last accessed February 23, 2021).

32. Mike Baker, Thomas Fuller, and Sergio Olmos, "Federal Agents Push into Portland Streets, Stretching Limits of Their Authority," *New York Times*, July 25, 2020, https://www .nytimes.com/2020/07/25/us/portland-federal-legal-jurisdiction-courts.html (last accessed February 23, 2021).

33. "Acting DHS Secretary in Portland, Likely to Address Downtown Protests," *KGW8*, July 16, 2020, https://www.kgw.com/article/news/local/portland-protests-homeland-security -wolf-riot-anarchist-downtown-chapman-lownsdale/283-0026b198-fb45-4d55-bddo -ca05800d9379 (last accessed February 23, 2021).

34. Department of Homeland Security, "Acting Secretary Wolf Condemns the Rampant Long-Lasting Violence in Portland," Press Release, July 16, 2020, https://www.dhs.gov/news /2020/07/16/acting-secretary-wolf-condemns-rampant-long-lasting-violence-portland (last accessed February 23, 2021).

35. Stephen Vladeck and Benjamin Wittes, "DHS Authorizes Domestic Surveillance to Protect Statues and Monuments," *Lawfare Blog*, July 20, 2020, https://www.lawfareblog.com/dhs-authorizes -domestic-surveillance-protect-statues-and-monuments (last accessed February 23, 2021).

36. *Tuck Woodstock et al. v. City of Portland*, No. 3:20-cv-1035-SI, U.S. Dist., filed June 28, 2020, https://aclu-or.org/sites/default/files/field_documents/woodstock_portland_aclu_or _06282020.pdf (last accessed February 23, 2021).

37. "US Judge Blocks Trump's Health Insurance Rule for Immigrants," *Yahoo!* via Associated Press, November 3, 2019, https://news.yahoo.com/us-judge-blocks-trumps-health-222526673 .html (last accessed February 23, 2021).

38. *Index Newspapers LLC v. City of Portland, et. al.*, Temporary Restraining Order Enjoining Federal Defendants, filed July 23, 2020, https://www.courtlistener.com/docket/17301670/84 /index-newspapers-llc-v-city-of-portland/ (last accessed February 23, 2021).

39. Maxine Bernstein, "Judge Temporarily Bars Federal Officers from Using Force, Threats, Dispersal Orders against Journalists, Legal Observers," *Oregonian*, July 23, 2020, https://www .oregonlive.com/portland/2020/07/judge-inclined-to-restrain-federal-law-enforcement-from -using-force-threats-dispersal-orders-against-journalists-legal-observers.html (last accessed February 23, 2021).

40. Caroline Linton, "Tear Gas Deployed in Portland Protests as Oregon Officials Call for Federal Authorities to Leave," *CBS News*, July 18, 2020, https://www.cbsnews.com/news /portland-protests-tear-gas-oregon-officials-call-for-federal-authorities-to-leave/(last accessed February 23, 2021).

41. Quinn Owen, "Wolf Defends Feds in Portland Protests, Rebuffs Former Homeland Security Leaders," *ABC News*, August 6, 2020, https://abcnews.go.com/Politics/wolf-defends-feds-portland-protests-rebuffs-homeland-security/story?id=72213759 (last accessed February 23, 2021).

42. *Index Newspapers LLC v. United States Marshals Serv.*, 977 F.3d 817 (9th Cir. 2020).

43. Celina Tebor, Molly Harbarger, Maxine Bernstein, and Noelle Crombie, "Portland Protests Draw Thousands Thursday, No State, Federal Police in Sight," *Oregon Live*, July 30, 2020, https://www.oregonlive.com/portland/2020/07/changing-of-the-guard-oregon-state-troopers-start-duty-at-federal-courthouse-in-portland-quiet-so-far.html (last accessed February 23, 2021).

44. Chris McGreal, "Portland Sees Peaceful Night of Protests Following Withdrawal of Federal Agents," *The Guardian*, July 31, 2020, https://www.theguardian.com/us-news/2020/jul/31/portland-protests-latest-peaceful-night-federal-troops-withdrawal (last accessed February 23, 2021). Gillian Flaccus and Andrew Selsky, "Portland, Oregon, Protests Relatively Calm after US Drawdown," *USNews*, July 31, 2020, https://www.usnews.com/news/politics/articles/2020-07-31/oregon-police-try-to-tamp-down-nightly-portland-protests (last accessed February 23, 2021)

45. Department of Homeland Security, "Acting Secretary Wolf's Statement on Oregon Agreeing to Cooperate in Quelling Portland Violence," Press Release, July 29, 2020, https://www.dhs.gov/news/2020/07/29/acting-secretary-wolfs-statement-oregon-agreeing-cooperate-quelling-portland (last accessed February 23, 2021).

46. Karina Brown, "Judge to Rule Thursday on Press Claims against Federal Officers in Portland," *Courthouse News*, August 18, 2020, https://www.courthousenews.com/judge-to-rule-thursday-on-press-claims-against-federal-officers-in-portland/ (last accessed February 23, 2021).

47. Department of Homeland Security, MYTHS VS. FACTS: Cooperation and Receding Riot Activity in Portland, OREGON, Press Release, August 4, 2020, https://www.dhs.gov/news/2020/08/04/myths-vs-facts-cooperation-and-receding-riot-activity-portland-oregon (last accessed February 23, 2021).

48. Karina Brown, "Judge: Federal Agents Lack Authority to Clear Portland Streets," *Courthouse News*, August 20, 2020, https://www.courthousenews.com/judge-federal-agents-lack-authority-to-clear-portland-streets/#:~:text=Federal%20agents%20are%20still%20in,in%20Portland%20at%20augmented%20levels (last accessed February 23, 2021).

49. Lang et al., "Operation Diligent Valor." Maxine Bernstein, "Former U.S. Customs and Border Protection Chief Calls Federal Officers' Actions in Portland: 'Undisciplined, Unnecessary and Excessive Force,'" *Oregonian*, August 16, 2020, https://www.oregonlive.com/crime/2020/08/former-us-customs-and-border-protection-chief-calls-federal-officers-actions-in-portland-undisciplined-unnecessary-and-excessive-force.html (last accessed February 23, 2021).

50. Karina Brown, "Judge Extends Order Barring Assaults of Portland Journalists by Officers," *Courthouse News*, August 6, 2020, https://www.courthousenews.com/judge-extends-order-barring-assaults-of-portland-journalists-by-officers/ (last accessed February 23, 2021).

51. Brown, "Judge to Rule Thursday"; *Index Newspapers LLC v. United States Marshals Serv.*, 977 F.3d 817 (9th Cir. 2020), https://assets.documentcloud.org/documents/7041366/Index-Newspapers-PI-2.pdf (last accessed February 23, 2021).

52. *Index Newspapers LLC v. United States Marshals Serv.*, No. 20-35739, 2020 U.S. App. LEXIS 27408 (9th Cir. Aug. 27, 2020), https://www.courthousenews.com/wp-content/uploads/2020/08/Ninth-Order.pdf. "According to the website for the Ninth Circuit Court of Appeals, three-judge panels for motions like the one filed by the government in this case are being heard this month by McKeown, Judge Barry Silverman, who was also appointed by Clinton, and Judge Daniel Bress, a Trump appointee. But in an unusual move, Judge Eric Miller, a Trump appointee, apparently subbed in for Silverman." Karina Brown, "Feds in Portland Now Unrestrained in Removing Journalists at Protests," *Courthouse News*, August 27, 2020, https://www.courthousenews.com/feds-in-portland-now-unrestrained-in-removing-journalists-at-protests/ (last accessed February 23, 2021)

53. Luke Barr, "Trump Administration Has Taken a 'Belligerent, Aggressive Tone' with Oregon Officials: Former DHS Secretary Michael Chertoff," *ABC News*, July 22, 2020, https://abcnews.go.com/Politics/trump-administration-belligerent-aggressive-tone-oregon-officials-dhs/story?id=71925276 (last accessed February 23, 2021).

54. Greg Sargent, "Trump's Authoritarian Crackdown Is So Bad That Even Some in the GOP Are Blasting It," *Washington Post*, July 22, 2020, https://www.washingtonpost.com/opinions/2020/07/22/trumps-ugly-law-enforcement-crackdown-is-even-alienating-republicans/ (last accessed February 23, 2021).

55. Michael Chertoff, "The Hijacking of Homeland Security," *New York Times*, July 28, 2020, https://www.nytimes.com/2020/07/28/opinion/homeland-security-portland-trump.html (last accessed February 23, 2021).

56. Author interview with Brian Jenkins, December 30, 2020.

57. "Ridge: 'It Would Be a Cold Day in Hell' before I'd Let 'Uninvited' Federal Agents into Cities," *Pittsburgh Post-Gazette*, July 22, 2020, https://www.post-gazette.com/news/crime-courts/2020/07/22/homeland-security-portland-tom-ridge-philadephia-trump-federal-agents/stories/202007220076 (last accessed February 23, 2021).

58. "Richard Clarke on DHS, Governance, and the 2020 Presidential Election," *Vital Interests Podcast with Karen Greenberg*, October 13, 2020, https://open.spotify.com/episode/7aDnleKStRThTdcXo3i7l7?si=jQdE-GiGQhep-n_B3Y3olA (last accessed February 23, 2021).

59. Author interview with Brian Jenkins, December 30, 2020.

60. Senate Hearing on Role of Federal Law Enforcement in Protests across the U.S., C-SPAN, August 6, 2020, https://www.c-span.org/video/?474472-1/senate-hearing-role-federal-law-enforcement-protests-us (last accessed February 23, 2021).

61. "Former DHS Head Chertoff: GOP Being 'Hijacked,'" *PBS*, August 20, 2020, https://www.pbs.org/video/former-dhs-head-chertoff-gop-being-hijacked-bphvix/ (last accessed February 23, 2021).

62. Department of Homeland Security, "2020 State of the Homeland as Delivered by Acting Secretary Chad Wolf."

63. Katie Benner, "Barr Told Prosecutors to Consider Sedition Charges for Protest Violence," *New York Times*, September 22, 2020, https://www.nytimes.com/2020/09/16/us/politics/william-barr-sedition.html/ (last accessed February 23, 2021).

64. 18 U.S.C. § 2384 (1948) Seditious Conspiracy, https://www.govinfo.gov/content/pkg/USCODE-2011-title18/pdf/USCODE-2011-title18.pdf.

65. Mark Bray, "Five Myths about Antifa," *Washington Post*, September 11, 2020, https://www
.washingtonpost.com/outlook/five-myths/five-myths-about-antifa/2020/09/11/527071ac-f37b
-11ea-bc45-e5d48ab44b9f_story.html (last accessed February 23, 2021).

66. Jeffrey A. Rosen, "Memorandum to US Attorneys: Charging in Connection with Violent
Rioting, including U.S.C., § 2384," September 17, 2020, https://www.justice.gov/archives/opa
/page/file/1317916/download (last accessed February 23, 2021).

67. Benner, "Barr Told Prosecutors." Karina Brown, "Portland Defense Attorneys Doubtful
of Sedition Charges for Protesters," *Courthouse News*, September 18, 2020, https://www
.courthousenews.com/portland-defense-attorneys-doubtful-of-sedition-charges-for-protesters/
(last accessed February 23, 2021).

68. "Some Portland Law Enforcement Officers Have Been Deputized by the Federal Government: Here's What That Means," *KGW8*, September 30, 2020, https://www.kgw.com/article/news
/local/the-story/portland-police-officers-and-county-deputies-have-been-deputized-by-the
-federal-government-heres-what-that-means/283-dded3b33-3deb-4268-b324-afid4ba378c9 (last
accessed February 23, 2021). Karina Brown, "Feds Reject Oregon Demand to End Deputization of
Portland Police," *Courthouse News*, September 30, 2020, https://www.courthousenews.com/feds
-reject-oregon-demand-to-end-deputization-of-portland-police/ (last accessed February 23, 2021).

69. Karina Brown, "Feds Reject Oregon Demand to End Deputization of Portland Police."

70. *Index Newspapers LLC v. United States Marshals Serv.*, 977 F.3d 817 (9th Cir. 2020),
https://www.opb.org/pdf/20201009CourtOrder_1602345843220.pdf (last accessed February 23, 2021.

71. Everton Bailey Jr., "Portland Voters Approved Creating New Civilian-Run Police Oversight Board," *Oregonian/OregonLive*, November 3, 2020, https://www.oregonlive.com/politics
/2020/11/portland-voters-approve-creating-new-civilian-oversight-board-for-police.html (last
accessed February 23, 2021).

Chapter 9: The 2020 Elections

This chapter's epigraph derives from Libby Nelson, "Donald Trump's 'Rigged Election' Myth,
Explained," *Vox*, October 19, 2016, https://www.vox.com/2016/10/19/13308020/rigged-election
-donald-trump-voter-fraud.

1. Lawrence Wright, "The Plague Year," *New Yorker*, December 28, 2020, https://www
.newyorker.com/magazine/2021/01/04/the-plague-year (last accessed February 23, 2021).

2. Ibid.

3. CDC Fact Sheet, "Health Equity Considerations and Racial and Ethnic Minority Groups,"
updated July 24, 2020, https://www.cdc.gov/coronavirus/2019-ncov/community/health-equity
/race-ethnicity.html (last accessed January 21, 2021).

4. Daniel Wolfe and Daniel Dale, "'It's Going to Disappear': A Timeline of Trump's Claims
That Covid-19 Will Vanish," *CNN*, October 31, 2020, https://www.cnn.com/interactive/2020
/10/politics/covid-disappearing-trump-comment-tracker/ (last accessed February 23, 2021).

5. Christina Maxouris and Eliott C. McLaughlin, "Only Two US states Are Reporting a
Decline in New Coronavirus Cases," *CNN*, June 28, 2020, https://www.cnn.com/2020/06/28
/health/us-coronavirus-sunday/index.html (last accessed January 23, 2021).

6. Debbie Elliot, "While COVID-19 Stats Rise in Some States, Cases Drop in Others," *NPR*, June 18, 2020, https://www.npr.org/2020/06/18/879892205/while-covid-19-stats-rise-in-some-states-cases-drop-in-others (last accessed Jan. 23, 2021).

7. Wright, "The Plague Year."

8. Matthew Haag, "One-Third of New York's Small Businesses May Be Gone Forever," *New York Times*, August 3, 2020, https://www.nytimes.com/2020/08/03/nyregion/nyc-small-businesses-closing-coronavirus.html (last accessed January 21, 2021).

9. Maggie Haberman, Patricia Mazzei, and Annie Karni, "Trump Abruptly Cancels Republican Convention in Florida: 'It's Not the Right Time,'" *New York Times*, July 23, 2020, https://www.nytimes.com/2020/07/23/us/politics/jacksonville-rnc.html (last accessed January 21, 2021). Bryan Anderson, Gary D. Robertson, and Jill Colvin, "Trump Says GOP Is Pulling Convention from North Carolina," Associated Press, June 2, 2020, https://apnews.com/article/59c39a41260ec5e40fb8620d58e295b4 (last accessed January 21, 2021).

10. "First Presidential Debate," *C-SPAN*, September 29, 2020, https://www.c-span.org/debates/?debate=first (last accessed January 21, 2021). Michael M. Grynbaum and Shane Goldmacher, "Second Debate Canceled as Biden Condemns Trump for 'Reckless' Conduct,'" *New York Times*, October 9, 2020, https://www.nytimes.com/2020/10/09/us/politics/biden-nevada-debate.html (last accessed February 27, 2021). "Second Presidential Debate," *C-SPAN*, October 22, 2020, https://www.c-span.org/debates/?debate=second (last accessed January 21, 2021).

11. Donald J. Trump, Facebook, May 26, 2020, https://www.facebook.com/DonaldTrump/posts/there-is-no-way-zero-that-mail-in-ballots-will-be-anything-less-than-substantial/10164748538560725/ (last accessed January 1, 2021).

12. Donald J. Trump (@RealDonaldTrump), Twitter, July 30, 2020, 8:46:09 a.m.), https://twitter.com/realdonaldtrump/status/1288818160389558273 (last accessed January 1, 2021) available at "Donald Trump suggests delay to 2020 US presidential election," BBC, July 30, 2020, https://www.bbc.com/news/world-us-canada-53597975 (last accessed February 23, 2021). Eugene Kiely, Lori Robertson, Rem Rieder, and D'Angelo Gore, "The President's Trumped-Up Claims of Voter Fraud," *Factcheck.org*, July 30, 2020, https://www.factcheck.org/2020/07/the-presidents-trumped-up-claims-of-voter-fraud/ (last accessed January 21, 2021).

13. Miles Parks, "FACT CHECK: Trump Repeats Voter Fraud Claim about California," *NPR*, April 5, 2018, https://www.npr.org/2018/04/05/599868312/fact-check-trump-repeats-voter-fraud-claim-about-california (last accessed January 21, 2021).

14. Tom LoBianco, "Trump Falsely Claims 'Millions of People Who Voted Illegally' Cost Him Popular Vote," *CNN*, November 28, 2016, https://www.cnn.com/2016/11/27/politics/donald-trump-voter-fraud-popular-vote/index.html (last accessed January 21, 2021).

15. Andrew S. Bowen, "Russian Cyber Units," Congressional Research Service, IF11718, January 4, 2021, https://crsreports.congress.gov/product/pdf/IF/IF11718 (last accessed January 21, 2021). Seth G. Jones, "Russian Meddling in the United States: The Historical Context of the Mueller Report," CSIS, March 27, 2019, https://www.csis.org/analysis/russian-meddling-united-states-historical-context-mueller-report (last accessed January 21, 2021).

16. Michael Tackett and Michael Wines, "Trump Disbands Commission on Voter Fraud," *New York Times*, January 3, 2018, https://www.nytimes.com/2018/01/03/us/politics/trump-voter-fraud-commission.html (last accessed January 21, 2021).

17. Elizabeth Landers, Eli Watkins, and Kevin Liptak, "Trump Dissolves Voter Fraud Commission: Adviser Says It Went 'Off the Rails,'" *CNN*, January 4, 2018, https://www.cnn.com/2018/01/03/politics/presidential-election-commission/index.html (last accessed January 21, 2021).

18. Joseph P. Williams, "Trump Panel Finds No Voter Fraud," *US News*, January 10, 2018, https://www.usnews.com/news/national-news/articles/2018-01-10/trump-commision-on-election-integrity-found-no-evidence-of-voter-fraud (last accessed January 21, 2021).

19. Chris Cillizza, "Donald Trump Warns People to Beware of Non-Existent Voter Fraud," *CNN*, October 22, 2018, https://www.cnn.com/2018/10/22/politics/donald-trump-voter-fraud/index.html (last accessed Jan 21, 2021).

20. Donald J. Trump (@RealDonald Trump), Twitter, November 9, 2018, 11:52:19 a.m., https://twitter.com/realDonaldTrump/status/1060938144336367616?ref_src=twsrc%5Etfw (last accessed January 1, 2021), available at "Trump Calls Florida Vote Count a 'Disgrace' as Recount Looms in Senate Race," *NBC*, November 9, 2018, https://www.nbcnews.com/politics/white-house/trump-calls-florida-ballot-count-disgrace-nelson-scott-file-lawsuits-n934451 (last accessed February 23, 2021). Ken Stone, "Democrats' 'Best Election Stealing Lawyer' to Oppose Issa on Ballot Suit," *Times of San Diego*, June 10, 2020, https://timesofsandiego.com/politics/2020/06/10/democrats-best-election-stealing-lawyer-to-oppose-issa-on-ballot-suit/ (last accessed January 21, 2021).

21. Jane C. Timm, "Vote Fraud Fact Check: Trump's Bogus (So Far) Claims about Florida," *NBC*, November 12, 2018, https://www.nbcnews.com/politics/donald-trump/fact-check-trump-s-unsubstantiated-claims-voter-fraud-florida-n935461 (last accessed January 21, 2021).

22. Joe Hernandez, "N.J. Election Fraud Case Draws a Trump Tweet but Suggests Safeguards Are Working," *NPR*, July 1, 2020, https://www.npr.org/2020/07/01/885074932/n-j-election-fraud-case-draws-a-trump-tweet-but-suggests-safeguards-are-working (last accessed January 21, 2021).

23. Mattathias Schwartz, "William Barr's State of Emergency," *New York Times Magazine*, June 1, 2020, https://www.nytimes.com/2020/06/01/magazine/william-barr-attorney-general.html (last accessed January 21, 2021).

24. "Transcript: NPR's Full Interview with Attorney General William Barr," *NPR*, June 25, 2020, https://www.npr.org/2020/06/25/883273933/transcript-nprs-full-interview-with-attorney-general-william-barr (last accessed January 21, 2021).

25. Marshall Cohen, "Trump Spreads New Lies about Foreign-Backed Voter Fraud, Stoking Fears of a 'Rigged Election' This November," *CNN*, June 22, 2020, https://www.cnn.com/2020/06/22/politics/trump-voter-fraud-lies-fact-check/index.html (last accessed January 21, 2021).

26. Amy Gardner, "Election Officials Contradict Barr's Assertion That Counterfeit Mail Ballots Produced by a Foreign Country Are a 'Real' Worry," *Washington Post*, June 2, 2020, https://www.washingtonpost.com/politics/election-officials-contradict-barrs-assertion-that-counterfeit-mail-ballots-produced-by-a-foreign-country-are-a-real-worry/2020/06/02/5ac8d664-a43e-11ea-b619-3f9133bbb482_story.html (last accessed January 21, 2021).

27. Ibid. Rebecca Tan, "Md. Elections Officials Say Video's Allegation of Ballot Fraud Is Untrue. But It's Already Gone Viral," *Washington Post*, October 21, 2020, https://www.washingtonpost.com/local/md-politics/ballot-fraud-denied-montgomery-county/2020/10/21/aee4de64-13dd-11eb-bc10-40b25382f1be_story.html (last accessed January 21, 2021).

28. "Ten Things to Know about Trump's Post Office Scandal," *MooreNews*, August 20, 2020, https://moorenews.net/articles/4/5/6681/Ten-Things-to-Know-About-Trump-s-Post-Office -Scandal.html (last accessed January 21, 2021).

29. David Dayden, "Unsanitized: Does Amazon Rip Off the Postal Service?" American Prospect, May 15, 2020, https://prospect.org/coronavirus/unsanitized-does-amazon-rip-off-the -postal-service/ (last accessed January 21, 2021).

30. "House Oversight Committee Hearing on Postal Service Operations and Mail-In Voting," *C-SPAN*, August 24, 2020, https://www.c-span.org/video/?474917-1/house-oversight-commttee -hearing-postal-service-operations-mail-voting (last accessed January 21, 2021). "Postmaster General Louis DeJoy Testimony Transcript, August 24 2020: House Oversight Hearing," *Rev*, August 24, 2020, https://www.rev.com/blog/transcripts/postmaster-general-louis-dejoy-testimony -transcript-august-24-house-oversight-hearing (last accessed January 21, 2021).

31. Postmaster General Louis DeJoy Testimony Transcript, August 24 2020:

32. *New York v. Trump*, Case No. 20 Civ. 2340, Complaint, filed August 25, 2020, https://ag .ny.gov/sites/default/files/doc_1_complaint_usps.pdf (last accessed January 21, 2021).

33. *Pennsylvania v. Dejoy*, Case No. 20 Civ. 04096, Complaint, filed August 21, 2020, https://ncdoj .gov/wp-content/uploads/2020/08/1-Complaint-PA-v-DeJoy.pdf (last accessed Jan 21, 2021).

34. *Washington v. Trump*, Case No. 20 Civ. 03127, Order, filed September 17, 2020, https:// www.courtlistener.com/recap/gov.uscourts.waed.91975/gov.uscourts.waed.91975.81.0_1.pdf (last accessed Jan 21, 2021).

35. *New York v. Trump* (D.D.C. September 27, 2020). Luke Broadwater, "In Latest Legal Rebuke, Court Orders Postal Service to Prioritize Mail-In Voting," *New York Times*, September 21, 2020, https://www.nytimes.com/2020/09/21/us/politics/postal-service-mail-in-voting .html (last accessed January 21, 2021).

36. *Pennsylvania v. Dejoy*, Case No. 20 Civ. 04096, Order, filed September 28, 2020, https:// www.courthousenews.com/wp-content/uploads/2020/09/pa-dejoy.pdf (last accessed January 20, 2021).

37. Luke Broadwater, "In Latest Legal Rebuke, Court Orders Postal Service to Prioritize Mail-In Voting," *New York Times*, September 21, 2020, https://www.nytimes.com/2020/09/21 /us/politics/postal-service-mail-in-voting.html (last accessed February 28, 2021).

38. David Leonhardt, "There Have Been over 300 Lawsuits, in 44 States, over Voting Rules: Here's the Latest," *New York Times*, October 14, 2020, https://www.nytimes.com/live/2020/10 /28/us/trump-biden-election/there-have-been-over-300-lawsuits-in-44-states-over-voting -rules-heres-the-latest (last accessed January 21, 2021).

39. Sam Baker and Stef W. Kight, "How the Supreme Court Is Handling Election Cases," *Axios*, November 2, 2020, https://www.axios.com/supreme-court-2020-election-cases-1c45e752 -fb0c-490e-9aa4-f98e83ccf71f.html (last accessed January 21, 2021). Ian Millhiser, "The Supreme Court's Latest Decision Looks Like a Win for Voting Rights: It's Really a Threat," *Vox*, October 28, 2020, https://www.vox.com/2020/10/28/21539169/supreme-court-pennsylvania-republican -party-samuel-alito-mail-in-ballots-boockvar (last accessed January 21, 2021).

40. Daniel L. Byman and Colin P. Clarke, "Why the Risk of Election Violence Is High," *Brookings*, October 27, 2020, https://www.brookings.edu/blog/fixgov/2020/10/27/why-the -risk-of-election-violence-is-high/ (last accessed February 23, 2021).

41. Mark Milley, "Use of the Military for Political Gain," United States House of Representatives Armed Services Committee, Questions, QFR ID: HASC-22-010, https://sherrill.house.gov /sites/sherrill.house.gov/files/wysiwyg_uploaded/HASC%20Hearing%20QFR%20responses%20GEN%20Milley%20to%20Sherrill%20Slotkin%20200827.pdf (last accessed January 21, 2021). Jennifer Steinhauer and Helene Cooper, "At Pentagon, Fears Grow That Trump Will Pull Military into Election Unrest," *New York Times*, September 25, 2020, https://www.nytimes .com/2020/09/25/us/politics/trump-military-election.html (last accessed January 21, 2021).

42. Christianna Silva, "Gen. Mark Milley Says the Military Plays 'No Role' in Elections," *NPR*, October 11, 2020, https://www.npr.org/2020/10/11/922827554/gen-mark-milley-says-the -military-plays-no-role-in-elections (last accessed January 21, 2021).

43. Dave Philipps, "National Guard Readies for Election Day Deployment," *New York Times*, November 2, 2020, https://www.nytimes.com/2020/11/02/us/national-guard-election.html (last accessed January 21, 2021).

44. Jim Rutenberg and Nick Corasaniti, "National Guard Readies for Election Day Deployment," *New York Times*, October 27, 2020, https://www.nytimes.com/2020/10/27/us /kavanaugh-voting-rights.html (last accessed January 21, 2021).

45. Neil MacFarquhar and Shaila Dewan, "Ahead of Election, Police Prepare for Violence and Disruption," *New York Times*, November 1, 2020, https://www.nytimes.com/2020/11/01/us /election-police-violence.htm (last accessed February 23, 2021).

46. James M. Lindsay, "The 2020 Election by the Numbers," Council on Foreign Relations, December 15, 2020, https://www.cfr.org/blog/2020-election-numbers (last accessed February 23, 2021). Annie Goldsmith, "The 2020 Election Had the Highest Voter Turnout in Modern History," *Town and Country*, November 7, 2020, https://www.townandcountrymag.com /society/politics/a34574744/2020-election-voter-turnout-high/ (last accessed February 23, 2021).

47. "Donald Trump 2020 Election Night Speech Transcript," *Rev*, November 4, 2020, https://www.rev.com/blog/transcripts/donald-trump-2020-election-night-speech-transcript (last accessed January 21, 2021).

48. Rebecca Sinderbrand, "How Kellyanne Conway Ushered in the Era of 'Alternative Facts,'" *Washington Post*, January 22, 2017, https://www.washingtonpost.com/news/the-fix/wp /2017/01/22/how-kellyanne-conway-ushered-in-the-era-of-alternative-facts/ (last accessed January 21, 2021).

49. United States Attorney General, "Post-Voting Election Irregularity Inquiries," Memorandum, November 9, 2020, https://assets.documentcloud.org/documents/7327241/Attorney -General-Barr-Memo-Election.pdf (last accessed January 21, 2021).

50. Bill Chappell, "Head of DOJ's Election Crimes Unit Steps Down after Barr OKs Election Inquiries," *NPR*, November 10, 2020, https://www.npr.org/sections/live-updates-2020-election -results/2020/11/10/933395215/head-of-doj-s-election-crimes-unit-steps-down-after-barr-oks -election-inquiries (last accessed January 21, 2021). Matt Zapotosky and Devlin Barrett, "Barr Clears Justice Dept. to Investigate Alleged Voting Irregularities as Trump Makes Unfounded Fraud Claims," *Washington Post*, November 9, 2020, https://www.washingtonpost.com/national -security/trump-voting-fraud-william-barr-justice-department/2020/11/09/d57dbe98-22e6 -11eb-8672-c281c7a2c96e_story.html (last accessed January 21, 2021).

51. Letter from the Minnesota Attorney General et al. to the Attorney General, November 13, 2020, https://www.ag.state.mn.us/Office/Communications/2020/docs/AG_BarrLtr.pdf (last accessed January 21, 2021).

52. Cybersecurity and Infrastructure Security Agency (CISA), "Joint Statement from Elections Infrastructure Government Coordinating Council and the Election Infrastructure Sector Coordinating Executive Committees," November 12, 2020, https://www.cisa.gov/news/2020/11/12/joint-statement-elections-infrastructure-government-coordinating-council-election (last accessed January 21, 2021). CISA, "#Protect2020 Rumor vs. Reality," https://www.cisa.gov/rumorcontrol (last accessed February 23, 2021).

53. "Trump Fires Head of DHS Election Security Agency," *Spectrum News*, November 17, 2020, https://spectrumnews1.com/ky/northern-ky/news/2020/11/18/trump-fires-cisa-director-chris-krebs (last accessed February 27, 2021). Patrick Howell O'Neill, "After Trump Fires CISA's Director, the Agency Is Poised to Become Even More Powerful," *MIT Technology Review*, November 21, 2020, https://www.technologyreview.com/2020/11/21/1012422/after-trump-fires-cisas-director-the-agency-is-poised-to-become-even-more-powerful/ (last accessed January 21, 2021). Alex Marquardt and Geneva Stands, "Two Top Homeland Security Officials Forced to Resign by White House," *CNN*, November 12, 2020, https://www.cnn.com/2020/11/12/politics/dhs-officials-forced-resign-white-house/ (last accessed January 21, 2021). Jason Miller, "CISA's Ware Resigns: Is Director Krebs Next out the Door?" *Federal News Network*, November 12, 2020, https://federalnewsnetwork.com/people/2020/11/cisas-ware-resigns-is-director-krebs-next-out-the-door/ (last accessed February 23, 2021).

54. Rosalind S. Helderman and Elise Viebeck, "'The Last Wall': How Dozens of Judges across the Political Spectrum Rejected Trump's Efforts to Overturn the Election," *Washington Post*, December 12, 2020, https://www.washingtonpost.com/politics/judges-trump-election-lawsuits/2020/12/12/e3a57224-3a72-11eb-98c4-25dc9f4987e8_story.html (last accessed February 23, 2021).

55. Emily Bazelon, "Trump Is Not Doing Well with His Election Lawsuits: Here's a Rundown," *New York Times*, November 13, 2020, https://www.nytimes.com/2020/11/13/us/politics/trump-election-lawsuits.html (last accessed February 23, 2021). Alison Durkee, "Trump and the GOP Have Now Lost More Than 50 Post-Election Lawsuits," *Forbes*, December 9, 2020, https://www.forbes.com/sites/alisondurkee/2020/12/08/trump-and-the-gop-have-now-lost-50-post-election-lawsuits/?sh=fd225c29606d (last accessed February 23, 2021).

56. *Texas v. Pennsylvania*, Complaint, filed December 7, 2020, https://www.texasattorneygeneral.gov/sites/default/files/images/admin/2020/Press/SCOTUSFiling.pdf (last accessed February 23, 2021).

57. *Texas v. Pennsylvania*, Amicus Curiae, filed December 9, 2020, https://www.democracydocket.com/wp-content/uploads/sites/45/2020/12/20201209144840609_2020-12-09-Texas-v.-Pennsylvania-Amicus-Brief-of-Missouri-et-al.-Final-with-Tables.pdf (last accessed January 21, 2021).

58. *Texas v. Pennsylvania*, Brief, filed December 10, 2020, https://www.supremecourt.gov/DocketPDF/22/22O155/163367/20201210142206254_Pennsylvania%20Opp%20to%20Bill%20of%20Complaint%20v.FINAL.pdf (last accessed January 21, 2021).

59. "States Targeted in Texas Election Fraud Lawsuit Condemn 'Cacophony of Bogus Claims,'" *The Guardian*, December 10, 2020, https://www.theguardian.com/us-news/2020/dec

/10/us-election-texas-lawsuit-georgia-pennsylvania-michigan-wisconsin (last accessed January 21, 2021).

60. *Texas v. Pennsylvania*, No. 155, 2020 U.S. (December 11, 2020), https://www.democracydocket.com/wp-content/uploads/sites/45/2020/12/S.-Ct.-order-denying-Texas-election-lawsuit-12-11-2020.pdf (last accessed January 21, 2020).

61. Michael Balsamo, "Disputing Trump, Barr Says No Widespread Election fraud," Associated Press, December 1, 2020, https://apnews.com/article/barr-no-widespread-election-fraud-b1f1488796c9a98c4b1a9061a6c7f49d (last accessed January 21, 2021). Matt Zapotosky, Devlin Barrett, and Josh Dawsey, "Barr Says He Hasn't Seen Fraud That Could Affect the Election Outcome," *Washington Post*, December 1, 2020, https://www.washingtonpost.com/national-security/barr-no-evidence-election-fraud/2020/12/01/5f4dcaa8-340a-11eb-8d38-6aea1adb3839_story.html (last accessed January 21, 2021).

62. Office of the Attorney General, William Barr, Letter to the President, December 14, 2020, https://int.nyt.com/data/documenttools/attorney-general-william-barr-resignation-letter/b82836cfofe20bf8/full.pdf (last accessed January 21, 2021).

63. "Public Law 88-277," 78 Stat. 1964 (March 7, 1964), https://www.govinfo.gov/content/pkg/STATUTE-78/pdf/STATUTE-78-Pg153.pdf (last accessed February 23, 2021).

64. National Commission on Terrorist Attacks Upon the United States, "9-11 Commission Report," 2002–2004, https://9-11commission.gov/report// (last accessed February 23, 2021).

65. John Rollins, "2008–2009 Presidential Transition: National Security Considerations and Options," Congressional Research Service, April 21, 2008, https://fas.org/sgp/crs/natsec/RL34456.pdf (last accessed February 23, 2021). Glenn P. Hastedt and Anthony J. Eksterowicz, "Perils of Presidential Transition," *Seton Hall Journal of Diplomacy and International Relations* (Winter/Spring 2001), http://blogs.shu.edu/journalofdiplomacy/files/archives/eksterowick.pdf (last accessed February 23, 2021).

66. "Public Law 111–283," 124 STAT. 3045 (October 15, 2010), https://www.congress.gov/111/plaws/publ283/PLAW-111publ283.pdf (last accessed February 23, 2021). Henry Hogue, "Presidential Transition Act: Provisions and Funding," Congressional Research Service, 7-5700, RS22979, November 13, 2020, https://fas.org/sgp/crs/misc/RS22979.pdf (last accessed February 23, 2021).

67. Center for Presidential Transition, "Despite President's Comments, Transition Efforts Required by Law Are Underway," *Government Executive*, September 30, 2020, https://presidentialtransition.org/publications/transition-efforts-are-underway/ (last accessed February 23, 2021). *Government Executive*, "Trump Administration Redacts Meeting Minutes on the Presidential Transition," *Government Executive*, July 21, 2020, https://www.govexec.com/management/2020/07/trump-administration-redacts-meeting-minutes-presidential-transition/167073/ (last accessed February 23, 2021).

68. "Pentagon Blocks Visits to Military Spy Agencies by Biden Transition Team," *Washington Post*, December 4, 2020, https://www.washingtonpost.com/national-security/pentagon-blocks-biden-transition-team/2020/12/04/2e7042fa-3656-11eb-a997-1f4c53d2a747_story.html (last accessed February 23, 2021).

69. "Trump's Plan to Gut the Civil Service," *Lawfare*, December 8, 2020, https://www.lawfareblog.com/trumps-plan-gut-civil-service (last accessed February 23, 2021).

Conclusion

This chapter's epigraph derives from "Barack Obama on Trump's Defeat and Cooperation in a Divided America," *Consider This from NPR*, November 16, 2020, https://www.npr.org/transcripts/934498021 (last accessed February 23, 2021).

1. "Proceedings and Debates," *House Congressional Record*, 117th Cong., 1st Sess. (January 6, 2021), https://www.congress.gov/117/crec/2021/01/06/CREC-2021-01-06.pdf (last accessed February 23, 2021).

2. "Pro-Trump Mob Storms the US Capitol, Touting 'Stop the Steal' Conspiracy," *Tech Crunch*, January 6, 2021, https://techcrunch.com/2021/01/06/pro-trump-mob-storms-the-us-capitol-touting-stop-the-steal-conspiracy/ (last accessed February 23, 2021).

3. "Donald Trump Speech 'Save America' Rally Transcript January 6," *Rev*, January 6, 2021, https://www.rev.com/blog/transcripts/donald-trump-speech-save-america-rally-transcript-january-6 (last accessed February 23, 2021).

4. "Federal Agencies Respond to Riots at U.S. Capitol," *Government Executive*, January 6, 2021, https://www.govexec.com/management/2021/01/federal-agencies-respond-riots-us-capitol/171228/ (last accessed February 23, 2021).

5. Russ Feingold, "We Don't Need Another Patriot Act," *Wall Street Journal*, February 7, 2021, https://www.wsj.com/articles/we-dont-need-another-patriot-act-11612732869 (last accessed February 24, 2021).

6. "Proceedings and Debates," *House Congressional Record*, 117th Cong., 1st Sess. (January 6, 2021), https://www.congress.gov/117/crec/2021/01/06/CREC-2021-01-06.pdf (last accessed February 23, 2021).

7. "Missouri Congresswoman inside Capitol Says 'This Is 1,000 Times Worse' Than 9/11," *St. Louis Radio*, January 6, 2021, https://www.radio.com/kmox/news/local/missouri-congresswoman-wagner-says-protest-worse-than-9-11 (last accessed February 23, 2021).

8. "Being in Capitol Hill Chaos Felt 'Like I Was Back in Afghanistan': Congressman and Veteran," *MSN*, January 7, 2021, https://www.msn.com/en-us/money/smallbusiness/being-in-capitol-hill-chaos-felt-like-i-was-back-in-afghanistan-congressman-and-veteran/vi-BB1cyAKS (last accessed February 23, 2021).

9. "Proceedings and Debates," *House Congressional Record*, 117th Cong., 1st Sess. (January 13, 2021) https://www.congress.gov/117/crec/2021/01/13/CREC-2021-01-13-house.pdf (last accessed February 23, 2021).

10. *Senate Congressional Record*, 117th Cong., 1st Sess., pages S32-8 (January 6, 2021), https://www.congress.gov/117/crec/2021/01/06/CREC-2021-01-06-pt1-PgS32-2.pdf (last accessed February 23, 2021).

11. Ibid.

12. Liz Cheney, "Cheney: I Will Vote to Impeach the President," *Congresswoman Liz Cheney*, January 12, 2021, https://cheney.house.gov/2021/01/12/cheney-i-will-vote-to-impeach-the-president/ (last accessed February 23, 2021).

13. "Why We Need a January 6 Commission to Investigate the Attack on the Capitol," *The Rand Blog*, January 20, 2021, https://www.rand.org/blog/2021/01/why-we-need-a-january-6-commission-to-investigate-the.html (last accessed February 23. 2021).

14. Scott Wong, "Calls Grow for 9/11-Style Panel to Probe Capitol Attack," *The Hill*, January 23, 2021, https://thehill.com/homenews/house/535482-calls-grow-for-9-11-style-panel-to-probe-capitol-attack (last accessed February 23, 2021).

15. Nancy Pelosi, "Dear Colleague: Security, Security, Security," January 15, 2021, https://www.speaker.gov/newsroom/21521-0 (last accessed February 27, 2021). Hope Yen, "Pelosi Says Independent Commission Will Examine Capitol Riot," *AP*, February 15, 2021, https://apnews.com/article/7ebcbaedd6985537dec0c3918cbf06d9 (last accessed February 27, 2021).

16. Joseph R. Biden Jr., "Inaugural Address by President Joseph R. Biden Jr.," The White House, January 20, 2021, https://www.whitehouse.gov/briefing-room/speeches-remarks/2021/01/20/inaugural-address-by-president-joseph-r-biden-jr/ (last accessed February 23, 2021).

17. "'The Process Is Working': Biden Urges Patience as Vote Counting Drags On," *Politico*, November 5, 2020, https://www.politico.com/news/2020/11/05/the-process-is-working-biden-urges-patience-as-vote-counting-drags-on-434469 (last accessed February 23, 2021).

18. "Here's the Full List of Biden's Executive Actions So Far," *NBC*, January 25, 2021, https://www.nbcnews.com/politics/white-house/here-s-full-list-biden-s-executive-actions-so-far-n1255564 (last accessed February 23, 2021).

19. "Pentagon Clears Out Advisory Boards to Oust Last-Minute Trump Picks," *Wall Street Journal*, February 2, 2021, https://www.wsj.com/articles/defense-chief-clears-out-pentagon-advisory-boards-to-oust-last-minute-trump-picks-11612289262 (last accessed February 23, 2021).

INDEX

Nelson, Bill, 178

Netanyahu, Benjamin, 123

New York Times, 8, 34, 41, 165

9/11 Commission Report, 42–43, 195, 204

Nixon, Richard M., 10, 12, 62, 74, 137, 209

Noonan, Peggy, 41

norms, disruption of, 51, 208; Barr and, 71, 119; Capitol insurrection, 202; election pushback, 191; presidential transfer of power, 199–200; Supreme Court nomination, 186; Trump and, 53

norms, violation of: D.C. protests and, 151; military and law enforcement blurred, 153–54, 167; Portland protests, 170; Secretary of Defense, 56–58, 207; travel ban, 89

Obama, Barack, 3; AUMF language, 20–21; Comey appointment, 63; drone strikes and, 23–25; immigration policies, 85, 101–3; Iran policies, 131; OLC and executive privilege, 60; transparency and secrecy, 69. *See also* Joint Comprehensive Plan of Action (JCPOA); Obama Framework

Obama, Barack, executive orders and memoranda: closing of Guantanamo, 3, 25; "Transparency and Open Government," 66, 81; transparency and secrecy goals, 66

Obama administration: Anti-Nepotism Statute and, 59; counterterrorism efforts, 23; Iran and nuclear weapons, 122–23. *See also* Authorization for the Use of Military Force (2001) (AUMF)

Obama Framework, 133–35, 144

Obey, David, 44–45

O'Brien, Robert, 131, 139

Office of Homeland Security (OHS), 40, 42–43

Office of Immigration and Citizenship, 108

Office of Legal Counsel (OLC): executive staff testimony, 78; Obama and, 67, 69; role and duties, 59; secret memo on immunity from testifying, 76–77; sitting

president memo, 74; staff of, 15–16, 54–55; Stellar Wind, warrantless surveillance, 66; Trump and, 60

Office of Refugee Resettlement (ORR), 112–113

Office of the Director of National Intelligence, 38, 196, 206. *See also* Director of National Intelligence.

Olsen, Matt, 153

Oppenheimer, J. Robert, 9

Orwell, George, 7, 10

Owens, Annie, 59–60

Oxley, Michael, 28

Papachristou v. City of Jacksonville, 32

Paterson, NJ, special election, 179

Paxton, Ken, 192

Pelosi, Nancy, 76, 204

Pence, Mike, 25, 54, 65, 78, 161, 177, 199

Pennsylvania v. DeJoy, 184

Petraeus, David, 126, 128–29

PEW Research Poll, 1

Pilger, Richard, 190

"Politics and the American Language" (Schlesinger), 10

"Politics and the English Language" (Orwell), 10

Pompeo, Mike, 55–56, 78, 122–26, 130, 139–41

Portland protests, 155–58; DHS role, 162; Don't Shoot Portland, 156; election day experience, 172; journalists lawsuit, 159–64, 170–71; Operation Diligent Valor, 157; "phased withdrawal" of federal troops, 161–62; secrecy and confusion of, 163; Temporary Restraining Order (TRO), 156–60, 162, 171

Posse Comitatus Act, 149, 153

post 9/11 policies, 3, 41, 45, 53, 84, 91, 202–4, 208

Postal Regulatory Commission (PRC), 181, 183–84

Postal Reorganization Act (1970), 180

A NOTE ON THE TYPE

This book has been composed in Arno, an Old-style serif typeface in the classic Venetian tradition, designed by Robert Slimbach at Adobe.